CROSS
and
CRESCENT

Praise for *Cross and Crescent*

'Colin Chapman's book is intended as a guide for Christians who find themselves encountering Muslims for the first time. The book would be useful for Christians of any theological persuasion ... especially for those who are basically scared of Islam, afraid even of picking up a copy of the Qur'an ... Colin Chapman's book will quickly enable them to move on constructively from such a crude and negative view.'

Hugh Goddard, University of Nottingham

'It is a rich resource ... not intended as an academic textbook. Rather, it is something of a manual for Christians who want to develop worthwhile and well-informed relationships with Muslims. This practical aim is never far from view ...'

David Marshall, Oxford

'I recommend this book to all who need to understand the phenomenon of Islam, and anyone who seriously wants to relate to Muslims should buy a copy.'

John Meadowcroft, Bible College of New Zealand

'... Colin is an able teacher. This book does not just give us facts about Islam, but Colin has thought long and deeply about his readership. He is aware of the sense of threat that many Christians feel and the attitude to Muslims that results. This is one of the best books on Islam available today.'

Bryan Knell, *Christian Herald*

CROSS
and
CRESCENT

Responding to the challenge
of Islam

Colin Chapman

Inter-Varsity Press

INTER-VARSITY PRESS
38 De Montfort Street, Leicester LE1 7GP, England
Email: ivp@uccf.org.uk
Website: www.ivpbooks.com

First published 1995
Reprinted 1996, 1998, 1999
This edition in new format 2002

British Library Cataloguing in Publication Data
A catalogue record for this book is available from the British Library.

ISBN 0-85111-494-6

Set in Linotron Palatino

Typeset in Great Britain by Parker Typesetting Service, Leicester

Printed in Great Britain by Creative Print and Design (Wales), Ebbw Vale

Inter-Varsity Press is the publishing division of the Universities and Colleges Christian Fellowship (formerly the Inter-Varsity Fellowship), a student movement linking Christian Unions in universities and colleges throughout Great Britain, and a member movement of the International Fellowship of Evangelical Students. For information about local and national activities write to UCCF, 38 De Montfort Street, Leicester LE1 7GP, email us at email@uccf.org.uk, or visit the UCCF website at www.uccf.org.uk.

Acknowledgments

For permission to quote from the following publications IVP expresses its gratitude to:

The Church Missionary Society (CMS) for extracts from *Uncharted Journey* by Roger Hooker.
The Fellowship of Faith for the Muslims and the author for extracts from *The Life of Muslim Women* by Vivienne Stacey.
The Islamic Book Foundation for extracts from *Christian Mission and Islamic Da'wah* by Isma'il al-Faruqi.
The Islamic Foundation, Markfield, Leicester, LE67 9RN, for extracts from *The Holy Qur'an, Translation and Commentary* by A. Yusuf Ali.
Israel Academic Committee on the Middle East for the extract from *Islam and the Minorities* by Ronald L. Nettler.
MARC (a division of World Vision International) and the author, Bill Musk, for the diagram from *The Gospel and Islam: A 1978 Compendium*, edited by Don M. Curry.
Masihi Isha'at Khana, Lahore, Pakistan, and the author for extracts from *Christ Supreme Over Satan* by Vivienne Stacey.
The Muslim Educational Trust, London N4 3RZ, for extracts from *Islam: A Brief Guide*.
John Murray (Publishers) Limited and the author for the table from *Approaches to Islam* by Richard Tames.
The Open University for extracts from *Islam and the Muslim* by Kenneth Cragg.
Oxford University Press for extracts from Khursh'd Ahmad's contribution to *Voices of Resurgent Islam* edited by John L. Esposito (1983) and from *The Life of the Prophet: A Translation of Ibn Ishaq's Sirat Rasul Allah* by A. Guillaume (1970).
Ta Ha Publishers Limited for extracts from *Islam in Britain* by Zaki Badawi.

Unwin Hyman, an imprint of HarperCollins Publishers Limited, and the authors for extracts from *Islam and The Destiny of Man* by Charles Le Gai Eaton and from *The Meaning of the Glorious Koran* by Mohammed Marmaduke Pickthall.

Penguin Books India (P) Ltd and the author for the extracts from *The Struggle Within Islam* and *Muhammed and the Qur'an* by Rafiq Zakaria.

Contents

Introduction

'Cross' and 'crescent'

It is not hard to understand why the cross has been a major symbol – if not *the* major symbol – of Christianity since the beginning.

But what of the crescent? The moon is important for Muslims because they follow a lunar calendar, and have their own names for the twelve months of the year. So, for example, the first sighting of the new moon at the beginning of the ninth month of the Islamic calendar signals the start of the fast of Ramadan. Since a new moon is increasing, the crescent symbolizes something that is growing in strength.

The symbol of the crescent, however, has a strange history. The people of Byzantium (Constantinople) used to have a myth that the city had been founded by Keroessa, the daughter of the moon goddess, Io-Hera. They therefore used the crescent as a symbol for the city. It continued to symbolize Byzantium when it became the capital of the eastern half of the Holy Roman Empire. For centuries, therefore, it was the major symbol of a Christian empire. In other cultures the crescent has symbolized 'the Great Mother', 'the Queen of Heaven'.

It was then taken over by the Muslims some time after they conquered the city in AD 1453, and for several centuries it was regarded as a Turkish symbol. Since the beginning of the nineteenth century, however, the crescent, usually combined with a star, has come to be regarded as the emblem *par excellence* of the faith and community of Islam all over the world.

Just as Christians often put a cross on the spire or dome of a church, so Muslims put a crescent on top of the minaret or the dome of a mosque. The symbol of the crescent clearly does not play the same role in Islam as the cross does in Christianity. But by putting *'cross'* and *'crescent'* together in the title, we are simply bringing together the symbols of two major world religions.

Why speak of Islam as a challenge?

The word 'challenge' appears in the sub-title of this book. It is a popular word which we use in sport, politics and many other areas of life. It conveys the feeling that we are being invited to a contest or a duel. We cannot remain neutral and are forced to react in one way or another, since ignoring or refusing the challenge amounts to surrender, and making an inadequate response means certain defeat.

Christians who live in predominantly Islamic societies, such as the Copts in Egypt, tend to have all the fears of a minority community, and feel themselves to be at best tolerated and at worst persecuted. Since in many cases they have lived in this kind of situation for centuries, they have worked out ways of adapting, which often involve having as little close contact with Muslims as possible. Their concern is not so much with the growth of the church as with its survival, and the religion of Islam is perceived as a threat to their very existence.

Christian expatriates working in the Gulf and Saudi Arabia come face to face with Islam in every area of their life and work. They cannot fail to see how Islam is practised all around them and how it is presented for their benefit on television. They are only too aware that the authorities want them to gain greater sympathy for Islam, even if they do not actually become Muslims.

Christians in the western world, who are gradually becoming aware of the growing Muslim communities in their inner cities and the increasing number of mosques, can easily feel threatened by what they see as an alien religion. They cannot avoid asking fundamental questions about the uniqueness of the Christian faith, and wondering if Islam is set to win the world.

Many of these Christians would feel that the word 'challenge' is entirely appropriate, while others would feel that it is too weak, and prefer the word 'threat'. This latter group find it hard to agree with other Christians who adopt a 'live and let live' attitude to other faiths, or who think simply in terms of 'mutual sharing' between Muslims and Christians. They believe that Islam has its own clear agenda, and that in one way or another it continues to throw down the gauntlet to the Christian world.

How is the challenge perceived?

If we are thinking simply in terms of *numbers*, the feeling is that 'Islam is growing and spreading'. We know that Islam has been a missionary religion ever since the time when the Prophet Muhammad brought the tribes of Arabia into the house of Islam. We have heard of the glories of the Islamic civilization. Islam is very obviously here to stay, and it seems incredible to us today that as recently as 1916 Samuel Zwemer, an American missionary in the Middle East, could write a popular book entitled *The Disintegration of Islam*. Muslims claim that Islam is the fastest-growing religion in the world, with about 1,000 million adherents, and that it is now poised for the conversion of Europe and North America. Here, then, in what is said to be a pluralist world, we have a missionary religion which would like to convert the world; and while the Christian church seems to be contracting in the West, Islam seems to be expanding.

If we are thinking in terms of *culture*, the typical reaction of Christians is that 'Muslims are different; their culture is alien to us'. When westerners think of Muslims, they tend to think of Arabs, Asians, Africans or Turks rather than of white Europeans or Americans. When Muslims keep their wives in purdah, want their children to go to Muslim schools, or insist on halal meat, they seem to be foreigners trying to maintain their own kind of culture and society in 'our' country. The smells of their cooking and the way they dress make us feel that we are dealing with a totally different culture. They do not seem to follow the saying, 'When in Rome, do as the Romans do.'

When we come to think of *politics and economics*, the feeling seems to be that 'Islam wants to conquer the world'. Since Muhammad regarded himself as both prophet and statesman, his followers have always believed that 'Islam must rule'. The assumption was that the territory occupied by Islam (*dar al-Islam*) would eventually overcome and absorb the territories as yet outside the control of Islam (*dar al-harb*). Within a hundred years of his death, the Islamic Empire had spread as far as Spain in the West and China in the East. If Charles Martel had not stopped their advance at the Battle of Tours in AD 732, they might have conquered the whole of Europe. In 1453 the Muslim armies captured Constantinople, and in 1683 they were battering on the gates of Vienna.

Coming nearer to our own time, we think of Idi Amin attempting to turn Uganda into an Islamic country, or of the Ayatollah Khomeini wanting to export the Islamic revolution to other Islamic countries from Iran. We can never forget the way the Arab world used its oil as a political weapon in 1973, and we are aware of many countries in which Muslims are working to establish an Islamic state. And don't some of them even say that they want Britain to be an Islamic state? When we're told that 'the Arabs are buying up the whole of London', and hear rumours that 'Arab hotel-owners are throwing the Gideon Bibles into the dustbin', it is understandable that all the alarm bells start ringing in our minds, and we begin to imagine the worst: 'The Muslims are coming!' If we are no longer afraid of 'Reds under the beds', we begin to think that the Muslim world has taken over from the Communist world as *the* major threat to the western world.

If we are thinking of *the intellectual and theological* challenge of Islam, we can sum it up in the words, 'Here is a religion that offers an alternative to Christianity and humanism.' Islam seems to be saying to the Christian world, 'You've got it all wrong about Jesus! Your Trinity of three persons in one God is impossible to understand, let alone explain. Islam is a simple creed without any dogmas, and this belief in one Creator God includes all that had previously been revealed in Judaism and Christianity. It leads to a unified worldview which embraces every aspect of life, and can draw people of all races together without discrimination.'

When these four perceptions are put together, the word 'challenge' can seem more than justified. But before we get carried away by such feelings, it may be wise to look more critically at this kind of language, asking what it may be doing to us.

Is 'challenge' the right word?

We need to acknowledge, in the first place, that the word 'challenge' is grossly overworked. We are in danger of being numbed into a state of apathy and indifference because of all the issues that confront us. We cannot possibly face all these 'challenges' at the same time; so why bother with any of them?

Secondly, many Muslims would say that Islam is *not* wanting to challenge anyone – least of all the Christian world. They would quote the verse from the Qur'an which says, 'There is no compulsion in religion' (2:256), and point out that the word used by Muslims to describe their missionary activities is *da'wa*, a word which simply means 'calling' or 'invitation'. While they recognize that there are Muslim missionaries working all over the world, they would say that most of them are working among Muslims. The vast majority of ordinary Muslims simply want to keep their own community together, and are not trying to convert people of other faiths to Islam. We may or may not agree with such a generous interpretation of the intentions of Islam; but we do need to be willing to hear the many different voices within the Muslim community.

Thirdly, the language of 'challenge' can easily become provocative and sensational. So, for example, we speak of the 'clash of the Titans' to describe the encounter between Christianity and Islam in Africa. This language tends to harden the 'them/us' division; it also implies that it is always the Muslims who are challenging us, the Christians. As Christians we are therefore made to feel like the young, defenceless David, faced by the Goliath of Islam.

As a result of this process, we begin to think that if this is how Islam is challenging the Christian world, we must respond in the same terms. We therefore use statistics to prove that Muslims do not outnumber Christians; we present Christianity as a superior culture; we think that we must use political weapons to resist the spread of Islam; and we argue back, trying to prove that Christianity is more reasonable than Islam.

Should we therefore hesitate to speak about 'the challenge of Islam', or abandon this kind of language altogether? Each of us will have to answer this question for himself or herself. But one reason for using the word 'challenge' in the sub-title and for starting at this point is that this is how many Christians in Europe and North America perceive Islam.

This book will show that Islam puts very real questions to us as Christians which we *have* to answer. But as we do so, we ought to realize that there may be more than one way of answering these questions and responding to this faith and to the people who live by it.

What is involved in a Christian response to Islam?

Each of the five parts of this book deals with a vital element in a genuinely Christian response to Islam.

Part 1, 'Knowing our Muslim Neighbours', focuses on the way we relate to Muslims. We begin at this point because relating to people is more important than acquiring information or mastering new ideas. This means appreciating Islamic culture and reflecting on some of the difficulties that we experience in our relationships with Muslims. Many of the examples used relate to situations in the western world. One chapter here, however, looks at a wide variety of situations all over the world in which Christians live alongside Muslims.

Part 2, 'Understanding Islam', covers basic Islamic beliefs, the practice of Islam, the life of Muhammad and the Qur'an. The study of Islam cannot stop at this point in time, however, and we need to take note of developments in Islam since the beginning up to the present day. In all this we are not simply trying to absorb facts and information. Our aim is to try to understand Islam 'from within' as far as possible. We want to put ourselves into the shoes of Muslims, and learn to sit where they sit.

Part 3, 'Entering into Discussion and Dialogue', deals with some of the main issues that tend to come up in discussions between Muslims and Christians. Some of these are very practical (such as 'Why do you eat pork?'), while others are more theological (for instance, 'Why do you believe in the Trinity?'). Another group of questions is related to political and social issues (such as 'Why do Christians tend to support the state of Israel?'). We need to work out how to respond to these questions and objections, and think of what we should be aiming at in our discussions with Muslims.

Part 4, 'Facing Fundamental Issues', begins by considering some of the difficult theological questions which come to the surface sooner or later when Christians start engaging with Muslims and Islam (for instance, 'Is the God of Islam the same as the God of Christianity?'), and looks at some of the most fundamental differences between the Christian faith and Islam. One chapter explores what is involved in thinking biblically about Islam. Two further sensitive issues are the cost of conversion and the political challenge of Islam.

Part 5, 'Sharing our Faith', attempts to get beyond the stage of argument and to concentrate on Christian witness. How can we share our faith in Jesus as the most complete revelation of the one true God? We look at one example of a situation in everyday life, and at ways of responding to aspects of 'folk Islam'. We then turn to three different examples of how the Christian Scriptures can be used with Muslims. In the next chapter, three themes that are important for both faiths are studied first in the Qur'an and then in the Bible. This part ends with an agenda that Christians, as individuals and as groups, may need to work through in their relations with Muslims and their response to Islam.

In the Conclusion we reflect on what it may mean for us as Christians to be walking the way of the cross in responding to the challenge of Islam.

Notes

■ The material is designed for both individual and group study.

■ Some of the material in certain chapters (especially in Parts 1 and 2) is in note form.

■ In several chapters (especially in Part 2) there is a section entitled 'For further study'. This often includes examples of texts that can be studied.

■ Bibliographies are given at the end of each of the five parts under the heading 'Resources for further study'.

■ The main translation of the Qur'an used is *The Meaning of the Glorious Koran: An Explanatory Translation* by Mohammed Marmaduke Pickthall (Mentor, New American Library). References in the Qur'an are given as follows: 4:3 means *sura* 4, verse 3.

■ Arabic words and other Islamic technical terms are given with widely accepted English spelling, but without the diacritical points often used for greater accuracy (*e.g.* Qur'an rather than Qur'ān). Quotations from other sources may use slightly different transliterations.

Part 1

Relating to our Muslim neighbours

If we are to make any progress in dialogue with Muslims we must first of all get inside the world of Islam and make ourselves welcome as guests and friends . . . There is also a need for some of us to get inside the Muslim world and meet Muslims on their own territory where they are most at home, and, perhaps, most truly themselves.

Roger Hooker[1]

I am not reaping the harvest; I can scarcely claim to be sowing the seed; I am hardly ploughing the soil; but I am gathering out the stones.

Robert Bruce, nineteenth-century missionary to Persia[2]

The emphasis in Part 1 is on the relationships of Christians with Muslims. Before asking what Muslims believe or how they practise their faith, we think about how we relate to them as people and as neighbours in the different situations in which we find ourselves anywhere in the world.

1

Meeting face to face

1.1 'Hello! How are you?'

This was the short answer of a speaker to the student who asked: 'How should I approach a Muslim?' No doubt the questioner had a particular idea in his mind of what Muslims are like, and expected that he had to learn some special techniques which would enable him to communicate with Muslims.

The simple answer sums up the basic point that we approach Muslims as human beings. We meet them as people before we meet them as Muslims. We greet them as individuals with a name before we think of them as representatives of a great world religion. We extend the hand of friendship as neighbours before we self-consciously announce that we are Christians. Perhaps it is a sad reflection on our culture and on the state of the western Christian world that something as obvious as this needs to be said! But unless it is understood and put into practice, all our study of Islam and all the talk about sharing our faith with Muslims are worthless.

1.2 Starting where we are

If we are in contact with Muslims at the present time, we may need to take stock of our situation and think how we can build on the relationships that we already have. Whom do we know? What is the context in which we meet? How well do we know each other? What kind of relationships are they – do we know each other as neighbours, colleagues at work, teachers, students, or casual acquaintances?

If we do not already have any natural contact with Muslims in our own situation, we may need to ask ourselves some questions. Are there any situations where we could get to know any Muslims in a natural way – talking with other parents at the school gates, or chatting with colleagues at work, or being involved in some kind of social work in the community, for example? The great advantage of relationships of this kind is that they can be utterly natural; there need not be anything forced or artificial about them.

If we have no contacts of this kind in our different situations, are there ways in which we can take the initiative and go out to meet Muslims – for instance, by visiting a mosque or a Muslim bookshop, by talking to a Muslim shopkeeper, or by inviting a Muslim student to our home? If we do decide to take initiatives like these, we need to be aware of our motives in doing so. Is it pure curiosity? Are we wanting to be good neighbours? Are we wanting to 'share the gospel' with them? All of these motives can be good and appropriate in their own way. But it can be valuable for us to put our motives into words and discuss them with others.

1.3 The secret of real dialogue

Assuming, then, that we have some kind of relationship with Muslims in our society, that we are getting to know them *as people*, are we aiming at anything more?

Luke's description of Jesus in the temple at the age of twelve gives us a picture of what is involved in any genuine dialogue that gets beneath the surface. His parents find him 'sitting among the teachers, listening to them and asking them questions; and all who heard him were amazed at his understanding and his answers' (Luke 2:46–47, RSV). It is obvious that the situation of Jesus relating in this way to the religious leaders of Judaism is not exactly comparable to that of Christians in any country relating to their Muslim neighbours. But the value of Luke's brief picture is that it shows us what is involved in *any* meeting of minds when people are exploring each other's faith.

Jesus would have learned his faith in the home and the synagogue. But now he is in the capital city, and talking to some of the religious leaders of Judaism. He is *sitting among them* and *listening* to what they are teaching. He genuinely wants to know what they think, and how they teach the faith of their fathers. When he *asks questions*, it is not to trip them up and embarrass them, but to draw them out into real dialogue. What impresses the observers about Jesus is that he seems to have *understanding* (as distinct from intelligence or knowledge), and is able to grasp the important issues. When he offers *answers*, therefore, it is in response to actual questions which people are asking.

What would it mean to see this as a model for dialogue between Christians and Muslims? 'Sitting among them' might mean visiting Muslims in their homes, or spending time with them socially. For a student in a university or college it might mean plucking up courage to attend meetings of the Islamic Society and getting to know Muslim students. For Christians who have grown up as members of a minority community in a Muslim country overseas, it might mean working through their fears and trying to relax a little more in the company of Muslims.

'Listening' could mean listening to Muslim neighbours and friends, not just to find out about their faith, but to get to know and understand them as people. In some cases it could mean reading a magazine, a tract or a book offered by a Muslim friend, going to a Muslim bookshop, or watching a video about Islam in a Muslim home. 'Asking questions' may at first produce very basic and elementary answers. But as we continue to probe gently, it should become obvious that we are not trying to score points, but doing all we can to see the world as Muslims see it.

If this kind of deeper exchange is going to be fruitful, we will need that understanding which enables us to discern the most important issues. And if we reach the stage of being able to offer any answers, they will then be answering genuine questions in the minds of Muslims, and not simply the questions which *we* think they ought to be asking.

1.4 Greetings

The problem for most of us is that we find it hard to break the ice, and, for reasons which are perfectly understandable, we are reluctant to cross barriers of language, culture and religion.

Muslims all over the world, whatever their mother tongue, are taught the following Arabic greeting: one person says *'assalamu 'alaikum'* ('Peace be upon you'), and the other replies *'wa'alaikum assalam'* ('And upon you be peace'). Is there any reason why we should not learn the greeting, whatever country we are living in, and use it to greet any Muslims we meet? Some may not be pleased to hear Christians using a greeting which is generally thought to be a greeting for fellow Muslims. But others will be pleasantly surprised to be greeted in this way by non-Muslims, and delighted to feel that we have taken the trouble to learn something which is part of their religion and their culture. And it could be even more significant for ourselves if we discover that greetings are more than a mere formality, because they convey something about our whole attitude to the other person.

1.5 Visiting

Most westerners think of their homes as a place to which to retreat for privacy, and feel they are intruding if they call on someone without an invitation. This is not, however, the mentality of the East and most of the Muslim world. An Egyptian sums up the way most easterners think about the custom of visiting in this way: 'In this country, and throughout the East, you honour people more by visiting them in their homes than by inviting them to yours.'

In this respect it is probably true to say that it is we in the West who are out of step with the rest of the world. Throughout the East, in Africa and in Latin America, hospitality is regarded almost as a sacred duty. If someone visits me in my home, I must drop whatever I am doing, however urgent I think it is, because welcoming and entertaining my guests has priority over every other obligation. I will offer them something to drink and perhaps even something to eat, and they will have to think twice before refusing what I offer.

What might this mean in practice in relating to Muslims? It may mean that I need to put to one side western ideas of etiquette. So if I meet a Muslim and want to get to know him or her better, it might be natural to say, 'Can I visit you in your home?' rather than 'Will you come to mine?'

Once we have taken the plunge and begun to feel relaxed and comfortable in their homes, it will be natural to think of other occasions when visits would be appropriate. What about visiting them, for example, during one of their feasts? And why not visit after the birth of a child, when someone has returned from a journey, or when there is a wedding or a bereavement?

Another way to meet Muslims is to visit a mosque. With some mosques it is wise to make an appointment before you go. But in most mosques in the West this is not necessary, and one can simply turn up at almost any time. (See chapter 4.)

If we want to work out in advance where it is all going to lead, the chances are that there is still something wrong in our own attitudes. In the teaching of Jesus, the command to love our neighbours is prior to the command to go out and make disciples of all the nations. It makes little sense to calculate how we are going to share the gospel with our Muslim neighbours if we have not begun to know them, love them and care for them as our neighbours. There needs to be genuine meeting between people.

But how does this emphasis on relationships work out in practice? The following three quotations come from entirely different situations and illustrate different kinds of response to initiatives in friendship.

In the first, Roger Hooker describes an important breakthrough in his attempts to get to know his Muslim neighbours while he was working in India:

> When we came to live in Bareilly in October 1968 I determined to make contact with the Muslim community, which was obviously a large one. But how to set about it? In Agra I had once paid a visit to the Jama Masjid, but had been asked to leave after about 10 minutes. In Allahabad I had asked a *durzi* if I could visit his mosque to watch the worship, but this was not allowed. Soon after we got to Bareilly I wrote to the principal of the local Muslim college to ask if I could see round his institution, but I got no reply. One afternoon in February 1969, in sheer desperation, I went for a walk in the old city and climbed the steps of the first mosque I came to. I asked if I could see the *maulana*. After some time he appeared and asked me what I wanted. I said that I wanted to see round his mosque. He showed me round but of course there was not very much to see, so he invited me to sit down and have a cup of tea. We chatted for about half an hour. He asked me who I was and what I was doing in India. I told him I was a missionary. He said that he, too, had wanted to be a missionary in Africa but his parents wouldn't let him go. We also discovered that we each had a son of the same age and that our respective wives were expecting a second child. As I went down the mosque steps he asked me to come again.

For me this was one of the most thrilling moments I had known since arriving in India four years before. At last I had managed to penetrate into the house of Islam, and had met a Muslim as a fellow human being.[1]

The second comes from a Muslim who had been welcoming groups of Christian students to his mosque in a British city over a period of years. At the end of a helpful time of questions and discussion, someone said to him: 'Would you and any of your community be interested in visiting a church or coming to our college to hear how we understand our faith?' The answer was polite but clear:

> There are too few of us looking after our own community, and we don't really have the time to meet with people of other faiths. What's more, it might be confusing for any Muslims who are not sure of their faith. But for those of us who are sure about our faith, there's nothing we can learn from Christians, because it's all there in the Qur'an. We've got it all in Islam.

The third is from an Arabic-speaking Christian from the Middle East living and working in another country in the region, who describes his experience of mixing with his friends and colleagues during the month of Ramadan:

> The month of Ramadan has just finished. Particularly on this occasion I am having first-class contact with Islam and its practices. The legalism, the Judaism, salvation by works and hypocrisy is [sic] just killing. Being invited to so many dinners I eat so much during this month, but also suffer so much spiritually. I find myself completely helpless being evangelized rather than evangelizing. It is a faith so much rooted in the hearts of people. Anything else contradicting their Book is false because God has actually and verbally spoken.

This person had moved beyond the one-off and superficial contacts, and had begun to get beneath the surface. He had also discovered that there is nothing romantic in dialogue at this deeper level, and had begun to experience some of the pain involved in relating face to face.

2

Appreciating Islamic culture

2.1 What do we mean by 'culture'?

Here are five different attempts to define what is meant by this important word 'culture':

The way we do things here.[1]

Culture is to a society what personality is to an individual.[2]

Culture is a *way of life*; culture is the *total* plan for living; it is functionally organized into a system; it is *acquired through learning*; it is the way of life of a *social group*, not of an individual as such.[3]

Culture is an integrated system of beliefs (about God or reality or ultimate meaning), of values (about what is true, good, beautiful and normative), of customs (how to behave, relate to others, talk, pray, dress, work, play, trade, farm, eat, etc.), and of institutions which express these beliefs, values and customs (government, law courts, temples or churches, family, schools, hospitals, factories, shops, unions, clubs, etc.), which binds a society together and gives it a sense of identity, dignity, security, and continuity.[4]

When we speak of culture in its broadest sense, we are speaking about the sum total of ways of living which shape (and are also shaped by) the continuing life of a group of human beings from generation to generation. We are speaking about the language which enables them to grasp, conceptualize, and communicate the reality of their world; about law, custom, and forms of social organization, including marriage, family, and nation; we are talking also about art, science, technology, and agriculture. These things shape the life of each member of the society. They are also shaped, modified, and developed from generation to generation by the members of the society. From the point of view of the individual member they are given as part of the tradition into which he is born and socialized. But they are not changeless absolutes.[5]

2.2 Why think about culture?

It may seem strange to raise this subject so near the beginning. Why put culture before creed? There are four basic reasons why it may be more helpful to consider how Muslims live before we study what they believe.

1. We want to relate to Muslims as people, as individuals, as families and as communities, rather than as representatives of the religion of Islam. Concentrating too much on doctrines and beliefs can easily create barriers and make it harder for us to accept them as people. Developing cultural sensitivity is an important part of our obedience to the commandment 'Love your neighbour as yourself'.

2. Since culture and creed are so interwoven in Islam, an awareness of the culture can provide us with a helpful way into the study of doctrine and beliefs.

3. Looking at the culture of Muslims ought to make us aware of our own cultural bias. We may find that some of the things that we find difficult in Islam have more to do with culture than with religion. If their culture looks strange to us, we can be quite certain that *our* culture looks strange to *them*!

4. When we come to think about communicating the basic Christian message to Muslims, we will need to be aware of the vitally important distinction between the gospel and culture. What we think of as 'the Christian way of life' may owe more to our culture than it does to the gospel. We must avoid giving the impression that conversion to Christ means rejecting everything in Islamic culture and adapting to a foreign culture (see chapter 30, 'Counting the Cost of Conversion').

2.3 How can we begin to appreciate their culture?

One way is to allow Muslims to explain their culture in their own words. Here, therefore, is an outline of the Muslim way of life as described by a Muslim for non-Muslims, taken from *Islam: A Brief Guide*.

Festivals

These celebrations are observed to seek the pleasure of Allah. There is no concept of a festival for pleasure's own sake in Islam; but there are occasions of joy and happiness. The happiest occasion of a Muslim's life is to see the laws of Allah established in their totality on the earth. *Idul Fitr* and *Idul Adha* are the two major festivals in Islam.

IDUL FITR is observed on the first day after the month of Ramadan. On this day, after a month of fasting, Muslims express their joy and happiness by offering a congregational prayer, preferably in an open field. They express their gratitude to Allah for enabling them to observe the fast. Special food is prepared, and it is customary to visit friends and relatives and to give presents to children to make the occasion lively and special for them.

IDUL ADHA begins on the 10th day of the month of *Dhul Hijjah* and continues until the 12th. This celebration is observed to commemorate the willing-ness of Abraham when he was asked to sacrifice his own son, Ishmael. Abraham showed his readiness and Allah was very pleased. A lamb was sacrificed instead of Ishmael on Allah's command. Muslims offer congregational prayer on the day, and afterwards they sacrifice animals such as sheep, goats, cows and camels to seek the pleasure of Allah. The meat of the sacrificed animal is shared amongst relatives, neigh-bours and the poor.

Some other occasions to remember include the beginning of the **Hijrah** (migration of the Prophet), **Lailatul Miraj** (Night of the Ascension) and dates of Islamic battles fought by Muhammad (pbuh). There is a night of special significance in Ramadan known as **Lailatul Qadr** (Night of Power). It occurs in one of the odd numbered nights of the last ten days of the month of Ramadan. The Qur'an mentions it as a night 'better than a thousand months'.

Islamic festivals are observed according to the Islamic Calendar, which is based on lunar months. The lunar year is about 10 days shorter than the solar year. Festival dates are determined by the appearance of the moon.

Marriage and family life

Marriage is the basis of family life in Islam. It is a solemn and yet simple contract between a man and woman. Muslim marriages are generally arranged by parents, but must be with the consent of the son and daughter, as required by Islamic law (*Shari'ah*). Marriages are performed in a simple ceremony in the presence of relatives, friends and neighbours.

Islam does not allow free mixing of men and women; nor does it allow sex before marriage. Extra-marital sex is severely punished. No discrimination is made on the basis of sex. Husband and wife are equal partners of the family and play their part in their respective fields. Divorce is permitted but is regarded as the action most displeasing to Allah.

Diet

Muslims are encouraged in the Qur'an to eat what is good and wholesome for them, and are specifically forbidden to eat certain foods. A Muslim is not allowed to eat:

- animals which died of natural causes or of a disease;
- animals slaughtered without invoking the name of Allah;
- animals strangled to death;

24

- pigs;
- carnivorous animals;
- animals devoured by wild beasts;
- the blood of animals.

Fish and vegetables are permitted. Islamic law requires an animal to be slaughtered by a sharp knife penetrating the inner part of the animal's neck, to allow maximum drainage of blood. Invoking the name of Allah is obligatory at the time of slaughter. All varieties of alcoholic drinks, such as beer, wines and spirits are prohibited. These rules aim at rooting out the evil effects of food and drink in society.

Dress

Muslims must cover their bodies properly and decently. No particular dress is recommended. Outlines for guidance include:

- For men, covering from the navel to the knees is a must.
- For women, covering the whole body except the face and hands is compulsory, and according to some jurists women above the age of puberty should cover the face when going out or meeting strangers. A woman must not wear a dress which arouses man's base feelings, e.g. transparent, skin-tight or half-naked dress.
- Pure silk and gold are not allowed for men.
- Prohibition of women's clothes for men and vice versa.
- Symbolic dress from other religions is not allowed.

Simplicity and modesty are encouraged. Dress expressing arrogance is disliked. The style of dress depends on local customs and climate.

Social manners

Islam teaches decency, humility and good manners. A Muslim greets another Muslim by saying:

As-salamu 'Alaikum (peace be upon you)

and the reply is:

Wa'alaikumus salam (peace be on you too).

Keeping promises, truthfulness, justice, fair play, helping the poor and needy, respect for parents, teachers and elders, love for children and good relations with neighbours are the most valued virtues of a Muslim. Islam condemns enmity, back-biting, slander, blasphemy, ridicule, use of offensive names, suspicion and arrogance. Muslims must not adopt these bad habits.[6]

Notes

Allah is the ordinary Arabic word for 'God'. It is not associated exclusively with Islam, since it is the word for 'God' used by up to fourteen million Arabic-speaking Christians all over the Middle East. When Muslims are speaking English they generally prefer to speak of 'Allah' rather than 'God'. This is partly because it is important for them that the revelation given by God in the Qur'an was in Arabic, and partly because they are afraid of the possible confusion between the one true God and concepts of God or gods in other religions.

Idul Fitr is the Feast or Festival of Fitr. The word *Id* is used for all the main feasts in the Muslim year.

Ishmael: Muslims believe that Ishmael was the son whom Abraham was prepared to sacrifice. The story is found in the Qur'an (37:83–113). It is important to note, however, that the Qur'an does not explicitly say that the son concerned was Ishmael. For some centuries there was a debate among Muslim scholars, some saying it was Isaac and others that it was Ishmael, and it wasn't until some centuries later that it became a fixed belief among Muslims that it was Ishmael.

The Hijra is the Migration of the Prophet, *i.e.* his migration from

Mecca to Medina in AD 622. This is regarded as the most significant event in the life of the Prophet (apart from his receiving of the Qur'an), and years in the Islamic calendar are all dated from this central event (*e.g.* 1994 is the years 1414/1415 AH, *i.e. Anno Hegirae*).

Lailatul Miraj (Night of Ascension) is referred to in the Qur'an (17:1). Some Muslims believe that the Prophet was taken physically from Mecca to Jerusalem and from there taken up to heaven by night, while others believe that it was simply a mystical or spiritual experience like that described by Paul in 2 Corinthians 12:1–4.

Pbuh stands for 'Peace be upon him'. Muslims show their respect for all the prophets by using this expression whenever they mention their names.

Festivals. Since the dates of festivals are based on the lunar year, they occur approximately eleven days earlier each year. So, for example, the approximate dates of the two main feasts are as follows:

1995	2 March	10 May
1996	20 February	29 April
1997	9 February	18 April
1998	29 January	7 April
1999	18 January	27 March
2000	7 January	16 March

Questions: We may well want to ask Muslims to explain these beliefs and traditions more fully. If we ask, for example, what is the basis for them, we will find that in some cases they are based on the teaching of the Qur'an (*e.g.* the prohibition of pork in 5:3). In others they are based on the teaching or the example of the Prophet (*e.g.* according to Muslim tradition Muhammad did not wear silk, and forbade Muslim men to wear silk).

2.4 What is special about Islamic culture?

Some of the aspects of the culture of Islamic communities which are most obvious to people in the West can be listed as follows:

1. The 'family' means the extended family rather than the

nuclear family. Children are bound to respect and obey their parents and elders.

2. People are more aware of their obligations to their family and their society than of their rights as individuals. Personal interests and personal views and opinions should be subordinate to those of the group. Religion has to do more with the community than with the individual.

3. Great respect is shown to old people and to any who are older than oneself.

4. 'Honour' is a very important concept, especially the honour of the family and the whole community. The word used in Urdu is *izzat*.

5. Hospitality is an almost sacred obligation. It is so important that one should never normally turn a visitor away.

6. Education tends to rely more on rote learning than it does in the West. Acquiring knowledge is more important than thinking independently or questioning other people's opinions.

7. God is concerned about the whole of life – not just about the 'religious' parts of life. There should be no distinction between areas of life that are 'secular' and areas that are 'sacred'.

It needs to be recognized, however, that *none* of these attitudes and customs is *exclusively* Islamic. They are regarded as part of the Muslim way of life and are undergirded by Islamic moral teaching (*e.g.* about respect for parents, hospitality, *etc.*). But several of them are part of the culture of Africa and of the East – in other words of *most* of the world except the West. There are many Christians living in Islamic societies, therefore, whose way of life is very similar to that of their Muslim neighbours in these respects. This means that these cultural differences have little or nothing to do with the religion of Islam.

Other aspects of Islamic culture, however, are very clearly based on the teaching of Islam. Some are based directly on the teaching of the Qur'an:

■ The prohibition of eating the blood of an animal and certain kinds of animals (2:168; 2:173; 5:3; 6:145; 16:115).

- The prohibition of alcohol (5:90–91).
- The possibility of marrying up to four wives (4:3).

Others are based on the example of the Prophet:

- The Prophet Muhammad instructed his followers to eat with the right hand and to wash their hands before meals.
- The Prophet did not allow men to wear silk or clothes decorated with gold. (See further chapter 12, 'Tradition'.)

Others are based on Islamic tradition:

- Muslims should begin their meals by saying the Arabic words *Bismillahi rrahman irrahim* ('In the name of God, the most Merciful and the most Kind'); and end by saying, *Al hamdu lillahi ladhi at'amana wa saqana wa ja'alana minal muslimin* ('All praise be to God who gave us to eat and to drink and made us Muslims').
- Dogs are regarded as unclean and are not normally kept as household pets.

We need therefore to be careful about any generalization about 'Islamic culture'. Some of the dangers in making sweeping statements about 'Islamic culture' and 'Islamic society' are pointed out by Albert Hourani:

> There is no such thing as 'Islamic society'; there are societies partly moulded by Islam, but formed also by their position in the physical world, their inherited language and culture, their economic possibilities and the accidents of their political history. Before Islam was, they existed, and if Islam has shaped them, they also have shaped it, each in a different way.[7]

2.5 What do they think about *our* culture?

Another way of appreciating their culture is to try to understand what they feel about *our* culture. While recognizing the danger of relying on stereotypes, we might say that the following are examples of the kind of general comments that Muslims (as well as people of other faiths) often make about western culture:

1. *'Your families in the West are all broken up and fragmented. You think of yourselves as individuals, and are concerned about your own happiness and fulfilment. You emphasize the nuclear family, while we think of the extended family.'* This is not a peculiarly Islamic view, since most cultures, except in the western world, have the same ideas about the family.

2. *'You don't show enough respect for old people. In our religion and our culture, we are taught to show respect for anyone who is older than ourselves. We can't understand, for example, how you shut your old people away in old people's homes.'* Here again we are dealing with an attitude that is strongly supported by Islam, but is not exclusively Muslim. Westerners probably need to be deeply challenged by observations and criticisms of this kind!

3. *'We don't agree with free mixing between the sexes. We prefer Muslim girls to go to single-sex schools, and we don't allow our teenage daughters to go to discos, or at least we strongly discourage them from doing so.'* Many Muslims take this view because they want their young people to marry within their own community, and because they want to protect them from harmful influences in the society around them. Not all Muslim families in the West, however, are as strict in their attitudes, and some allow their children considerable freedom.

4. *'We don't like the kind of moral standards that we see on TV and in videos. We are shocked by all the sex, the violence and the blasphemous language.'* This reaction is similar to the reaction of many Christians. In some cases Muslims go further than some Christians, and refuse to watch any films or TV, because they believe that the Qur'an's prohibition of idols extends to the representation of the human form both in art and in films.

In some of these examples we have seen that these reactions have little or nothing to do with Islam, but are common to people of all faiths in the East. The deeper problem in understanding Muslim reactions to other cultures is that they focus on the culture of the society *as a whole*, and find it hard to distinguish between that and the lifestyle of committed Christians.

2.6 Some basic do's and don'ts

The following are basic guidelines which may be of help to any who have little or no experience of meeting with Muslims or with people from an eastern culture. Here again, however, we need to enter a strong word of caution, since not all of these points are relevant for *all* Muslims or *all* Asians. We will need to be guided by people who have more experience than ourselves in relating to the Muslim community in our area.

■ Men should not visit women in their homes when they are alone, or be alone with women in other situations.

■ Men should not be surprised if the women in the family retire to a back room and do not sit with the men of the family and other guests in the front room.

■ A man should not try to look a woman in the eye.

■ A man should not shake the hand of a Muslim woman unless she takes the initiative by holding out her hand.

■ You should not receive a present or eat with your left hand, since the left hand is associated with functions that are regarded as unclean.

■ You should not sit with your legs folded if you are in the presence of an older person.

■ If you are sitting on the floor, you should not sit with the soles of your feet facing another person.

■ You should show respect for any copy of the Qur'an *and* of the Bible. It should not, for example, be left lying on the floor or under a pile of other books. Muslims show respect for the Qur'an and often keep it wrapped in a special cloth. They are also supposed to go through the ritual of washing before opening the Qur'an. They are therefore surprised and shocked when they see how Christians often treat their holy book.

■ It is best not to admire anything in a person's home too much, or to admire someone's child. In the minds of people of some cultures this can be regarded as a kind of coveting and associated with the 'evil eye'.

■ If you are entertaining Muslims in your home, you will obviously never offer them pork or alcohol. Strict Muslims will eat only meat that is halal, that is, killed by a Muslim with the proper ritual and using the name of Allah. There need be no embarrassment about asking them if they prefer to have a vegetarian meal.

■ If Muslims offer you meat in their home, there is no reason why you as a Christian should refuse to eat it. Most Christians would say that Paul's teaching about food offered to idols (1 Corinthians 8) is not relevant at all to this situation.

2.7 What is the relationship between culture and worldview in Islam?

The five circles in the diagram on the next page represent five major elements in the culture and worldview of Islam.

Basic realities

Every worldview has its own way of describing 'the way things are' in the universe, and this is how Muslims might describe these areas:

God/gods: For Islam the spiritual, unseen, supernatural world is very real. There is only one God, and there is no room for any lesser gods or goddesses. But there are also spirits and powers of different kinds – both good and evil.

Nature: Since Muslims have a strong belief in creation, their way of looking at the world is very close to that of Jews and Christians.

Humanity: Islam, like Judaism and Christianity, sees human beings as created by God and responsible to him.

Time: Here again Islam is like Judaism and Christianity in that it has a linear or historical view of time, and thinks of history as working towards an end.

Loyalties and values

These are some of the most basic convictions which express what is of greatest importance for Muslims and ultimately determine fundamental values:

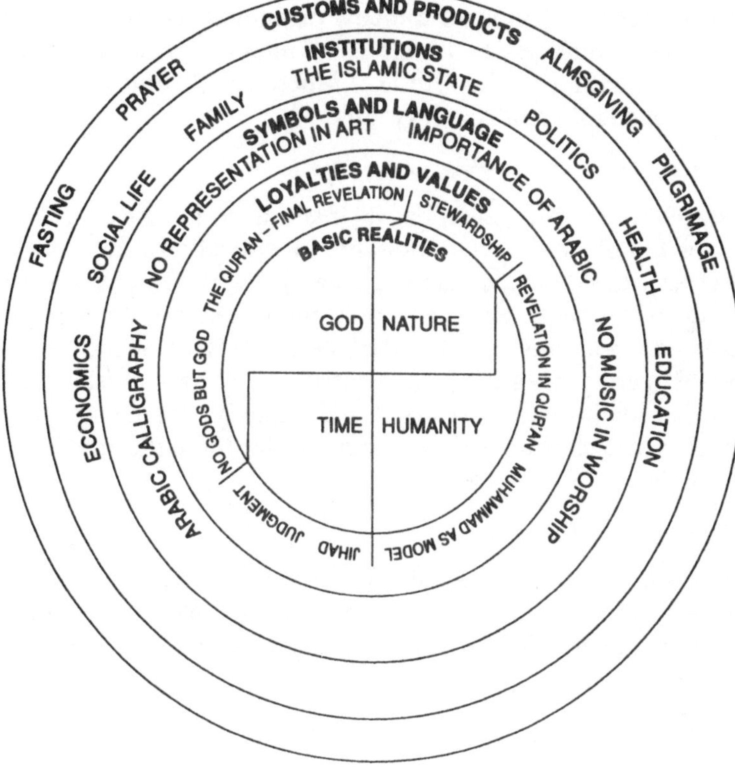
CUSTOMS AND PRODUCTS
PRAYER
ALMSGIVING
FASTING
PILGRIMAGE
INSTITUTIONS
THE ISLAMIC STATE
FAMILY
POLITICS
SOCIAL LIFE
HEALTH
ECONOMICS
EDUCATION
SYMBOLS AND LANGUAGE
NO REPRESENTATION IN ART
IMPORTANCE OF ARABIC
ARABIC CALLIGRAPHY
NO MUSIC IN WORSHIP
LOYALTIES AND VALUES
THE QUR'AN - FINAL REVELATION
STEWARDSHIP
NO GODS BUT GOD
REVELATION IN QUR'AN
MUHAMMAD AS MODEL
JUDGMENT
JIHAD
BASIC REALITIES
GOD
NATURE
TIME
HUMANITY

'There is no god but God: Muhammad is the apostle of God. The Qur'an is the final revelation of the will of God.'

'We are stewards of the natural world, and responsible to God for the way we care for it.'

'God's will for humanity is revealed in the Qur'an; and Muhammad provides us with a model for humanity to follow.'

'Every human being will appear before God on the day of judgment. Muslims must work and struggle (in *jihad*) for the extension of the rule of God in the world.'

Symbols and language

Here we see how the Muslim understanding of basic realities, loyalties and values is expressed in symbols and language. In this context, therefore, we note the importance of the fact that the Qur'an was revealed in the Arabic language. This is why Muslims are required to say the prescribed prayers in Arabic. No artistic representation of humans or animals is allowed (except by Shi'ite Muslims); and no music is allowed in worship (except in the chanting of the Qur'an). Much artistic energy has been channelled into Arabic calligraphy.

Institutions

Like every culture, Islam has its institutions for the organization of the family, society and the state, for education and health, and for activities that are 'religious' in the narrow sense. Islam is always insistent, however, that there can be no separation between 'religious' and 'secular', between 'sacred' and 'secular'. Since every part of life comes within the sphere of Islam, every human institution, whether it is the family, the mosque or the state, must be regarded as coming under the authority and rule of God.

Customs and products

In this final category we have four of the five 'pillars' of Islam, all of which are customs prescribed for all Muslims – prayer, fasting, almsgiving and pilgrimage (*hajj*. See pp. 72ff., 'Five basic duties of Islam').

3

Examining our attitudes

Once we have begun to develop genuine relationships with Muslims and to appreciate their culture, we may need to look more closely at some of our basic attitudes towards them. Some of these attitudes are related to theology and what we believe as Christians, while others are related to psychology, culture and politics. It is important that we should face up to them at an early stage in our study, since we are dealing with our reactions to a religion which challenges Christianity at many points. But many of us are also dealing with our gut reactions as white western Christians to a growing community of Asians and Arabs who have settled in our midst.

If we are honest with ourselves and can articulate these attitudes, we can then try to examine them in the light of the gospel. The following are examples of these attitudes:

3.1 'If Christianity is true, then Islam is false.'

If Christianity is *true*, the argument goes, doesn't it follow that Islam is *false*? If Jesus is the only way to God, doesn't it mean that Muslims can't know God in a personal way? Although we do not have the space to cover the very delicate and complex question of Christian attitudes to other faiths in any detail, we must at least notice that there are many passages in the Bible which express a very negative attitude towards 'other faiths' (*e.g.* Deuteronomy 12:1–3, 29–31; 32:17; Psalm 96:5; 1 Corinthians 8:4–6). On the other hand, there are other passages which reflect a much more positive and open approach to people of other faiths (*e.g.* Genesis 14:18– Malachi 1:10–11, rsv; Acts 10:30–43; 17:16–31). At the very least, therefore, we need to get beyond the simplistic view that if Christianity is completely true, Islam and all other faiths must be completely false. We can hardly say that they contain no understanding of God, of his creation or of humanity.

We also need to look again at the crucial verse, John 14:6, and ask if it really is as exclusive as it sounds. The key to a proper understanding of these words may be to recognize that Jesus is speaking here about people coming 'to the Father'. When he says 'I am the way', he means 'I am the way to the Father; no-one comes to the Father but by me.' We can therefore fill out the rest of the verse in this way: 'I am the truth about the Father; no-one can know the truth about the Father except through me. I am the life of the Father; no-one can live in fellowship with the Father except through me.'

If this is the thrust of what Jesus is saying, he can hardly mean that a person who does not believe in him knows nothing about God and has no relationship with him. But he does seem to be saying that people cannot know God *as Father*, and enjoy all the blessings of the father–child relationship, unless they recognize and trust Jesus as the Son. The testimony of Bilquis Sheikh in *I Dared to Call Him Father*[1] bears out the fact that Muslims generally believe it is quite wrong to think of God as 'Father'. Their denial of the sonship of Jesus is therefore linked with their denial of the fatherhood of God.

Quite apart from the exegesis of this important verse, however, we need to recognize that our attitudes may be influenced not only by our desire for correct doctrine. The story of Abraham and his wife Sarah and their dealings with Abimelech in Genesis 20:1–18 exposes some of our attitudes to people of other communities for what they really are. Abraham wants to protect Sarah, but gets her into a difficult situation because he is less than honest in the way he explains who she is. He also suffers from a subtle form of pride which makes him feel that no-one apart from himself and his family has any real relationship with God: 'I thought that there would be no-one here who fears God.' When God eventually speaks to Abimelech in a dream and Sarah is restored to Abraham, the painful lesson that Abraham has to learn is that some people outside the covenant *do* have a real reverence for God, and are even able to hear and respond to a direct communication from God.

A similar story in the New Testament is the account of how Peter's racial and religious prejudices are challenged through all the events leading up to his meeting with Cornelius (Acts 10). Peter has to allow the Holy Spirit to expose and root out these pernicious prejudices before he, as a Jew, can share the good news with a God-fearing person of a different nationality: 'God has shown me that I should not call any man impure or unclean' (verse 28).

If we as Christians suffer from a feeling of superiority that makes us look down on people of other faiths and other races as if they were inferior, we may need the same kind of upheaval to humble us and enable us to say with Peter: 'I now realise how true it is that God does not show favouritism but accepts men from every nation who fear him and do what is right' (verses 34–35). Reaching this point does *not* mean concluding that 'people of other faiths are all right as they are' and 'there's no need any longer to share the good news about Jesus with them'. (It is significant that immediately after these words Peter goes on to speak of 'the message God sent to the people of Israel, telling the good news of peace through Jesus Christ, who is Lord of all', verse 36.) But it *does* mean that in the process of sharing the good news, or perhaps even before we can be in a right frame of mind to do so, we may have to allow the Holy Spirit to do some painful things to deal with attitudes of pride in our conscious and unconscious minds.

3.2 'Islam needs to be strongly resisted in the West.'
'Muslims are aiming to conquer the world.'

The immediate answer to this must be: 'Yes – some of them are!' But for every Muslim in the West who has a strong missionary vision, there are dozens who are interested only in the survival of the present Muslim community in these countries. They are so concerned to hold on to their young people and protect them from the influence of our godless society that they have little interest in spreading the message of Islam. There *are* many groups which are actively spreading the message of Islam; and the church needs to be aware that they are not interested in the kind of open-ended dialogue which many Christian leaders are calling for.

It may be worth adding that among those in the West who have embraced Islam, many have been attracted by Sufism, the mysticism of Islam. Others have converted through marrying Muslims. Many Christians feel that it is unlikely that large numbers of white westerners will become Muslims, largely because Islam still appears so culturally foreign in the West.

'They're using their oil wealth to finance the spread of Islam.'

Once again we must say: 'True!' But how much did the modern missionary movement owe to the wealth created by the Industrial Revolution in Europe? And are the Muslims doing anything *in principle* that Christians have not done? When the Archbishop of Kenya expressed concern some years ago about petro-dollars being used to win Christians to Islam, Professor Ali Hillal Dessouki of Cairo University replied by pointing out that Muslims were only behaving in a similar way to the first Christian missionaries in Africa: 'Like Muslims today . . . the early missionaries used all available human and material resources, including money, to conduct their evangelistic work.' He went on to argue that Muslims had as much right as Christians to spread their faith and to Islamize Africans.

'They have no right to ask for the implementation of Islamic law in the West.'

Here again it depends very much what we are talking about. It is difficult to see any reason, either legal or theological, why they should not be allowed to have halal meat in schools and prisons. Indeed, it seems to be a situation in which we are called to act by the Golden Rule: 'In everything, do to others what you would have them do to you, for this sums up the Law and the Prophets' (Matthew 7:12). If we were living as Christians in a Muslim society, we would like the government to respect the feelings of our community. It is therefore our obligation as Christians to show the same kind of respect towards Muslim communities in the West. We may want to ask at the appropriate time whether the implementation of Islamic law in Muslim countries would allow Christian minorities the same kind of rights that they are demanding in the West. But the teaching of Jesus demands that we take the initiative, and that we do so not out of weakness, but out of love.

When a certain kind of Muslim rhetoric, however, calls for a country such as Britain to become an Islamic state, we may need to do some straight speaking. There is absolutely no way that a minority Muslim community could turn any European country into an Islamic state, however much they would like to do so.

But when Christians are taken in by such rhetoric and suggest that the Muslim community is actually planning to have the whole legal system in these countries abolished and the *shari'a* (Islamic law) adopted in its place, these Christians are playing on people's fears about 'the thin end of the wedge' and 'the domino theory'. Muslims in these countries at the present time are in a very strange and un-Islamic situation, because they live as a minority in post-Christian, secular, pluralist democratic states. The Qur'an never envisaged Muslims living in this kind of situation, and, while Judaism has had to develop a theology of Diaspora (Dispersion), Muslims are only beginning to develop a theology to explain the situation in which they find themselves in the West. We are not in the Sudan, Pakistan or Malaysia, and the total Islamization of western states which is held up by many Christians as the end of the slippery slope could never take place unless the vast majority of the country were to convert to Islam.

'They should adapt to our culture; when in Rome . . .'

But is this how westerners have behaved when they have gone overseas? If we seldom adopt this principle when we live and settle overseas, do we have any right to expect that Muslims should do the same when they become citizens in our country?

'The government should resist the spread of Islam.'

One Christian leader in Britain is known to have expressed the wish in private that the government would turn all mosques in this country into public conveniences! This sentiment is probably based on the story in 2 Kings 10:25–27, where we are told that after a temple of Baal had been torn down on the orders of Jehu, 'people have used it for a latrine to this day'. When this incident is related to Islam today, the assumptions seem to be (1) that our governments are in the same position as the kings of Judah in the Old Testament period (*i.e.* rulers of a theocracy); and (2) that Christian attitudes to Islam should be the same as the attitudes to Canaanite religion called for in parts of the Old Testament. If some Muslims are behaving in such a way as to threaten law and order in our society, there is every reason for governments to be concerned. But there is no other reason why we as ordinary citizens could possibly expect governments to resist the spread of Islam. And since as Christians we live after the incarnation,

Pentecost, and Paul's address at the Areopagus, some expressions of this view seem to represent a sad regression to a way of thinking that is less than Christian.

'Islam has no right to be here!'

Even if it is never expressed in these terms, this is probably the feeling which lies near the heart of many of our responses. What right have they got to bring their foreign religion into the Christian West? If we had a better understanding of history, however, perhaps instead we should be saying: 'Now at last we ought to know what it has been like for them to be at the receiving end of our missionary work for 200 years! Are they doing anything in principle in our country which we haven't done in theirs?' While therefore we must not be naïve about what is happening in the West, we need to be aware of the opposite danger, which is to appeal to people's fears of a great, sinister conspiracy. It is important that those who are involved in discussion of these issues with Muslim leaders should have had some experience of living in Muslim countries, and know what it is like for Christian minorities there. At certain times it may be right for us to say to Muslim leaders, 'Do the governments in Muslim countries grant to their Christian minorities these same rights which you are demanding for yourselves here in the West?' But if we do so, we must be certain of our facts and aware of all the implications. And if we are looking in the Old Testament for guidance about our basic attitudes to the spread of Islam in the West, the best place to find it is probably not in the commands to tear down the altars of Baal (*e.g.* Deuteronomy 12:1–3), but in the command to love the stranger (Leviticus 19:33–34; Exodus 22:21; 23:9).

3.3 'It's impossible to convert Muslims, and we shouldn't try to anyway.'

Sometimes this view springs from the simple 'live and let live' attitude: 'We have our religion, they have theirs – so why can't we just accept the situation as it is?' At other times it arises from the conviction that all religions are basically the same, and that it is sheer arrogance for Christians to think that their faith is 'more true' or 'better' than any other. In other cases, however, this is the conclusion which Christians have reached because of the many problems they face in relating to Muslims, and the terrible cost that often has to be paid by Muslims who recognize Jesus as more than a prophet.

One book in the Bible which speaks to these attitudes is the book of Jonah, which has been described as the 'high-water mark' of mission in the Old Testament. Jonah takes some time to realize that God wants him and needs him to convey his message to the people of Nineveh. One reason for his reluctance to answer the call is the feeling that 'if God wants to convert them, he can do it perfectly well without *me*'. Jonah therefore has to learn that God uses people in his purposes of love for the world. After he obeys the call and preaches the message of judgment and mercy, he is amazed to find how responsive the people of Nineveh are. He expects them to be hardened pagans, and can hardly believe that they actually believe his message and express their repentance in a dramatic way!

At the end of the book there is a further challenge to Jonah, the reluctant and unloving missionary, when God has to say to him, 'You've been faithful in condemning all that was wrong in Nineveh. But have you secretly enjoyed it all? Do you really care for these people whose faith and way of life are so different from your own? Do you really *want* them to turn to me in repentance and faith?' (*cf.* Jonah 4:1–11). Could it be therefore that the book of Jonah has a powerful message, not just to individual Jonahs today who try to run away from God's call, but to the whole Christian church which runs away from the challenge of Islam?

It is also worth pointing out that it is not *we* who do the 'converting'. In the New Testament we have in Paul an example, almost larger than life, of how God can change the direction of a person's life. The Christians of Judea got the message that 'the man who formerly persecuted us is now preaching the faith he once tried to destroy' (Galatians 1:23). And writing towards the end of his life, Paul sees his conversion as proof of how God in his love and patience can turn the hardest hearts: 'For that very reason I was shown mercy so that in me, the worst of sinners, Christ Jesus might display his unlimited patience as an example for those who would believe on him and receive eternal life' (1 Timothy 1:16). If God could change someone as hostile as Saul, is there any reason why he cannot help people of any faith today to change their ideas about Jesus?

3.4 'Muslims seem to be very prejudiced and have closed minds.'

Yes, maybe they sometimes do. But often it is a case of the pot calling the kettle black! And people in glass houses shouldn't throw stones! It is always easier to accuse others of being prejudiced than to admit that we Christians have prejudices. We may not be able to change their prejudices; but we do have to start with our own, and we can do something about them.

Once we have made the admission and called these prejudices by their proper name, it can be a relief to find that the New Testament has so much to say on this subject. It is reassuring to know, for example, that the prejudices which many Christians have towards Muslims are very similar to the prejudices of Jews towards Samaritans at the time of Jesus. Just as John had to say, 'Jews have no dealings with Samaritans' (John 4:9; they 'do not associate with Samaritans', NIV), so in many situations today it is sadly true that 'Christians have no dealings with Muslims', or at least have as few dealings as possible.

When we try to explain these prejudices in the minds of the Jews, we find that there were at least three major reasons. The first was *racial*. The Jews despised the Samaritans for their mixed ancestry which resulted from intermarriage between people in the northern kingdom of Israel and Assyrians who were brought into the area after the fall of Samaria in 721 BC (2 Kings 17:24–41). The second was *religious*. The Samaritans had their rival temple on Mount Gerizim and recognized the Torah (the Pentateuch) but not the Prophets and the Writings. The third reason for these prejudices was *political*. There had been tensions and rivalries between the two communities over many centuries.

If we as Christians today think of Muslims in anything like the same way as the disciples thought of the Samaritans, we will have to learn that loving our neighbour involves putting aside our prejudices, and doing something very positive to overcome the social, political, cultural and religious barriers which separate us from Muslims. We may need to see how Jesus dealt with the prejudices in the minds of his disciples:

By example. The disciples were surprised, for example, that Jesus spoke to a *woman* at Jacob's well, and no doubt doubly surprised that she was a *Samaritan* (John 4:1–42, especially verse 27). He was not prepared to be bound by all the social and religious prejudices of his fellow Jews.

By his teaching. It can hardly have been an accident that Jesus chose a Samaritan as the main character in the story which we know as 'the parable of the good Samaritan'. His Jewish listeners would have been shocked to find that the priest and the Levite come out so badly in the story, and that the hero is from that despised and heretical community up in the north! If we wanted to capture the original impact of the parable, we would need to say that if Jesus were telling the parable today to a white audience in South Africa, the person who helped the injured man would be black. If he were addressing Protestants in Northern Ireland, he would have been a Catholic; and if he were speaking to Palestinian Arabs, the person who so unexpectedly showed kindness would have been a Jew. In this way Jesus was, among other things, encouraging his disciples to reject such terrible stereotypes, and to believe that sacrificial love often comes from sources which we in our arrogance think most unlikely.

By sending the Holy Spirit. Jesus specifically mentions Samaria as one of the places where his disciples are to take the good news: 'You will be my witnesses in Jerusalem, and in all Judea *and Samaria . . .*' (Acts 1:8) A few chapters later we learn how this worked out in practice. Luke tells us that when the apostles in Jerusalem heard that Samaria 'had accepted the word of God, they sent Peter and John to them' (8:14). It seems that the leaders of the church may have felt that the coming of the gospel to Samaria was such a significant development that they had to send an official apostolic delegation to the city to welcome the new believers. In view of all the animosities between Jews and Samaritans in the past, some public gesture was called for, to show to all the world that in the church there would be no place for any bad feeling between Jewish and Samaritan believers.

4

Visiting a mosque

4.1 Why visit a mosque?

One motive may be simple curiosity; we want to know what it looks like and what happens in a mosque. Another reason could be that we want to meet devout, practising Muslims, and want to understand them and their faith as much as we can. It is not appropriate to visit a mosque in order to 'evangelize Muslims', although such a visit can sometimes lead to opportunities to share our faith with Muslims. We need to remember that we are visitors, enjoying the hospitality that is extended to us in someone else's place of worship. If a group of Muslims were to visit our church, we would expect them to come primarily to listen and to learn, rather than to preach to us!

4.2 What is the mosque for?

The word is an anglicized version of the Arabic word *masjid*, a place of prostration, *i.e.* in worship. In addition to being a place of worship, the mosque is regarded as a kind of community centre, and many important social functions are held in the mosque or in a hall attached to the mosque. It is also a place for education, and in many cases classes for teaching Islam and the Qur'an are held regularly in the mosque.

4.3 What should you do before going?

The leader of the group should make personal contact before going, either with the imam, or some other leader of the community, or a member of the mosque committee.

Women should wear a scarf to cover their heads. They may sometimes be asked to wear a long skirt or loose trousers, and to have their arms covered. Some mosques may ask that women should not visit during menstruation. Men are sometimes expected to cover their heads. You should be prepared to take your shoes off before going into the main prayer room of the mosque.

During your visit your hosts will probably want to talk about the mosque and explain their faith to you, perhaps at some length. There will usually also be opportunities for you to ask questions. It can be helpful to think out in advance some of the questions you may want to ask.

You should be prepared to stay for at least an hour, and not be in a hurry to leave. You may be served with refreshments, and there may be an opportunity for you to ask further questions. If the leader of your group knows the mosque well, he or she should know how long the visit is likely to take.

If any members of your group have reservations about visiting a mosque, they should not feel obliged to do so. It may be helpful, however, if they can be encouraged to express their feelings openly and discuss them with the rest of the group.

4.4 What can you do and what can you see at the mosque?

You may be welcomed by the imam, whose position is roughly similar, but not identical, to that of the minister, pastor, or priest in a Christian church. It is worth asking about the responsibilities of the imam, and finding out how they differ from those of a Christian minister or priest. It is possible, however, that you will be welcomed and shown round by any member of the community, who may not have studied Islam in any depth.

You may be able to see the place where those who come to the mosque carry out their ablutions, *wudu*, the ritual washing of the hands, arms, face, nose and feet, before they pray. Your hosts may be very willing to demonstrate to you how they say their prayers, and what the ritual means for them.

In the prayer room or prayer hall itself, you will see the *mihrab*, the alcove in the wall which marks the direction of Mecca, the central shrine of Islam, and thus indicates the direction which Muslims face to pray. They generally do not mind if visitors watch them from behind when they are saying the prayers, and are often willing to demonstrate for visitors the special postures that they adopt during their prayers.

The *minbar* is the pulpit with steps, usually made of wood, from which the imam gives a sermon at the Friday prayers.

There is often Arabic writing on the walls. This could be

the name of God, Allah
the name Muhammad
the Fatiha (the first *sura* of the Qur'an; see p. 66).
other verses from the Qur'an (*e.g. sura* 112).

There may be a series of clocks indicating the times for prayer each day, and the Friday prayers.

There may or may not be a minaret. In a Muslim country, the call to prayer, the *adhan* (pronounced *azan*) would be heard from the minaret, often magnified by a loudspeaker. In most mosques in Britain the call to prayer is heard only inside the mosque, and special permission has to be given by the local Council if it is to be broadcast outside the building.

There may or may not be a separate women's prayer room. If there is no special room, there may be a gallery or a curtained area in the main prayer hall which is used by women.

In many mosques there is a special room which is used for Qur'an classes. Children come here for an hour or more after school each day to learn the Qur'an. It may be worth studying the pictures and posters on the walls.

There may be a hall attached to the mosque, which is used for social functions, like weddings and important festivals. There is sometimes a morgue.

4.5 What should you do after the visit?

It is important for members of the group to meet together, even if only for a short time, to share their impressions of the visit.

It may be appropriate to write to your hosts to thank them for their hospitality.

You should think together about the most appropriate way to follow up your visit. You cannot expect to make too much progress on your first visit, and may well want to arrange further visits to the mosque, or to visit your hosts in their homes. If you invite them to visit your church, don't be surprised or offended if there is some reluctance to do so, and try to work out the reasons for their reluctance.

5

Facing immediate issues

The following case studies – from Europe, Africa, North America and Asia – all raise basic questions about how Christians should think about Islam and relate to Muslims. All of them deal with real situations, and are either written by people with first-hand knowledge of the situation or based on material provided by such people. A situation is described, and some of the main issues explained. Each case study ends with a series of questions that could be discussed in a group.

The special value of case studies is that they enable us to focus on actual situations in which Christians have found themselves in different parts of the world in recent years, and then force us to think through the different issues involved. Even if we ourselves are not likely to face any of these situations, the discipline of putting ourselves into the shoes of others, apart from increasing our sympathy for them, can concentrate our minds and sharpen our thinking.

All these case studies raise major questions which we will look at again in one form or another in Parts 2–5.

5.1 Selling a redundant church to be used as a mosque

A considerable number of redundant churches in inner-city areas of Britain have been sold in recent years and turned into mosques, Hindu temples or Sikh temples (gurdwaras). You are a member of your church committee, and were told some weeks ago that the Muslim community in your area has made an offer for a church building belonging to your denomination which has not been used for several years and has been up for sale for some months. A special committee was set up to present the arguments for and against selling the building for this purpose. The following is a summary of their report.

Arguments for selling to the Muslims

1. Islam has much in common with Christianity: it is a monotheistic religion which owes much to Judaism and Christianity and recognizes only one God.

2. It would be better to sell a redundant church to be used as a place of prayer for another religious community than for it to be turned into a warehouse or demolished.

3. Selling the church should not be seen as a defeat, but rather as a simple recognition of demographic changes; if there are hardly any Christians living in the area and the majority are Muslims, the Christians need fewer churches in the inner city.

4. What would it say to the Muslim community if we were to refuse to sell it to them? It would suggest that we despise Islam, and that we would rather let the building be used for secular purposes than for it to be used as a place of prayer.

5. We must not think of the sale of the building as a final event. It needs to be seen in the context of the churches' relations with the Muslim community. Instead of thinking in terms of defeat and retrenchment, the local churches need to work out a strategy for their relations with the Muslim community over the next five, ten or twenty years.

Arguments against selling the church to Muslims

1. It would be dishonouring to the name of Christ for a building which has been used for Christian worship to be used for Muslim worship. We cannot avoid having a sense of shame, feeling that somehow the church has failed and Islam has won a victory.

2. White people living in the area, even if they are not churchgoers, have some feeling for the local church where baptisms, weddings and funerals take place. In the folk religion of these people, the church is important, even if they don't belong to the congregation. They are likely to feel some sadness if the church is sold to Muslims.

3. What would it say to the Muslim community if we do sell it to them? They would see the sale as a victory for Islam, and a defeat for Christianity. We don't want to give the Muslim community an opportunity to boast and rejoice in this way.

Questions

1. What do you personally think?

2. What do you think your church and other churches in the area can or should do in this situation?

5.2 State funding for Muslim schools in the UK

In recent years the Muslim community in Britain has been calling on the government to allow state funding for Islamic schools. There have been for some time private, independent Islamic schools, which are financed by fees and gifts from Muslim communities, and these schools are inspected regularly by inspectors from the Department for Education.

Muslims are now going further, however, in their requests and demands. They argue that if Anglican, Roman Catholic, Methodist and Jewish schools can be grant-aided and thus financed by the government, why can't Muslim schools enjoy the same status?

Arguments for Muslim schools within the state system

1. The Golden Rule suggests that we should extend to others the same privileges that we expect for ourselves. There is nothing except tradition and prejudice which prevents us having Muslim schools within the state system.

2. Allowing Anglican, Catholic, Methodist and Jewish schools has not turned these communities into ghettos.

Arguments against having Muslim schools within the state system

1. It is in most cases only a few Muslim leaders who are making these requests. The majority of the Muslim community do not want to come under the control of their imams, and would prefer their children to go to existing state schools, whether church schools or not.

2. Allowing state funding for Muslim schools would make Muslim communities even more inward-looking and self-contained than they already are. They would become more and more like ghettos, since children in Muslim schools have little or no contact with non-Muslims.

3. Muslim schools would teach only Islam. In grant-aided church schools, Christian and Muslim children are exposed to the teaching of faiths other than their own. Muslims, however, would probably never allow their children to be taught other religions such as Christianity.

Questions

1. How should the government respond to these requests/demands? What will be the factors that the government will take into consideration in determining its policy?

2. Should there be, and can there be, a distinctively Christian response on this issue?

3. What should be the attitude of the churches? How should they make their views known, and how should they be engaged in the debate?

5.3 The controversy about the wearing of the veil in France

Jamilah is a seventeen-year-old French pupil from a Moroccan family who needed to change from one secondary school to another in a major city in France. Her first school had permitted her to wear the *hijab* (a long scarf or veil covering all but her face). But the second school raised a storm of protest. Many teachers refused to admit her to their classes unless she removed the scarf. When the problem was brought before the disciplinary council, she was excluded from studying at the school.

Finally an appeals commission worked out a compromise with the family, the regional Muslim Association, and the school administration. Jamilah would wear a turban in those classes where the teachers complained about the *hijab*, and leave her scarf on where they were not opposed. She felt some reluctance, but decided to continue her studies on these conditions.

The wearing of the scarf is imposed by God and not by man;

we cannot change his Word,' declared Jamilah. 'It is to protect women from being looked at by men. Girls who do not wear it are not good Muslims. Those who speak of the inferiority of the woman do not know Islam. Today it is the second religion of France. Where is tolerance?'

The first school was able to accept Jamilah and her *hijab* on the basis of her faithful attendance and her discretion in not proselytizing among her fellow students. These teachers felt it was important to consider her as an individual and not to obstruct her search for identity and spiritual life. For them a secular educational system should emphasize tolerance rather than forbid religious expression.

The second school, however, saw the problem differently. Many of the teachers and parents there believed that anything touching on religion should be kept out of government schools. Religious symbols should not be in evidence, since they make distinctions between pupils.

Questions

1. If you were a teacher in the second school, what would you do – accept Jamilah with a turban, or with a scarf (*hijab*), or fight for tolerance, or oppose all signs of religion in a government school? Why?

2. How would you relate to her and her family in your community? By supporting them in their rights (if so, how?), or by seeking to change their opinions (if so, how?)?

3. Suggest ways of sharing the message of Christ with committed 'fundamentalist' Muslim women and their families.

5.4 The dilemma concerning emigration from the Middle East

An engaged couple in a Middle Eastern country comes to you for counselling. The young man is a committed Christian believer from a Christian background, who has been active in outreach and evangelism throughout his time at university. He is just about to graduate and is thinking and planning for his future. He comes from a wealthy family and has very good prospects for future employment in his family business. He wants to work with the church in his country and in the Arab world, and is very committed to working for the economic development of his country. He is the kind of person who is likely to be a great asset to both his country and his church.

The young woman comes from a Muslim background and has been a committed Christian for several years. She has been ostracized by her family, and has had a difficult time since becoming a believer. Yet she has had a great impact on her friends and has helped others to come to faith. She too is a gifted person, and, like her fiancé, has much to contribute both to the church and to the country.

They have discovered that since they come originally from different religious communities, they cannot legally be married in their country. A person cannot officially change his or her Muslim faith, and a Muslim woman is not allowed by law to marry a Christian man. Thus, although she is a practising Christian, she is considered by law to be a Muslim, and they cannot get married. They therefore want desperately to emigrate to the West.

The dilemma is even more acute since they realize that there is no country to which they can go. For the past year they have been working hard to find a country that will accept them as religious refugees, but all the doors are closed to them. They love the Lord and they love each other. They love their country and have been effective in ministry to their fellow countrymen. They feel strongly called to get married, but do not know what to do.

Question

If you were able to counsel the couple, how would you speak to them?

5.5 Islamization in Nigeria?

The population of Nigeria includes approximately 600 ethnic groups, the most significant of which are the Hausas in the north (almost entirely Muslim), the Yorubas in the south-west (partly Christian and partly Muslim), and the Ibos in the south-east (largely Christian). Much of the north was converted to Islam as it spread south across the Sahara between the tenth and nineteenth centuries. The south became largely Christian through the work of Christian missionaries in the nineteenth century. Islam is therefore strong in the north, Christianity is strong in the south, and in the area in between both religions are competing for converts. The total population is around 120 million, of which approximately 49% are Christian, 45% Muslim and 6% animist or of tribal religions.

The Constitution of 1963 guaranteed freedom of religious belief and practice, which included not only freedom to observe, teach and propagate one's faith, but also freedom to change one's religion. In 1967 the country was divided into twelve states. A new Constitution accepted in 1979 described Nigeria as a multi-religious society, and prohibited the federal government or the government of any of the states from declaring any religion the state religion. The most recent Constitution (adopted in 1989) includes the same article prohibiting the establishment of any religion in either the federal or the state government.

Relations between Muslims and Christians in Nigeria in the past have generally been good. Inter-religious marriage has been common, and families often include Muslims, Christians and people of traditional religions. In recent years, however, tensions between Muslim and Christian communities have increased. The following are some of the main factors contributing to these tensions:

1. In 1983 Nigeria obtained observer status in the Organization of the Islamic Conference (OIC), an organization that links together almost all nations with Muslim majorities. Early in 1986, however, it was rumoured that Nigeria had become a full member. Christians and others protested strongly because they claimed that it amounted to declaring Nigeria a Muslim state and seemed to be part of a secret process of Islamization. Members of the government who were not Muslims were not consulted about the decision. The President was forced to admit that Nigeria had become a full member of the OIC, but emphasized that the reasons had to do with culture and religion rather than with politics. When a Commission of twenty members including Muslims and Christians was set up to discuss the issue, the Christian members demanded the immediate withdrawal of Nigeria from the OIC. Early in 1992 the government announced that it had withdrawn from membership.

2. Christians (especially in the north) have complained of discrimination against them in religious education in schools, in the media and in the courts. They say they have difficulties in getting permission to build new churches, and point out that new mosques have been built very close to churches. Muslims also complain of discrimination. An article in a Muslim magazine after the riots in 1991 made the following charge: 'The combined efforts of the Christian elites in the private sectors, Army and the police and the contacts in the media have subjected Muslims and Islam to terrible victimization. While the private leaders of the Church initiate violent provocations against Islam and the Muslims, the police and the Army move with military precision to unleash terror on Muslims, destroying innocent lives and properties.'

3. Muslims have felt threatened by certain Christian evangelistic activities, such as student missions in universities and colleges, and missions in the north led by foreign evangelists.

4. In addition to tribal and religious differences, economic factors have sometimes been significant. Disadvantaged social groups feel resentful against the rich and against the system which leaves them caught in the poverty trap.

5. Christians have felt threatened by Muslim requests and demands for the imposition of *shari'a* law. Before the coming of the British, parts of the north were under *shari'a* law from early in the nineteenth century. The British, however, reduced the powers of the *shari'a* courts until they covered only family and divorce laws for Muslims. When Nigeria became independent in 1960, a *shari'a* Court of Appeal was set up for the *whole* of northern Nigeria. Later a similar Court of Appeal was set up in each of the ten northern states. When Muslims began to demand that a federal *shari'a* Court of Appeal should be set up, the Constituent Assembly voted against the proposal by 190 to 60, but gave each state the right to establish *shari'a* courts *for Muslims*. Christians in Nigeria suspect that having a federal *shari'a* Court of Appeal would lead to the implementation of *shari'a* law over the whole country, and that this would make Christians second-class citizens. *Shari'a* law is recognized in the present Constitution, but applies only to Muslims.

As a result of these tensions, many riots have taken place since 1980, especially in the north. These have led to the destruction of many churches and mosques (in one case fifty-two churches and five mosques), to looting, maiming, killing, and making many homeless. In one case the riot was started when a Muslim claimed that a Christian butcher had sold him pork. In other cases the riots have been sparked off by the different tensions already described.

In many of the earlier disturbances, the Christians either turned the other cheek or ran for their lives. In more recent riots, however, some Christians have begun to defend themselves and even to organize themselves in 'defence squads', arming themselves with knives, iron rods, sticks and broken bottles, attacking Muslims and destroying property.

Questions

1. Is there enough evidence for believing that Muslims have a deliberate policy of Islamization?

2. How should Christians respond to the political challenge of Islam in this situation?

3. Should Christians be prepared to defend themselves in civil disturbances, by force if necessary?

4. What kind of constitution is appropriate for a state and for a federation of states in which there are different proportions of Muslims and Christians?

5.6 Conversion and family loyalties

A pastor from East Africa writes:

> I am a pastor in an area where the population is 75% Muslim. I am often able to go into schools to take evangelistic meetings. I was once invited to a school and took with me a group of Christians who played gospel music, and I then gave an evangelistic address. At the end of the address I invited any of the girls who wanted to know more about the gospel to come and see me afterwards. One who wanted to see me was a Muslim girl, and as I talked with her on her own after the meeting she said she wanted to take the next step and

to know what she must do. We therefore prayed together and she accepted Christ as her Saviour. She then asked how she must go on from here, and when I told her that I was the pastor of a nearby church, I suggested that she should come to the church next Sunday.

Very soon, however, her family began to show strong opposition to what she was doing. At one stage I had to invite her to come and live with us in our home because of the difficulties she faced in her home. I also had to get in contact with the police and the chief of the tribe in order to explain the situation. Eventually the opposition of the family was so strong that they moved her completely from the school to a different school. Later when it was found that she was having contact with Christians in that school, her parents moved her again, this time to a school in another county. Soon after this her parents married her to a Muslim man. She had to discontinue her studies at school, and as far as I know she has lost all contact with Christians.

Some time later my cousin made contact with an old lady who was a Muslim. When she expressed an interest in becoming a Christian, he prayed with her. She then asked what she must do as a Christian. His first answer was that she must take off the Muslim veil and the special clothing that she was wearing. These clothes were then burned publicly to express her rejection of Islam. Very soon this lady had difficulties with her husband, and although for a short time she was attending the church, my cousin lost contact with her.[1]

Questions

1. How should the pastor have dealt with the Muslim girl? Did he do anything wrong when he spoke to her on the first occasion after the evangelistic meeting? Was she simply suffering opposition and persecution for the sake of the gospel?

2. How should the pastor's cousin have approached this lady when she expressed an interest in the gospel?

5.7 The Islamization of the law in Malaysia

Muslims in Malaysia are approximately 55% out of a total of 17 million. The remaining 45% are approximately 30% adherents of Chinese religions, 7.5% Hindus and 7.5% Christians.

The situation is complicated, however, by the delicate balance between the different ethnic communities: the Malays (about 50%), the Chinese (about 35%), the Indians (about 10%), and other tribal groupings in East Malaysia (about 5%). Most Christians are from Chinese, Indian or tribal backgrounds.

Since the mid-1980s many Muslims in Malaysia have expressed their desire to see the integration of the Islamic *Shari'a* courts and the civil courts. Both the federal and state governments have agreed to this in principle, although they have said that the changes should be brought in gradually. Thus the Lord President Tun Hajj Sallah Abas is reported to have said in 1986, 'The best changes are those which are imperceptible. Drastic changes would cause confusion, a lot of unhappiness, and it would also make people uncertain.' Among the politically dominant Malay Muslims, therefore, there is a tendency to want to further the influence of Islam in the public life of the whole nation.

The feelings of some Malaysian Christians in this situation have been expressed in this way: 'We Christians and all non-Muslim Malaysians feel like a frog. Put a frog into cold water and it will swim contentedly in it. If you heat the water slowly, the frog will adapt itself to the warm water and will not leap out. But if you drop a new frog into this warm water, it will jump out. We non-Muslims feel like the frog in the water that is being slowly heated up. We feel that we are not wanted in a Muslim country; we don't feel that we are consulted before new decisions are made silently and then implemented.'

Some Christians also point to particular developments which create anxiety. They say that hotels have been asked to remove all Bibles and biblical verses that have been placed by the Gideons, and that schools have been asked to remove crosses and other Christian symbols from outside their schools, and to replace the cross with a star on school badges. Other Christians, however, recognize that in seeking to further the role of religion in public life, the government, especially in its 2020 programme, is essentially trying to ensure that ethical standards are preserved in society, and that Christians should not feel threatened by these developments.

Muslims reassure non-Muslims that their status is completely secure, and that they have nothing to fear. One spokesman said recently, 'Islamic laws can be implemented in a plural society, as there are sufficient provisions for the well-being of all, including the non-Muslims.'

Questions

1. How should Christians react in this situation?

2. What precisely is the status of non-Muslims in a country in which Islam is officially the state religion, and where some Muslims are seeking to implement Islamic law?

3. Do Christians have good reason to be afraid of these developments? Should they resist them, and if so, how? Or should they accept them, while trying to make sure that adequate safeguards are built into the laws and the Constitution at every stage?

5.8 The pros and cons of public debates in the USA

Christians in universities in the USA have been discussing whether a Christian group should join with a Muslim group to co-sponsor a debate (or dialogue) as a form of public interaction between Christians and Muslims on campus. The debate format is attractive to many Muslims because it enables them to put forward one of their star promoters and apologists of Islam (usually a representative of one of the more prominent Muslim centres developing in many cities).

Arguments for

1. This format provides an opportunity for a genuine educational experience and exchange of views.

2. The process of setting up the debate enables Muslim and Christian leaders to get to know and trust one another. Careful attention needs to be given to working out details of the programme, such as timing, publicity, and choice of speakers, chairperson and topic.

Arguments against

1. Planning the debate can consume a great deal of time and energy. It may attract only a small number of people.

2. Dialogues or debates do not necessarily establish warm relationships and friendship between Muslims and Christians.

3. Some public debates that have taken place in recent years have been staged almost like a boxing match. There are generally far more Muslims than Christians who attend, and they are often vocal in supporting their speaker.

4. The Christians, often naïvely, ask one of their local pastors to present and defend the Christian gospel, hoping that sincerity and fairness will prevail. But with some exceptions these debates have failed to do much more than confirm already held convictions, with little genuine listening to the other side. Sometimes the presenter is unable to respond adequately to the skilled argument or tactics of the other participant, who has superior knowledge.

5. Videos of the debates that have been made by Muslims have been carefully edited in favour of the Muslim side and distributed widely all over the world.

Questions

1. Do the arguments *for* outweigh the arguments *against*, or *vice versa*?

2. Would debates of this kind be possible in other countries and other situations? If not, why not?

3. If Christian speakers are not generally effective in such debates, what does this say about Christian responses to Islam? (Note: Debates were staged by chapters of the InterVarsity Christian Fellowship and Muslim student groups on campuses in the USA in 1992. Detailed information is available from IVCF, PO Box 7895, Madison, WI 53711, USA.)

Resources for further study

Zaki Badawi, *Islam in Britain* (Ta Ha Publishers, 1981)

Colin Chapman, 'Going Soft on Islam? Reflections on Some Evangelical Responses to Islam', *Vox Evangelica* XIX (1989), pp. 7–31

Anne Cooper, *Ishmael My Brother* (MARC, 1985), chapter 2, pp. 20–31

Roger Hooker, *Uncharted Journey* (Church Missionary Society, 1973)

———, *Journey into Varanasi* (Church Missionary Society, 1978)

Roger Hooker and Christopher Lamb, *Love the Stranger: Christian Witness in Multi-Faith Areas* (SPCK, 1986)

Philip Lewis, *Islamic Britain: Religion, Politics and Identity among British Muslims* (I. B. Tauris, 1994)

Jorgen Nielsen, *Muslims in Western Europe* (Edinburgh University Press, 1992)

Mohammad S. Raza, *Islam in Britain, Past, Present and Future* (Volcano Press, 1991)

Edward W. Said, *Covering Islam* (Routledge, 1981)

Andrew Wingate, *Encounters in the Spirit* (WCC, 1988)

Part 2

Understanding Islam

Great Spirit, grant that I may never criticize a man until I have walked a mile in his moccasins.

An American Indian prayer

One tries to get inside the mind and heart of Islam, to get the feel of it, to be at home within it.

Roger Hooker[1]

You have got to know and yet never try to teach a Muslim his own religion.

Jens Christensen[2]

The intention is to describe, rather than to pass judgement, on the phenomena of religion . . . Our first need is to understand.

Ninian Smart[3]

I was profoundly conscious that they [the missionaries] did not understand the Muslims because they were not properly trained for the work – were in fact, as far as Islam was concerned, horribly ignorant . . . . The result for me was that I made up my mind if ever I could do anything to train missionaries to Muslims to know Islam, I would put my back into it.

D. B. Macdonald, writing about a visit to Cairo in 1907[4]

Our aim in Part 2 is to try to understand Islam as much as possible *from the point of view of Muslims*. We want to describe the faith and practice of Islam in a way that Muslims will recognize as accurate and fair, so that we can put ourselves, as it were, into the shoes of Muslims and understand their worldview.

We are not at this stage trying to compare Islam with Christianity, except where there is some similarity or difference that can help us to appreciate better some aspect of Islamic belief and practice. We are not trying to show that Christianity is superior to Islam, and we are not yet at the stage of answering Muslim objections to Christianity. We are simply trying to understand Islam as a world faith in its own right, resisting the temptation as far as possible to interpret it in Christian categories or to see it through Christian spectacles.

Much of the material is presented in note form, with quotations from different writers, Muslim, Christian or secular, to illustrate important points. Brief texts are included in several sections to encourage students to go on to study original sources. The later chapters are longer and deal with more complex issues.

6

Muslims at prayer

One way of attempting to understand Islam is to try to enter sympathetically into the mind and heart of Muslims at prayer. This means that before studying what they believe (in chapter 8), we should try to find out how they pray. Instead of looking on critically as spectators, we try to appreciate what they are doing and saying when they pray.

Constance Padwick's classic *Muslim Devotions: A Study of Prayer Manuals in Common Use* illustrates powerfully the value of this approach, which is based on the conviction that

> in Islam, as in any other faith, a stranger desiring not to remain a stranger could best feel the pulsing life of religion through a study of the devotions actually in use . . . We should desire to have worship, Muslim or Christian, judged not by what it means to the lukewarm and the untaught, but by what it gives to those who try to enter fully into its life. This is not only a fairer procedure for the understanding of the life of devotion but it is also probable that in learning what devotion means when carried to intensity we best learn also to understand the diffused and weakened religious ideas of the masses.[1]

6.1 The 'call to prayer'

The following is a translation of the call to prayer (*adhan* – often pronounced *azan*) which is chanted in Arabic five times a day, with some variations, from mosques throughout the Islamic world:

> God is most great, God is most great, I bear witness that there is no god except God: I bear witness that Muhammad is the Apostle of God. Come ye unto prayer. Come

ye unto good. Prayer is a better thing than sleep. Come ye to the best deed. God is most great. God is most great. There is no god except God.[2]

It may be helpful for those who hear the call to prayer regularly to be able to recognize some of the key phrases:

allahu akbar	'God is most great'
la ilaha illa Allah	'There is no god but God'
hayya 'ala-ssalah	'Come to prayer'
hayya 'ala-lfalah	'Come to good'

Christians living in the Muslim world who hear the call to prayer regularly could ask themselves whether there are any ways in which they too can hear these words as a call to prayer, and pray with and for Muslims whenever they hear it.

6.2 The ablutions

Muslims are required to say a prescribed form of prayers five times a day, either in the mosque or wherever they happen to be at the time. The five times are: (1) between dawn and just before sunrise; (2) between midday and afternoon; (3) between late afternoon and just before sunset; (4) between sunset and dark; (5) at night before midnight or dawn.

They must prepare themselves to offer prayer by carrying out the ritual ablution (*wudu*). These are the different stages they must go through:

wash both hands up to the wrists three times
rinse the mouth three times
sniff water into the nostrils
wash the tip of the nose three times
wash the face three times
wash the arms three times from wrist to elbow
pass the wet hand over the head and both hands over
    the back of the head to the neck
wash inside and behind the ears with wet fingers
wash both feet thoroughly up to the ankles

6.3 The compulsory prayers (*salat*)

The following are the main stages in the basic sequence of the ritual prayer (called a *raka'a*), which is repeated with variations three or four times at the different times of prayer, together with an English translation of words that have to be said in Arabic:

1. Stand upright on the prayer mat, facing the Ka'ba, the Black Stone, in Mecca, and say some words expressing your 'intention' (*niyya*) either aloud or silently: *e.g.* 'I intend to say four *raka'as* of the dawn prayers for Allah facing the Ka'ba.'

2. Raise your hands to your ears and say, 'God is most great' (*allahu akbar*). Place the right hand on the left just below the navel or on the chest and say: 'O Allah, glory and praise are for you, and blessed is your name, and exalted is your Majesty; there is no god but you. I seek shelter in Allah from the rejected Satan. In the name of Allah, the most merciful, the most kind.'

3. Recite the *Fatiha*, the first *sura* of the Qur'an (see 1.4), and recite any other verse(s) of the Qur'an.

4. Bow from the waist, saying, 'God is most great'; and place your hands on your knees saying, 'Glory to my Lord, the Great.' Then stand up, saying, 'Allah hears those who praise him. Our Lord, praise be to you.'

5. Prostrate on the floor, with forehead, nose, both palms and knees touching the ground, say 'God is most great. Glory to my Lord, the Highest.' Then stand up again, saying, 'God is most great.' Sit upright with knees bent and palms on the knees. Prostrate again, say, 'God is most great.' Then get up again, saying, 'God is most great.'

6. Other prayers (called *du'a*), either memorized or extempore, can be said at this point; *e.g.* 'O Allah, I have been unjust to myself and no-one grants pardon for sins except you; therefore, forgive me with your forgiveness and have mercy on me. Surely you are the Forgiver, the Merciful.'

7. Turn your face to the right (whether or not there is someone praying beside you), saying, 'The peace and mercy of Allah be upon you,' and then to the left with the same words.

In observing the postures which Muslims adopt for their prayers, Christians should remember:

- that Muhammad may well have learned some of these postures from Syrian Christian monks;

- that prostration is found in the Bible (*e.g.* Ezekiel 1:28);

- that Muslims are trying to express their total submission to God in a physical way;

- that Muhammad first taught Muslims to pray towards Jerusalem, like the Jews. It was only when his message was rejected by the Jews that they changed the direction to Mecca in accordance with a Qur'anic revelation.

6.4 The 'Fatiha' (the opening *sura* of the Qur'an)

This is Kenneth Cragg's English translation of the prayer which is always included in every form of ritual prayer. Pickthall suggests that it sums up 'the essence of the Qur'an',[3] while the Christian Islamicist W. Montgomery Watt describes it as 'the quintessence of Islamic doctrine'.[4]

> In the name of the merciful Lord of mercy.
> Praise be to God, the Lord of all being,
> The merciful Lord of mercy,
> Master of the Day of Judgment,
> Thee alone we worship
> And to Thee alone we come for aid.
> Guide us in the straight path,
> The path of those whom Thou hast blessed,
> Not of those against whom there is displeasure,
> Nor of those who go astray.[5]

Questions

1. What are the main elements in the prayer?

2. What are the similarities and differences between the Fatiha and the Lord's Prayer? Are there any sentiments in the prayer which Christians could not share?

6.5 For further study

1. *Look up the following verses about prayer in the Qur'an*

The command to pray (2:43–46)
Times for prayers (17:78–79)
Prayers to be said facing Mecca (2:149–150)
Purification before prayer (5:6)
The Friday prayers (62:9–10)
Circumstances when one is excused from prayers
(4:101–103)
The value of prayer (29:45)

2. *Informal prayer (du'a)*

The word *du'a*, which means literally 'a cry' or 'a call', is used to refer to prayers of petition or intercession other than the prescribed prayers which must be said as part of the ritual prayers. It can be used either for prayers which are found in books of prayers, or for extempore prayers using one's own words (*e.g.* a prayer for healing or protection).

Roger Hooker gives the following example of a prayer which is attributed to a grandson of the Prophet Muhammad:

> Praise be to him who when I call on him answers me,
>   slow though I am when he calls me.
> Praise be to him who gives to me when I ask him,
>   miserly though I am when he asks a loan of me.
> Praise be to him to whom I confide my needs
>   whenever I will and he satisfies them.
> My Lord I praise for he is of my praise most worthy.[6]

He then quotes a prayer written by Lancelot Andrewes, an Anglican bishop in the seventeenth century, and asks if there is any obvious difference in spirit between the two prayers:

> How truly meet and right, and comely, and due
>   In all and for all,
>   In all places, times and manners,
>   In every season, every spot,
>   Everywhere, always, together,
> To remember thee, to worship thee,

To confess to thee, to praise thee,
To bless thee, to give thanks to thee,
 Maker, Benefactor, Protector of all.[7]

7

Basic Muslim beliefs and practices

In this chapter we consider the basic 'creed' of Islam (*i.e.* basic Muslim beliefs) and the 'five pillars' (*i.e.* the five 'basic duties') of Sunni ('orthodox') Islam.

In each case, two summaries are presented. The first is written by a Muslim, and comes from *Islam: A Brief Guide*. The second is an attempt to summarize these same beliefs and practices, including some details not mentioned in the Muslim document.

7.1 Basic beliefs
Islam

Islam is a complete way of life. It tells man about the purpose of his creation and existence, his ultimate destiny, his place among other creatures and, most importantly, it provides him with Guidance to lead a balanced and purposeful life which will enable him to avoid the Hell-fire and be rewarded with a place in Paradise in the life after death.

The Arabic word 'Islam' means voluntary surrender to the will of Allah and obedience to His commands. Allah, also an Arabic word, is the proper name of God. Muslims prefer to use Allah rather than God. The Islamic way of life is based on total obedience to Allah. This is the way to obtain peace both here and in the hereafter; hence, Islam also means peace.

Muslim

A person who freely and consciously accepts the Islamic way of life, and sincerely practises it, is called a Muslim.

Basic beliefs

The three fundamental Islamic beliefs are:

Tawhid – the oneness of Allah;
Risalah – prophethood;
Akhirah – life after death.

TAWHID is the most important Islamic belief. It implies that everything in existence originates from the one and only Creator, who is also the Sustainer and the sole Source of Guidance. This belief should govern all aspects of human life. Recognition of this fundamental truth results in a unified view of existence which rejects any divisions of life into religious and secular.

Allah is sole source of Power and Authority, and therefore entitled to worship and obedience from mankind. There is no scope for any partnership with the Creator. Tawhid is pure monotheism. It tells man that Allah is not born, nor is anyone born of Him. He has no son or daughter. Human beings are His subjects. He is the Real and the Ever-lasting; He is the First and the Last; and He is Allah, the One.

Belief in Tawhid brings a total change in a Muslim's life. This belief makes him bow down only to Allah, Who is ever-watchful over all of his actions. He must work to establish the laws of the Creator in all areas of his life, in order to gain the pleasure of Allah.

RISALAH means prophethood and messengership. Allah has not left man without Guidance (*Hidayah*) for the conduct of his life. Since the creation of the first man, Allah has revealed His guidance to mankind through His prophets. The prophets who received books from Allah are called messengers. The message of all the prophets and messengers is one and the same; they urged the people of their time to obey and worship Allah alone and none other. Whenever the teachings of a prophet were distorted by people Allah sent another prophet to bring human beings back to the Straight Path (*Siratul Mustaqim*). The chain of Risalah began with Adam, included Noah, Abraham, Ishmael, Isaac, Lot,

Jacob, Joseph, Moses, and Jesus, and ended with Muhammad (peace be upon them all). Muhammad is the final messenger of Allah to mankind.

The revealed books from Allah are: the Torah (*Tawrat*), the Psalms (*Zabur*), the Gospel (*Injil*) and the Qur'an. The Qur'an, which was revealed to Prophet Muhammad (peace be upon him), is the final book of Guidance.

AKHIRAH means life after death. Belief in Akhirah has a profound impact on the life of a believer. We are all accountable to Allah on the Day of Judgement, when we will be judged according to how we lived our lives. A person who obeys and worships Allah will be rewarded with a permanent place of happiness in Paradise (*Jannah*); the person who does not will be sent to Hell (*Jahannam*), a place of punishment and suffering.

Allah knows man's every thought and inner-most intention, and angels are recording all his actions; if he always keeps in mind that he will be judged on his actions, he will try to make sure that he acts according to the Will of Allah. Many of today's problems would disappear if man had this awareness and acted accordingly.

The articles of faith (iman)

The messenger believeth in that which hath been revealed unto him from His Lord and (so do) the believers. Each one believeth in Allah and His Angels and His scriptures and His messengers . . . (2:285).[1]

According to tradition, Muhammad summarized the basic articles, which a Muslim must believe, as follows: 'God, and his Angels, and His Books, and His Apostles; the Last Day, and the Decree of both good and evil.'

1. *God:* He is One; his nature and qualities are chiefly revealed in his ninety-nine 'Most Beautiful Names'.

2. *His angels:* these include four archangels (*e.g.* Gabriel) and an indefinite number of ordinary angels. There are also creatures

between angels and men called *jinn*, some of which are good and some evil.

3. *His books:* Scriptures were revealed to Adam, Seth, Enoch and Abraham, but these have now been lost. These are the main Scriptures:

a. The Pentateuch (*tawrat*)
b. The Psalms (*zabur*)
   (Both of these are said by Muslims to have been corrupted or misinterpreted by the Jews.)
c. The Gospel (*injil*)
   (said by Muslims to have been corrupted or misinterpreted by the Christians)
d. The Qur'an, revealed to Muhammad.

4. *His apostles:* The Qur'an names twenty-eight apostles, most of whom are biblical characters. The six greatest are Adam, Noah, Abraham, Moses, 'Isa (Jesus) and Muhammad.

5. *The Last Day:* the day of judgment, when all will be judged according to their deeds, and admitted to Paradise or to hell.

Some summaries add the following two doctrines:

6. *The predestination* of good and evil by God.

7. *The bodily resurrection* of all people at the last day.

7.2 Basic practices
Five basic duties of Islam

Islam has five basic duties, often called the 'pillars of Islam'. Performed regularly, correctly and sincerely these duties will transform a Muslim's life, bringing it into line with the wishes of the Creator. Faithful practice of these duties should inspire him to work towards the establishment of justice, equality and righteousness (*Ma'ruf*) in society, and the eradication of injustice, falsehood and evil (*Munkar*).

1. SHAHADAH, the first of the five basic duties, is the declaration, knowingly and voluntarily, of:
La ilaha illal lahu Muhammadur rasulul lah

'There is no god except Allah, Muhammad is the Messenger of Allah'

This declaration contains the two basic concepts of Tawhid and Risalah. This is the basis of all actions in Islam, and the four other basic duties follow this affirmation.

2. SALAH (compulsory prayer) is offered five times a day, either individually or in congregation. It is a practical demonstration of faith, and keeps a believer in constant touch with his Creator. The benefits of Salah are far-reaching, long-lasting and immeasurable. Salah prepares a Muslim to work towards the establishment of true order in society, and the removal of falsehood, evil and indecency. It develops in a believer the qualities of self-discipline, steadfastness and obedience to the Truth, leading him to be patient, honest and truthful in the affairs of his life.

Five times a day, Salah provides a wonderful opportunity for a Muslim to improve his life. It is a system of spiritual, moral and physical training which makes him truly obedient to his Creator.

The five daily prayers are:

FAJR	between dawn and sunrise
ZUHR	between midday and mid-afternoon
ASR	between mid-afternoon and sunset
MAGHRIB	just after sunset
ISHA	between nightfall and daybreak

3. ZAKAH (welfare contribution) is a compulsory payment from a Muslim's annual savings. It literally means purification, and is an annual payment of 2.5% on the value of cash, jewellery and precious metals; a separate rate applies to animals, crops and mineral wealth. Zakah is neither a charity nor a tax: charity is optional, whilst taxes can be used for any of the needs of society. Zakah, however, can only be spent on helping the poor and needy, the disabled, the oppressed, debtors and other welfare purposes, as defined in the Qur'an and Sunnah.

Zakah is an act of worship. It is one of the fundamental principles of an Islamic economy, which ensures an equitable society where everybody has a right to contribute and share. Zakah should be paid with the conscious belief that our wealth and our property belong to Allah, and we merely act as trustees.

4. SAWM is the annual obligatory fast during the month of Ramadan, the ninth month in the Islamic calendar. From dawn to sunset every day of this month a Muslim refrains from eating, drinking, smoking and from sex with his marital partner, seeking only the pleasure of Allah. Sawm develops a believer's moral and spiritual standards, and keeps him away from selfishness, greed, extravagance and other vices. Sawm is an annual training programme which increases a Muslim's determination to fulfil his obligations to the Creator and Sustainer.

5. HAJJ (pilgrimage to the House of Allah) is an annual event, obligatory on those Muslims who can afford to undertake it at least once in their lifetime. It is a journey to the House of Allah (*Al-Ka'bah*) in Makkah, Saudi Arabia, in the month of *Dhul Hijjah*, the twelfth month of the Islamic calendar. Hajj symbolises the unity of mankind; Muslims from every race and nationality assemble, together in equality and humility to worship their Lord. The pilgrim, in the ritual clothing of *Ihram*, has the unique feeling of being in the presence of his Creator, to Whom he belongs, and to Whom he must return after death.[2]

The practice of Islam (din)

The basic essentials in the practice of Islam are summed up in the 'Five Pillars':

1. Recital of the creed (*shahada*): 'There is no god but God, and Muhammad is the apostle of God.' Reciting this creed with sincerity qualifies a person to be called a Muslim. It is repeated in every act of ritual worship.

2. Prayer (*salat*): the recital of the ritual prayers five times a day, with the prescribed postures. Friday is a special day of prayer (17:78–79).

3. *Almsgiving* (*zakat*): the legal alms to be given away, amounting to around a fortieth of one's earnings (2:271–273).

4. *Fasting* (*sawm*): prescribed during the month of Ramadan for all except the sick, travellers, pregnant women, nursing mothers and young children. The fasting is between first light in the morning until sunset (2:183–187).

5. *Pilgrimage* (*hajj*): all Muslims who are able to are required to make the pilgrimage to Mecca once in their lifetime. The *ka'bah* in Mecca is a sacred shrine because Muslims believe that it was built by Adam, and later rebuilt by Abraham and Ishmael after the flood (2:196–197).

7.3 For further study

1. If you were asked to summarize the main articles of the Christian faith under seven main headings, how would you do it? What are the seven most basic things that you believe? This may seem at first sight an impossible or unreasonable task! But if you can summarize simply and clearly what you believe, it may help you to communicate it to a Muslim.

If, when you have done this, you feel that such an outline does not convey all that you believe, and does not communicate anything about Christian experience or what it feels like to be a Christian, this should help you to appreciate the limitations which a devout Muslim sees in any short summary of Muslim beliefs and practices.

2. Similarly, if you were asked to explain what are 'the five pillars of Christianity', what would you say? You may resist the demand to compress the whole of the Christian life into five words or activities, because you do not accept the idea that Christianity can be reduced to five basic 'duties' laid upon us by God. But if you were forced to make this kind of statement, what would you say are the five most important things *for you* about the *practice* of Christianity?

8

The Qur'an

It is essential for Christians to realize that *the Qur'an is to Muslims what Jesus is to Christians*. It is a mistake to make a direct comparison between the role of Jesus in Christianity and the role of Muhammad in Islam, or between the place of the Bible in Christianity and the place of the Qur'an in Islam. This point is made forcefully by Wilfred Cantwell Smith:

> Muslims and Christians have been alienated partly by the fact that both have misunderstood each other's faith by trying to fit it into their own pattern. The most usual error is to suppose (on both sides) that the roles of Jesus Christ in Christianity and of Muhammad in Islam are comparable . . . If one is drawing parallels in terms of the structure of the two religions, what corresponds in the Christian scheme to the Qur'an is not the Bible but the person of Christ – it is Christ who is for Christians the revelation of (from) God.[1]

8.1 A Muslim description of the Qur'an

The Qur'an is the sacred book of the Muslims. It is the last book of guidance from Allah, sent down to Muhammad (pbuh) through the angel Gabriel (*Jibra'il*). Every word of the Qur'an is the word of Allah. It was revealed over a period of 23 years in the Arabic language, and contains 114 Surahs (chapters) and 6236 verses. Muslims learn to read it in Arabic and many memorise it completely. Muslims are expected to try their best to understand the Qur'an's meaning and practise its teachings.

The Qur'an is unrivalled in its recording and preservation. The astonishing fact about this book of Allah is that it has remained unchanged even to a letter over the past fourteen centuries.

The Qur'an deals with man and his ultimate goal in life. Its teachings cover all aspects of this life and the life after death. It contains principles, doctrines and directions for every sphere of human activity. The theme of the Qur'an broadly consists of three fundamental concepts: Tawhid, Risalah and Akhirah. The success of human beings on this earth and in the life hereafter depends on obedience to the Qur'anic teachings.[2]

8.2 Further questions about the Qur'an
Was Muhammad illiterate?

Muslims believe that the revelation of the Qur'an was itself a miracle, since Muhammad himself was not able to read or write. This belief is summed up by the Arabic word *i'jaz*, meaning the incomparability of the Qur'an. It is based on such verses in the Qur'an as these:

Those who follow the messenger, the Prophet who can neither read nor write, whom they will find described in the Torah and the Gospel (7:157).

And thou [Muhammad] wast not a reader of any scripture before it, nor didst thou write it with thy right hand, for then might those have doubted, who follow falsehood (29:48).

Muslims have generally understood an Arabic word used in the Qur'an (*ummi*) to mean 'illiterate', and for this reason Pickthall translates the phrase 'the Prophet who can neither read nor write'. Muslim apologetic has made much of this point to argue for the miraculous nature of the Qur'an. How, they argue, could someone who could neither read nor write compose out of his own mind such beautiful Arabic? According to the Qur'an, the Prophet never performed any miracles. When challenged to perform a miracle to authenticate his claim to be a prophet, he simply pointed to the incomparable nature of the revelations he had received. No-one, he said, could produce verses of the same quality.

A number of Christian scholars, however, have suggested that this was not the original meaning of the word. A. J. Arberry translates it 'the Prophet of the common folk',[3] and Kenneth Cragg suggests 'the unlettered prophet', 'the prophet to the people without a book', meaning those who are as yet without Scriptures.[4] If this was the original meaning of the word, it would mean that Muhammad was aware that the Jews and Christians had their own Scriptures, and that he saw himself as the Prophet called by God to give the Arabs their own Scriptures in their own language of Arabic.

How was the Qur'an written down and collected?

According to the Qur'an and later tradition, many of the revelations came to Muhammad with the command, 'Recite . . .' (as in 96:1). He recited the revelations to his followers, who memorized them all carefully. Some of the revelations had probably been written down by the middle of the period when Muhammad was still in Mecca (*i.e.* before the *Hijra*). And it is likely that Muhammad used secretaries during the time he was in Medina.

Much of the Qur'an had probably therefore been written down in one form or another during the lifetime of Muhammad. He himself no doubt brought together many different passages and arranged them in a special order, which was then kept by his Companions. These collections would have included the main part of each *sura*.

One strong tradition reports that during the so-called 'Wars of Apostasy' (AD 632–634), 'Umar, who later became caliph (successor of the Prophet), was concerned about the fact that many of those who could recite parts of the Qur'an had been killed. Fearing that much of the Qur'an might be lost if more of them were killed, he urged the first caliph, Abu Bakr, to make an official 'Collection'. Abu Bakr was unwilling to do so at first, since he had received no authorization from Muhammad. Later, however, he agreed and commissioned Zayd ibn Thabit, one of Muhammad's secretaries, to carry out the task. The tradition goes on to say that he collected the verses 'from pieces of papyrus, flat stones, palm-leaves, shoulder-blades and ribs of animals, pieces of leather and wooden boards, as well as from the hearts of men'.

These same Islamic sources report that during the caliphate of

'Uthman (644–656), disputes about the reading of the Qur'an arose among the Muslim troops from Syria and Iraq who were engaged in expeditions into Armenia and Azerbaijan. These disputes were so serious that the general had to report the problem to the caliph 'Uthman. After consulting some of the senior Companions of the Prophet, he commissioned Zayd ibn Thabit to make a further 'Collection' of the Qur'an. He and three members of noble families in Mecca worked on the principle that wherever there were differences of reading, they should follow the dialect of Quraysh, the tribe to which Muhammad belonged. In this way the whole of the Qur'an was revised, and this became the authoritative text of the Qur'an.

The next stages in the process are described by Richard Bell:

> A number of copies were made and distributed to the main centres of Islam. As to the exact number of these standard codices, and the places to which they were sent, the account varies; but probably one copy was retained in Medina, and one was sent to each of the towns Kufa, Basra and Damascus, and possibly also to Mecca. Previously existing copies are said to have been destroyed, so that the text of all subsequent copies of the Qur'an should be based upon those standard codices.[5]

Evidence for the existence of these other readings can be found in most of the larger early commentaries, such as those of al-Tabari and al-Zamakhshari. Although the majority of the variant readings concern vowels and pronunciation, there are occasional differences in the consonants, and the order of the *suras* is sometimes different. Short vowels in Arabic are indicated by diacritical points above or below the letters. These were not introduced into the Arabic language until after the Qur'an had been distributed.

Can the Qur'an be translated?

Since the Qur'an was revealed in Arabic, the Arabic of the Qur'an is an essential part of the message, and part of the appeal of the Qur'an for Muslims lies in the beauty of the Arabic. Since it is thought of as the Word of God revealed in Arabic, and since much of the quality of the original is lost in translation, translating it into other languages is even harder than attempting to translate Shakespeare into another language.

In the past, translations were generally discouraged, if not actually forbidden. Today, however, they are being allowed, and some have the approval of Muslim scholars, although they are regarded as a kind of paraphrase and have to be given titles such as *The Meaning of the Glorious Qur'an*.

What is the place of the Qur'an in the experience of Muslims?

Since the Qur'an was first communicated orally by Muhammad to his followers, the Qur'an for Muslims is first and foremost a book to be recited, and it is from the Arabic word for 'recite' (*qara*') that the word 'Qur'an' is derived. Although the Qur'an needs to be read and studied, nothing can take away from the importance of the *recitation* of the Qur'an. 'Muslims see the reciting of the Qur'an', says Jan Slomp, 'as a way of communion with God.'[6] Moreover, learning the text by heart is extremely important, and public recitations of the Qur'an are popular, particularly at the time of certain festivals. Slomp also highlights a crucial difference between Islam and Christianity when he says that whereas starting a Qur'an school has often been a major priority for Muslim missionaries in different parts of the world, Christian missionaries have set about translating the Bible into the local language.

How do Muslims expound the Qur'an?

Muslims have always tried to interpret verses of the Qur'an by studying them in their original context. To do this they have asked questions such as these: what do we know about incidents in the life of the Prophet that help us to interpret the meaning of a particular passage? What do we know from the sayings of the earliest Companions of the Prophet that can help us to interpret the text?

The first great exegete of the Qur'an was Ibn Abbas, a cousin of Muhammad. The earliest important commentary on the Qur'an which exists today was written by al-Tabari (died 923) and gathered together all that was best in the earlier commentaries. Two other well-known commentators were al-Zamakhshari (died 1143) and al-Baidhawi (died 1286).

The following example of a discussion about the context of a revelation comes from Ibn Ishaq's *Life of the Apostle of God*. It refers to two different explanations of the context in which important passages concerning Christians (28:53–55 and 5:82–83) were revealed:

> It is said that these Christians came from Najran, but God knows whether that was so. It is also said, and again God knows best, that it was in reference to them that the verses [were revealed] 'Those to whom we brought the book aforetime, and they believe in it. And when it is read to them they say We believe in it. Verily it is the truth from our Lord. Verily aforetime we were Muslims,' as far as the words, 'We have our works and you have your works. Peace be upon you; we desire not the ignorant.' [*Sic.*]
>
> I asked Ibn Shihab al-Zuhri about those to whom these verses had reference and he told me that he had always heard from the learned that they were sent down concerning the Negus [Christian ruler of Abbysinia] and his companions and also the verses from the *sura* of The Table from the words, 'That is because there are of them presbyters and monks and because they are not proud' up to the words 'So inscribe us with those who bear witness'.[7]

One important principle used in exegesis of the Qur'an is 'Abrogation', which means that a revelation that came from God at one particular time could be 'abrogated', superseded or replaced by a new revelation given later. This principle is based on verses such as these:

> Such of our revelations as We abrogate or cause to be forgotten, We bring (in place) one better or the like thereof. Knowest thou not that Allah is able to do all things? (2:106).

> And when We put a revelation in place of (another) revelation, – and Allah knoweth best what He revealeth – they say: Lo! thou art but inventing. Most of them know not (16:101).

Richard Bell explains the doctrine of Abrogation as developed by Muslim scholars:

> The idea underlying the doctrine is that certain commands to the Muslims in the Qur'an were only of temporary application, and that when circumstances changed they were abrogated or replaced by others. Because the commands were the word of God, however, they continued to be recited as part of the Qur'an.[8]

8.3 Reading the Qur'an

It is probably just as hard for a Christian to read the Qur'an from beginning to end as for a Muslim to read the Bible from Genesis to Revelation! The following, therefore, are some of the points at which we can begin to read it.

(*Note:* The following verse numbers are from Pickthall's translation; in some other translations of the Qur'an the numbering of verses is slightly different. If the verses you have looked up in your translation do not seem to be the right ones, read a few verses *before* or *after*, until you find the right verses.)

1. *The shortest suras*
    Sura 1 – The Fatiha, often described as 'the essence of the Qur'an.'
        96 – said to be the first *sura* revealed to Muhammad.
        74 – said to be the second *sura*, revealed after some months.
        82, 84, 93, 101, 112, 113, 114
            – all short *suras* at the end of the Qur'an.

2. *Some well-known passages*
    2:255   – a well-known verse about the sovereignty of God.
    24:35–36 – a passage which has been a source of inspiration to mystics.
    2:256   – '. . . there is no compulsion in religion'.
    59:22–24 – verses about 'the most beautiful names' of God.

3. *Typical passages*
    – about the creation, 3:189–191; 13:2–4; 31:10–11; 32:4–9.

– about heaven and hell, 2:24–25; 38:50–60; 44:47–57.
– about prophets, 6:84–88.

4. Laws

– about marriage, 4:3.
       theft, 5:38.
       usury, 2:275–279.
       obedience to parents, 29:8.
       wine, 2:219.
       pork, 2:173.
– a summary of the moral law, 2:83; 2:177.

5. Use the index

. . . to look up subjects such as Abraham, marriage, divorce, Jews, Christians, Satan, adultery, *etc.*

6. Complete suras

12 – Joseph (compare and contrast with the story of Joseph in Genesis 37 – 50).

2 – The Cow – generally said to be the first *sura* revealed at Medina; one of the longer *suras*, but one which contains many important Qur'anic themes.

Look up the following verses in the Qur'an:

1. About the Qur'an itself

The Qur'an revealed in the Arabic language, 12:2; 46:12.
Muhammad 'the seal of the prophets', 33:40.
The Qur'an reveals clearly what Jews and Christians have hidden in their scriptures, 5:15.
Verses about 'Abrogation', the belief that some revelations to the Prophet can be superseded by later revelations, 2:106; 16:101; 22:52.

2. About the Bible

■ revelations in scripture recognized by the Qur'an:
       the *tawrat* (revealed to Moses), 2:87; 3:3.
       the *zabur* (revealed to David), 4:163.
       the *injil* (revealed to Jesus), 5:46–48.

- the Qur'an confirms the message of previous scriptures: 2:91; 3:1–4; 3:84; 4:47.

- God has protected the scriptures: 5:48; 18:28.

- Muhammad is to consult the scriptures already revealed if he is in doubt about what is revealed to him: 10:94–95.

- Jews and Christians are accused of tampering with their scriptures:
  a. they are ignorant of them, 2:78.
  b. they conceal them, 2:146, 159, 174; 5:15.
  c. they change them, 2:75.
  d. they sell false scriptures for gain, 2:79.
  e. they believe parts and disbelieve other parts, 2:85.

3. *About Christians*
  a. passages which are *sympathetic*: 2:62, 5:69, 82; 22:40.
  b. *appeals to Christians to accept Muhammad's message* because it confirms the *injil*, 3:64–71; 29:46.
  c. passages which are more *critical*: 5:14; 5:51; 9:29–31; 57:27.

4. *Passages about Jesus*
  a. the annunciation, and the birth of Jesus, 3:35–47; 19:16–35.
  b. the ministry of Jesus, 3:48–54; 5:110–117; 57:27; 61:6.
  c. the death of Jesus, 3:55; 19:33; 5:117; 4:155–159.
  d. Jesus and God, 3:59; 4:171–172; 5:72–75, 116–117; 9:30–31.

8.4 For further study

The following extract is a single verse of the Qur'an with an English translation and commentary by A. Yusuf Ali. This edition of the Qur'an is published by the Islamic Foundation, and is distributed widely by Islamic organizations in the West. The passage is from *sura* 4:171 and includes the words which the Prophet is to address to Christians in persuading them to change their beliefs about Jesus:

يَتَأَهْلَ ٱلْكِتَبِ لَا تَغْلُوا۟ فِى دِينِكُمْ وَلَا تَقُولُوا۟ عَلَى ٱللَّهِ إِلَّا ٱلْحَقَّ

إِنَّمَا ٱلْمَسِيحُ عِيسَى ٱبْنُ مَرْيَمَ رَسُولُ
ٱللَّهِ وَكَلِمَتُهُ أَلْقَنهَا إِلَى مَرْيَمَ وَرُوحٌ
مِنْهُ فَآمِنُوا بِٱللَّهِ وَرُسُلِهِ
وَلَا تَقُولُوا ثَلَنثَةٌ ٱنتَهُوا خَيْرًا لَكُمْ إِنَّمَا
ٱللَّهُ إِلَـهٌ وَٰحِدٌ سُبْحَـنَهُ أَن يَكُونَ
لَهُ وَلَدٌ لَّهُ مَا فِي ٱلسَّمَـوَٰتِ وَمَا فِي
ٱلْأَرْضِ وَكَفَىٰ بِٱللَّهِ وَكِيلًا

171. O People of the Book!
     Commit no excesses[675]
     In your religion: nor say
     Of God aught but the truth.
     Christ Jesus the son of Mary
     Was (no more than)
     An apostle of God,
     And His Word,
     Which He bestowed on Mary,
     And a Spirit proceeding
     From Him: so believe
     In God and His apostles.
     Say not 'Trinity': desist:[676]
     It will be better for you:
     For God is One God:
     Glory be to Him:
     (Far Exalted is He) above
     Having a son. To Him
     Belong all things in the heavens
     And on earth. And enough
     Is God as a Disposer of affairs.

675. Just as a foolish servant may go wrong by excess of zeal for his master, so in religion people's excesses may lead them to blasphemy or a spirit the very opposite of religion. The Jewish excesses in the direction of formalism, racialism, exclusiveness, and rejection of Christ Jesus have been denounced in many places. Here the Christian attitude is condemned, which raises Jesus to an equality with God; in some cases venerates Mary almost to idolatry; attributes a physical son to God; and invents the doctrine of the Trinity, opposed to all reason, which according to the Athanasian Creed, unless a man believes, he is doomed to hell for ever. Let our Muslims also beware lest they fall into excesses either in doctrine or in formalism.

676. Christ's attributes are mentioned: (1) that he was the son of a woman, Mary, and therefore a man; (2) but an apostle, a man with a mission from God, and therefore entitled to honour; (3) a Word bestowed on Mary, for he was created by God's word 'Be' (kun), and he was; iii. 59; (4) a spirit proceeding from God, but not God: his life and his mission were more limited than in the case of some other apostles, though we must pay equal honour to him as a man of God. The doctrines of Trinity, equality with God, and sonship, are repudiated as blasphemies. God is independent of all needs and has no need of a son to manage His affairs. The Gospel of John (whoever wrote it) has put in a great deal of Alexandrian and Gnostic mysticism round the doctrine of the Word (Greek, Logos), but it is simply explained here, and our Sufis work on this explanation.[9]

9

Muhammad

In a recent book about Islam by Gai Eaton, an English Muslim, the chapter on 'The Messenger of God' begins like this:

> The encounter with the story of Muhammad's life, like the encounter with the Qur'an, requires a shift in perspective both on the part of the Christian and of the secularist . . . The Christian, if he wishes to understand Islam, must resist the temptation to compare Muhammad with Jesus, for these two had entirely different roles in the scheme of things . . . . This man [Muhammad] was what he had to be, did what he had to do, and said what he had to say in accordance with the divine intention . . . It follows that, from the Muslim point of view, the world into which Muhammad was born . . . was a world providentially designed to receive and to give both the message of the Qur'an and the message contained in the story of his life the precise shape and colouring they have. The gemstone was matched to its setting, as was the setting to the gem; and to suppose that either could have been other than they were is to introduce a concept of 'chance' which has no place in this context.[1]

9.1 A Muslim statement about Muhammad

Muhammad (pbuh), the final messenger of Allah and the best of creation, was born in Makkah, Arabia, in the year 571 CE (Christian Era). His father, Abdullah, died before his birth and his mother, Aminah, died when he was only six. He married Khadijah, a noble lady of Makkah, when he was twenty-five.

He began to receive revelation from Allah at the age

87

of forty, marking the beginning of his work as the messenger of Allah.

The people of Makkah at that time worshipped idols. The Prophet (pbuh) invited them to Islam. Some responded favourably and became Muslims, while others rebuked him and turned against him. Undaunted, he continued to preach the message of Allah and, gradually, the number of his followers increased. He and the early Muslims underwent terrible suffering and faced stiff opposition from the idolaters.

In the twelfth year of his prophethood, in 622 CE, Muhammad (pbuh) migrated from Makkah to Madinah. The people of Madinah accepted him as their leader and he established the first Islamic state there. The Islamic calendar begins from the day of the migration (*Hijrah*) of the Prophet (pbuh).

The Prophet (pbuh) organised the early Muslims and preached the message of Allah with unmatched patience and wisdom. Eventually Islam was established in the whole of the Arabian peninsula, and was set to make a tremendous contribution to the history and civilisation of the world. Within a very short time, the message of Islam spread from Arabia to most parts of the known world. Over a billion Muslims of the present day still bear testimony to the success of that message.

Islam, completed at the time of Prophet Muhammad (pbuh), can solve all human problems, and is the only hope for the present as well as the future. The need is to practise it faithfully.

Prophet Muhammad (described in the Qur'an as the 'blessing for the universe' and the 'perfect example to follow') died in 632 CE at the age of sixty-three. He left behind the Qur'an and his Sunnah as the sources of guidance for all generations to come.[2]

9.2 Arabia before the time of Muhammad

This period is known by Muslims as *al jahiliyya*, the 'Age of Ignorance'.

Political

Some of the tribes were nomadic bedouin of the desert; others were semi-nomadic, while others were permanently settled in smaller towns (such as Ta'if) or larger cities (such as Mecca and Medina). While individual tribes were united by alliances, there was no unity in the area as a whole. Blood-feuds between tribes were settled by the tribal ethic of revenge and reprisal.

Foreign powers

The two great world powers in Muhammad's time were the Byzantine Empire and the Persian Empire; Arabia was influenced by the power struggle between these two great powers. (See map overleaf.)

Byzantine Empire (Asia Minor, Syria, Egypt, SE Europe; capital in Constantinople). Fiercely 'Orthodox' (Christian) in doctrine, and strongly opposed to other 'heretical' doctrines such as Monophysitism and Nestorianism.

Supported the Ghassanid Dynasty in Syria as a buffer state against the Arabs.

Persian Empire under the Sassanid Dynasty (Iraq to Afghanistan; capital in Iraq).

Supported the Lakhmid Kingdom of Hira in Iraq as a buffer against the Arabs.

In 614 AD the Persians captured Jerusalem from Byzantine power; but in 628 the Byzantines defeated the Persians. Both empires were exhausted by the struggles, leaving a power vacuum at the time when Islam was beginning to spread.

Economic and social

There was a flourishing caravan trade along routes running north–south and east–west. Mecca had become an important commercial centre, as well as a centre of pilgrimage. There were many social evils – for instance, female infants were often buried alive, and women had little protection.

Religion

Although there is some evidence of belief in one supreme God (Allah), religious practices centred round a host of lesser deities. For instance, at Mecca three goddesses were worshipped:

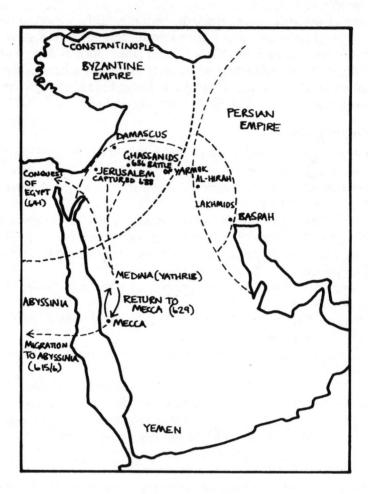

Manat, al-Lat, and al-Uzza. There were also many idol cults, and sacrifices were offered to spirits (of caves, trees, wells, stones *etc.*). Superstitious rituals were practised at many shrines, and there were annual pilgrimages to the major shrines such as the Ka'ba at Mecca. There was a strong belief in fate, and little or no belief in an after-life. A rich tradition of Arab poetry had developed.

Other religions

■ There were some *Jewish* communities or tribes, especially in and around Medina.

■ There were people called *hanif*. They were monotheists of a sort, but had little influence.

■ *Christians:* There were several nomadic tribes which had previously embraced Christianity. The area of Yemen in the south had been Christian since the fourth century.

In Mecca itself the Christians were mostly foreigners, such as black slaves from Ethiopia and labourers and traders from Syria. According to tradition, Muhammad's first wife Khadija had a cousin, Waraqa ibn Naufal, who had become a Christian.

Muhammad may well have had some contact with Syrian monks in the desert (see 9.6).

9.3 The life of Muhammad

AD c. 570	Birth of Muhammad; belonged to a tribe of Quraysh.
	Father died before he was born, and mother died six years later.
	Brought up by grandfather and uncle, Abu Talib.
c. 592	According to tradition began travelling to Syria with trading caravans, and on one of these journeys met Bahira, a Syrian Christian monk.
595	Married Khadija, a wealthy widow, and began working with her in her trading business.
610	Muhammad's first call to be a prophet, while meditating in a cave on Mount Hira near Mecca.
615/6	Persecution from his own tribe of Quraysh forced some of his followers to emigrate to the Christian kingdom of Abyssinia.
	Muhammad and his 'Companions' stayed in Mecca.

619	Death of Khadija, and of Abu Talib, Muhammad's uncle and protector. Muhammad's position now less secure in the tribe.
622	The Emigration (*Hijra*) to Medina in response to an invitation from a group of Muslim converts ('Helpers') for him to come to resolve the conflicts between the different communities in Medina. Beginning of the Muslim era.
624	Muslims began raiding caravans from Mecca, which led to a series of battles:
	Battle of *Badr* – Muslims (with 324 men) defeated Meccans (with 950 men).
625	Battle of *Uhud* – Muslims defeated by Meccans.
627	Battle of *Ahzab* (the Battle of the Trench) – Muslims repelled the Meccan attack on Medina.
628	The Treaty of Hudaibiya between Muhammad and the Meccans, which enabled him to return to Mecca for pilgrimage the following year.
629	Muhammad and the Muslims returned to Mecca on 11 January with 10,000 men. Meccans submitted without fighting. Muhammad declared a general amnesty. All idols in the *Ka'ba* destroyed.
	Muhammad returned to Medina. Beginning of mass movement of tribes embracing Islam.
631	Muhammad's last pilgrimage to Mecca.
632	Muhammad died in Medina.

9.4 The successors of Muhammad

The successors of the Prophet are known as 'caliphs', and the first four caliphs are known as the 'Rightly Guided' or 'Righteous' Caliphs. This period is regarded as the Golden Age of Islam.

632–634	1st caliph, Abu Bakr, chosen because he had been nominated by Muhammad to lead the prayers. Prevented many tribes from breaking away from the new Islamic state during the Wars of Apostasy. Byzantine army defeated in 634, and Islam spread into Syria, Iraq and Yemen.
634–644	2nd caliph, 'Umar, nominated by Abu Bakr. Authorized the collection of the *suras* of the Qur'an. Captured Damascus (634); defeated Byzantine army at Battle of Yarmuk, and captured Jerusalem (636), and Alexandria (641). Gained control of Syria, Egypt and Persia. Gave Jews and Christians the choice of conversion to Islam or leaving Arabia. Stabbed to death by a Persian Christian slave.

644-656	3rd caliph, 'Uthman. Established official text of the Qur'an and had other texts burned. A weak leader, accused of granting favours to relatives. His leadership provoked rebellion, and he was assassinated.
656-661	4th caliph, Ali, Muhammad's cousin and son-in-law. Fought against followers of 'A'isha, Muhammad's widow, at Battle of Camel; then against Mu'awiya, governor of Syria, who proclaimed himself caliph. After truce in 660, Mu'awiya ruled over Syria, and Ali over the rest of the Empire. Conflict over the succession after his death led to the split between Sunnis and Shi'ites (the 'party of Ali').

These four caliphs were succeeded by the Umayyad Dynasty which ruled in Damascus. In 750 power passed to the Abbasids, whose capital was Baghdad. The Fatimids had their own rival caliphate in Cairo from 909 to 1171.

9.5 Christianity at the time of Muhammad

The Christianity which Muhammad saw was basically a *foreign religion*. Most of the Christians with whom he came in contact were not Arabs but foreigners from the neighbouring countries, many of whom had settled in Arabia because they had been persecuted elsewhere. They kept themselves aloof from the Arabs; they continued to worship in their own languages. It is generally agreed that Muhammad cannot have had access to any books of the Bible in his own language of Arabic.

The Christian church was *deeply divided over doctrinal disputes*. Ever since the great Councils of Nicaea (AD 325) and Chalcedon (451), the churches in the East had been arguing about the doctrines of the Trinity and the person of Christ. Apart from those who accepted the doctrines of Chalcedon,

■ the Monophysites emphasized the divinity of Jesus, and gave the impression that Jesus was not fully human;

■ the Nestorians accepted the two natures of Jesus but thought that they were separate;

■ the Gnostics tended to think that matter was evil and that salvation depended on an experience of mystical enlightenment. They denied the incarnation, and some believed that Jesus was not crucified.

After nearly 300 years of being a persecuted minority religion, Christianity had become, since the conversion of Constantine in 312, a religion *associated with political power*. The Byzantine Emperors stood firmly for the orthodox faith and fiercely persecuted the different heretical sects. For many Arabs, therefore, Christianity was synonymous with Byzantine domination and fierce repression of any beliefs which differed from the religion of the state.

9.6 For further study

The word *sira* is used for accounts of the life of the Prophet written after his death.

The earliest of these 'Lives', called *The Life of Muhammad*, was written by Ibn Ishaq (707–773), who was born and grew up in Medina. He began collecting stories and legends about the life of the Prophet, but at some stage came into conflict with two religious leaders in Medina. He therefore went to Egypt at the age of thirty, and later, at the invitation of the Abbasid caliph, to Baghdad, where he died. His work was gathered into three volumes, which were incorporated into a Life of the Prophet written by Ibn Hisham, who died in 840 (67 years after the death of Ibn Ishaq).

The orientalist Alfred Guillaume believes that Ibn Ishaq has recorded the life of Muhammad 'with honesty and truthfulness and, too, an impartiality which is rare in such writings'.[3] The following extract from Ibn Ishaq's *Life* is his account of the journey which Muhammad made to Syria with his uncle while still a young boy, and his meeting with the Christian monk, Bahira. Christians may want to ask how far the account has been coloured by Muslim beliefs about the prophethood of Muhammad.

> When the caravan reached Busra in Syria, there was a monk there in his cell by the name of Bahira, who was well versed in the knowledge of Christians. A monk had always occupied that cell. There he gained his knowledge from a book that was in the cell, so they allege, handed on from generation to generation. They had often passed by him in the past and he never spoke to them or took any notice of them until this year, and when they stopped near his cell he made a great feast

for them. It is alleged that that was because of something he saw while in his cell. They allege that while he was in his cell he saw the apostle of God in the caravan when they approached, with a cloud overshadowing him among the people. Then they came and stopped in the shadow of a tree near the monk. He looked at the cloud when it overshadowed the tree, and its branches were bending and drooping over the apostle of God until he was in the shadow beneath it. When Bahira saw that, he came out of his cell and sent word to them, 'I have prepared food for you, O men of Quraysh, and I should like you all to come both great and small, bond and free . . .

When Bahira saw him he stared at him closely, looking at his body and finding traces of his description (in the Christian books). When the people had finished eating and gone away, Bahira got up and said to him, 'Boy, I ask you by al-Lat and al-'Uzza to answer my question.' Now Bahira said this only because he had heard his people swearing by these gods. They allege that the apostle of God said to him, 'Do not ask me by al-Lat and al-'Uzza, for by Allah nothing is more hateful to me than these two.' Bahira answered, 'Then by Allah, tell me what I ask'; he replied, 'Ask me what you like'; so he began to ask him about what happened in his sleep, and his habits, and his affairs generally, and what the apostle of God told him coincided with what Bahira knew of his description. Then he looked at his back and saw the seal of prophethood between his shoulders in the very place described in his book . . .

'You have told the truth,' said Bahira. 'Take your nephew back to his country and guard him carefully against the Jews, for by Allah! if they see him and know about him what I know, they will do him evil; a great future lies before this nephew of yours, so take him home quickly.'

So his uncle took him off quickly and brought him back to Mecca when he had finished his trading in Syria.[4]

10

Tradition (*hadith* and *sunna*)

The word *hadith* means literally a communication, a narrative, or a record. It came to be used for a record of the actions and sayings of the Prophet and his Companions.

The word *sunna* means literally a way, or a path. It therefore came to mean 'the way of the Prophet' or 'the Prophet's example', that is, the way the Prophet did something or said something, and so by extension the way that Muslims must follow.

Thus the *hadith* enshrines the *sunna*, and the two words have come to mean the same thing. 'The *hadith*' or 'the *sunna*' refers to the whole body of traditions about the Prophet, which were collected after his death. The importance of tradition as it was developed by his followers is summed up by Kenneth Cragg when he says, 'By *hadith/sunna* Muhammad shaped and ordered his community, we might say, from the grave.'[1] 'The *hadith* literature', in the words of Alfred Guillaume, 'is the basis of that developed system of law, theology and custom which is Islam.'[2]

10.1 A Muslim explanation of the *sunna*

The Sunnah is the example of Prophet Muhammad (pbuh). It is contained in the books of Hadith, which are collections of his sayings and actions and those actions done with his approval. The Hadith show how to put the Guidance of the Qur'an into practice. The Hadith were recorded meticulously by the Prophet's companions after his death. Six particular collections have become prominent and are regarded as the most authentic: *Bukhari, Muslim, Tirmidhi, Abu Dawud, Nasa'i* and *Ibn-i-Majah*.[3]

10.2 Further questions about tradition
How were hadith *and* sunna *recorded?*

Every *hadith* has two parts. (1) The names of the persons who handed it on. For example, 'A told me, saying that B said C had informed him, saying D mentioned that he heard E relate, "I heard F ask the Apostle of God such and such" . . .' This chain of authorities is known as the *isnad*, which means literally 'supports'. (2) The substance of the report of what the Prophet said or did (*matn*). In Muslim understanding only the *sunna* of the Prophet and the original Muslim community could supply a rule of conduct for believers.

How reliable is hadith?

In the 200 years after the death of Muhammad during which the genuine traditions about the Prophet were circulating widely, other traditions were circulated by people who wanted to gain authority for a particular view by attributing it to the Prophet himself. The Muslim community was therefore faced with the problem of how to distinguish between genuine traditions which could be traced back to the Prophet or his Companions and contradictory, doubtful or even spurious traditions invented later.

The problem was solved by the Collectors of *hadith*, who classified them in the following categories.

■ 'Sound': there are no weak links in the chain of authorities, and the content is not inconsistent with accepted Muslim belief.

■ 'Fair': the links in the chain of reporters are incomplete, or there is incomplete agreement about the reliability of the authorities.

■ 'Weak': some of the transmitters of the tradition are not regarded as reliable, or there are doubts about the content of the report.

How is hadith *used in the life of a Muslim?*

Gai Eaton explains why *hadith* is so important in the everyday life of Muslims:

If the Muslim is to tap that same source and become 'one who understands', he has no choice but to model himself upon this 'perfect exemplar', imitating Muhammad so far as he is able, both in his character and in his mode of action. Since the Prophet is 'closer to the believers than their [own] selves' (Q.33.6), it can be said that he is the believer's *alter ego* or – to take this a step further – more truly 'oneself' than the collection of fragments and contrary impulses which we commonly identify as the 'self'.

This is why the *ḥadīth* literature is of such immense importance in the everyday life of the Muslim; and the record is so extensive that it is always possible, even among learned people, for someone to astonish and delight his friends by quoting to them a 'Prophet story', or a saying of which they had not previously heard. The intimate knowledge we have of Muhammad's life (much of which we owe to 'A'isha) is, from a practical point of view, just as important as his religious teaching and the example he set in affairs of greater consequence. The believer feels close to him in life and hopes to be closer still after death, loving him not only as master and as guide but also as brother-man. It is in the light of this relationship that we may understand parts of the record which often appear trivial to the occidental, such as 'A'isha's meticulous account of the manner in which they washed from a single bowl after making love, and her added comment, 'he would get ahead of me and I used to say, "Give me a chance, give me a chance!"' . . .

Al-Ghazzali (d. AD 1111), who is one of the most widely accepted authorities, wrote of the true Muslim as one who 'imitates the Messenger of Allah in his goings out and his comings in, his movements and his times of rest, the manner of his eating, his deportment, his sleep and his speech'. So a man should sit while putting on his trousers and stand while putting on his turban, start with the right foot when putting on his shoes and, when cutting his nails, begin with the forefinger of the right hand; and al-Ghazzali mentions the case of a pious man who never dared eat a melon, much as he wished to do so, because he could not discover the precise manner in which God's Messenger ate melons. Did he cut them into segments? Did he perhaps scoop the flesh out with a spoon? We shall never know. But this outward observance is, of course, meaningless unless it both reflects and engenders a profound inward conformity to the perfect exemplar, given us by God as 'a mercy to mankind', a conformity of the believer's soul to the soul of Muhammad.[4]

10.3 For further study

The following examples illustrate the wide variety of subjects covered by *hadith* – details about the life of the Prophet, moral teaching, and regulations about clothes, eating, marriage, the pursuit of knowledge and apostasy.

'A'ishah said: The first revelation that was granted to the Messenger of Allah (peace and blessings of Allah be on him) was the true dream in a state of sleep, so that he never dreamed a dream but the truth of it shone forth like the dawn of the morning. Then solitude became dear to him and he used to seclude himself in the cave of Hira, and therein he devoted himself to divine worship for several nights before he came back to his family and took provisions for his retirement; then he would return to Khadijah and take more provisions for a similar period, until the Truth came to him while he was in the cave of Hira; so the angel (Gabriel) came to him and said, Read . . .

If a man goes an inch towards God, God will come a yard towards him. If he goes a yard towards God, God will come a furlong towards him.

Intentions count for more than actions.

The man who marries perfects half his religion.

Never did God allow anything more hateful to Him

than divorce. With God, the most detestable of all things allowed is divorce.

He who believes in Allah and the Last Day should honour his guest.

By Allah, I [Muhammad] ask Allah's forgiveness and turn to Him in repentance more than seventy times a day.

Modesty is part of faith.

Gold and silk are lawful to the women of my Umma and forbidden to the men.

The angels do not enter the house in which there is a dog or pictures.

Say Allah's name (Bismillah) and eat with your right hand and eat from near you.

If anyone has got an atom of pride in his heart, he will not enter Paradise.

The seeking of knowledge is a must for every Muslim man and woman.

No one of you (really) believes (in Allah and His religion) till he want for his brother what he wants for himself.

I have been commanded to wage war on the people till they testify that there is no deity save Allah, and that Muhammad is the Apostle of Allah, (till they) say the prayers and give the legal alms.

The blood of a man who is a Muslim is not lawful [*i.e.* it may not be lawfully shed], save if he belongs to one of three (classes): a married man who is an adulterer; one who owes his soul for another soul [*i.e.* a murderer]; one who abandons his religion, thus becoming one who splits the community.

11

Law (*shari'a*) and theology (*kalam*)

Christians will no doubt find it hard to understand why we need to give attention to law, since the concept of law seems foreign to Christians who are taught that salvation is by faith, not by works. While we recognize that each church has its own order and discipline, the only law we are conscious of is the law of the country in which we live.

The importance of law in Islam is summed up succinctly by Joseph Schacht when he says, 'Islamic law is the epitome of Islamic thought, the most typical manifestation of the Islamic way of life, the core and kernel of Islam itself.'[1]

Similarly Kenneth Cragg explains the role of law in Islam and the relationship between law and theology like this:

> Islam understands law as religion, religion as law . . .
> Law, rather than theology, has the prior emphasis in
> Islam. Broadly, it is obedience to the will of God, rather
> than fellowship in the knowledge of God's nature,
> which is paramount. Revelation is for direction of life,
> rather than disclosure of mystery . . . Islam is essentially
> submission, rather than 'communion'.[2]

Law (*shari'a*) in Islam, therefore, forms 'the constitution of the Muslim community, the pattern of its communal order'.[3] The process of formulating Islamic law took between 200 and 250 years. Thus, by about 850, 'Islam may be said to have reached the fully developed form in which it was to persist down to modern times. This full development was reached when the major items of belief and practice had been settled and an agreed body of authoritative sources had emerged.'[4]

11.1 The basis of law

The four sources (*usul*), principles or pillars of law in Sunni Islam are:

1. The *Qur'an*, which contains in principle the whole of the *shari'a* law;

2. The *sunna* (*hadith*), which clarifies or elaborates the teaching of the Qur'an;

3. The *consensus of the community* (*ijma'*). The word means 'convergence', *i.e.* of opinion. This principle is based on the saying of Muhammad, 'My community will never agree on an error.' The consensus of the community is reached in practice by the process of 'enterprise' (*ijtihad*), which is the activity of the scholars (*ulama*) who formulate legal precepts dealing with new situations, using all the sources of the law with a kind of logical reasoning or rational argument.

'The inner function of *ijma'*,' says H. A. R. Gibb, 'as the instrument by which the Community regulates its spiritual life, is to secure and to preserve the integral spiritual unity of all Muslims as a spiritually governed society.'[5] From about AD 900 it was felt that all essential questions had been finally settled, if a consensus had gradually emerged. All that remained to be done after this was the explanation, application and interpretation of the law that had been laid down.

4. The *principle of analogy* (*qiyas*). When there is no clear ruling that emerges from the Qur'an or the *sunna*, scholars try to find some comparable ruling that will suggest an appropriate parallel, relying on personal judgment (*ra'y*) and the application of discretion in legal judgments based on the 'good of the community' (*istihsan*).

The science of law is called jurisprudence (*fiqh*). The four main schools of law in the Sunni tradition differ according to the emphasis they place on each of the four sources. Each tends to be strong in certain countries or regions, and are 'schools' rather than 'sects'.

The Hanafi school was founded by Abu Hanifa (died 767) in

Iraq. Here the main emphasis is on the Qur'an, and the *sunna* is regarded as secondary.

The Maliki school was founded by Malik ibn Anas (died 795) in Medina. This is the oldest of the schools and is very conservative. It regards the Qur'an and the *sunna* as the main sources of authority, but allows some place for consensus.

The Shafi'i School was founded by Al-Shafi'i (died 820) who lived in Baghdad and Egypt. This position represented a compromise between the Maliki and Hanafi Schools, and rejected the role of private judgment.

The Hanbali School was founded by Ahmad ibn Hanbal (died 855) in Baghdad. This was the most conservative of all the schools, accepting only the Qur'an and the *sunna*, and rejecting both consensus and analogy. This is the school which is followed in Saudi Arabia today.

Alongside *shari'a* there developed a kind of unwritten Islamic custom, known as *'urf*. In addition to the *shari'a* courts, therefore, there existed in many countries *'urfi* courts to decide on questions related to customs.

The completion of this process of formulating Islamic law is described by Michael Nazir-Ali as follows:

> By the beginning of the third century after the Hijra, Muslim jurisprudence had been codified by the jurists of the four schools of law. The *ulama* now reached a consensus, which has only recently been challenged, that the four schools were 'final' and that the work of the jurists henceforward would be only the interpretation and application of the codified law.[6]

11.2 Theology

The following brief survey outlines some of the major theological issues that Islam has had to face during the past 1,400 years.

1. The question of succession: who were the rightful successors of the Prophet? How should the leaders of the community be chosen?

This was the fundamental issue that led to the split between Sunnis and Shi'ites. Should the successor of the Prophet be chosen by the community? Or should he be from the Prophet's family, as Ali (Muhammad's cousin and son-in-law) and the Shi'ites argued? Ali eventually became the fourth caliph; but when his first son Hasan renounced his claim to succeed his father, and his second son Husayn was killed in the Battle of Kerbala in 680, the family had no hope of competing with the claims of the Umayyad caliphs who were now ruling in Damascus.

2. *The definition of 'Muslim'*: what makes a person a Muslim?

When the centre of power in the Muslim world moved from the deserts of Arabia to the city of Damascus, and the Islamic Empire spread in every direction, the leaders of the Muslim community were exposed to all the temptations of power and wealth. Inevitably some protested against the worldliness and compromise that they felt were invading Islam, and challenged the community to define more carefully what makes a person a Muslim.

One group called *Kharijites* ('Seceders') were puritanical in their approach, and called for a strict definition of what it means to be a good Muslim. They argued that a Muslim who committed serious sin and refused to repent became automatically an unbeliever, an apostate. Another group called *Murji'ites* ('Postponers') took a more lenient view over moral standards, saying that only God could decide who was a good Muslim, and that he would give his verdict on the day of judgment. They argued that faith alone was sufficient for being a Muslim. While the Murji-'ites disappeared, the Kharijites continued as a distinct group.

3. *The challenge of rationalism*: what is the place of reason in faith?

As the Muslim community came in contact with Greek culture and civilization in such places as Damascus, they found they had to face all kinds of intellectual questions which might never have occurred to the first Muslims in Arabia. Islam had to come to terms with Greek philosophy, just as Christianity had been trying to do for centuries. These were some of the questions which were discussed:

- Is it reasonable to believe in God's predestination of *everything*, including both good and evil? Are there not many verses in the Qur'an which speak of human beings as responsible and free to choose for themselves?

- Can one prove the existence of God by reason alone?

- How are we to understand the language of the Qur'an? Are anthropomorphic expressions (*e.g.* about the 'face' or the 'hands' of God) to be understood literally or figuratively?

- If the Qur'an is the very Word(s) of God, how is it related to God? Was it created in time, or was it uncreated and eternal? Did it come into being as it was recited by Muhammad, or had it existed from eternity in heaven?

The *Mu'tazilites* took a position that might be described as 'rationalist' or 'modernist'. They questioned the more extreme expressions of predestination, and argued for the freedom of the will, insisting that individuals have power over their own choices and actions. They believed that if the Qur'an is thought to be eternal, it becomes something divine alongside God. They also taught that anthropomorphic language must not be understood literally.

Al-Ash'ari (873–935), after having been a Mu'tazilite theologian for some years, abandoned their philosophical method and returned to a more orthodox, traditional position. He rejected their teaching on freewill, for example, and taught that the Qur'an was *un*created. He came down strongly on the side of predestination, while allowing a place for human freedom and responsibility. He emphasized the transcendence of God, and in discussion of the problems of religious language frequently appealed to the formula *bi la kayf* (meaning 'without asking "how?"'). In emphasizing the qualitative difference between God and humanity, he believed that God's justice is different from any human concept of justice. His teaching 'determined the direction in which dogmatic Islam was to move for centuries' (Wensinck), and he is regarded as one of the greatest theologians in Islam.

At a later stage further challenges came from those who had been influenced by Greek philosophy, and believed that (1) the universe is eternal; (2) there is no resurrection of the body; (3) philosophy is more important than prophecy, and both are connected because they are related to the same human faculty of imagination. The person who demonstrated that these ideas were heretical and who re-established orthodox theology was al-Ghazali (died 1111), who came to be recognized as another of the greatest theologians in Islam (see also chapters 11.3 and 13.3.)

4. *The definition of orthodoxy*: what is unacceptable belief?

The Ahmadiyyah movement has raised this question for Muslims in an acute form in the twentieth century. Founded by Mirza Ghulam Ahmad Khan (1836–1908), it began as a reform movement, attempting to revitalize Islam from within. It had a strong missionary emphasis, and organized missionary work in many parts of the world. Its founder claimed to be a kind of Mahdi ('Messiah'). Because these claims seemed to question the finality of the Prophet Muhammad, the movement was declared non-Muslim by the government of Pakistan in 1974.

5. *The question of development*: to what extent can Islamic law and theology develop and change through time? How dynamic and progressive can they be?

It has generally been thought that the process of formulating Islamic law ended around the tenth century, and that only those who have been schooled in all the traditional disciplines of Islamic study can be called 'scholars' (*ulama*). In recent years, however, many Muslims have started questioning the idea that law cannot develop and evolve further since 'the gate of *ijtihad*' closed many centuries ago. They have also begun to ask whether lay people, who are not Islamic scholars in the technical sense, might have a contribution to make in these discussions.

6. *The status of* shari'a *law*: what should be the basis of law in Muslim countries?

When most of the Muslim world came under European colonial rule from the eighteenth century onwards, civil courts took over the powers of the *shari'a* courts, which then came to be responsible mainly for family law. Law codes were based on different kinds of western law (British or French, for example).

Many Muslims have argued that Islamic law should not need to be supplemented, let alone superseded, by legal systems which come from non-Islamic sources. This is the motive behind the 'fundamentalists', who want Muslim states to base their constitution and their law on the *shari'a*. Other Muslims, however, have resisted this attempt to go back to the *shari'a*, and want to see law codes based on a combination of *shari'a* and western law. Kemal Ataturk took the step of abolishing *shari'a* law altogether in Turkey in the 1920s.

11.3 For further study
Law

The concept of *law* embracing every aspect of life is summed up in this statement by a contemporary writer, Hammudah Abdal-ati, in *Islam in Focus*:

> The Qur'anic wisdom functions in three principal dimensions: inwardly, outwardly, and upwardly. Inwardly, it penetrates into the innermost recesses of the heart and reaches the farthest depths of the mind. It is aimed at the healthy cultivation of the individual from within. This inward penetration is different from and far deeper than that of any other legal or ethical system, because the Qur'an speaks in God's name and refers all matters to Him.
>
> The outward function of the Qur'an embraces all walks of life and covers the principles of the entire field of human affairs from the most personal matters to the complex international relations. The Qur'an reaches areas unknown to any secular system of law or code of ethics and inaccessible to any popular doctrine of religion. What is remarkable about the Qur'an in this respect is that it deals with human transactions in such a way as to give them a Divine flavor and a moral touch. It makes the presence of God felt in every transaction and acknowledges Him as the first source of guidance and the ultimate goal of all transactions. It is man's spiritual guide, his system of law, his code of ethics, and, above all, his way of life.
>
> In its upward function the Qur'an focuses on the One Supreme God. Everything that was, or that is, or that will be, must be channeled into and seen through this focus, the active presence of God in the universe.[7]

Theology

Al-Ghazali's theological treatise on *The Ninety-Nine Beautiful Names of God*, written at the end of the eleventh century, explains the meaning of all the names, such as 'Compassionate' and 'Merciful', that are given to God in the Qur'an and in Muslim tradition. One of the introductory chapters discusses whether or not it is possible to know God:

> Since there is no likeness of Him, He or 'His nature' is not known by other than Him. So al-Junayd – may God's mercy be upon him – was right when he remarked: 'Only God knows God' ... So, by God, no-one other than God knows God, in this world or the next ...
>
> This is the way in which one should understand the one who says 'I know God' and the one who says 'I do not know God'. If you were to show a piece of intelligible writing to a reasonable person and say to him: 'Do you know its writer?' and he said 'No', he would be speaking truly. But if he said 'Yes: its writer is a man living and powerful, hearing and seeing, sound of hand and knowledgeable in the practice of writing, and if I know all this from the sample how can I not know him?' – he too would be speaking truly. Yet the saying of the one who said 'I do not know him' is more correct and true, for in reality he does not know him. Rather he only knows that intelligible writing requires a living writer, knowing, powerful, hearing, and seeing; yet he does not know the writer himself. Similarly, every creature knows only that this ordered and precisely disposed world requires an arranging, living, knowing, and powerful maker ...
>
> Therefore, it is impossible for anyone other than God truly to know God most high.[8]

12

Sub-groups in Islam

The Muslim believes that there is much more unity among Muslims than there is among Christians. One of the reasons for this unity has been the authority and unanimity of orthodox theologians and jurists over the centuries. At the same time, however, there are many significant differences between the different branches of Islam and the different movements within Islam.

The two main branches of Islam

The break between the two branches goes back to AD 661 – the year that Ali, the fourth caliph, died.

THE SUNNIS ('Orthodox' Muslims)	THE SHI'IS ('Sectarian' Muslims)
The Sunnis accepted all the first four caliphs and accepted the claims of the Umayyad Dynasty in Damascus to take over the caliphate.	The Shi'ites accepted the fourth caliph, Ali, but did not accept the first three because they believed the line of succession from Muhammad should have been through Ali, the son-in-law of Muhammad. Therefore they wanted Ali's two sons Hasan and Husayn to succeed to the caliphate; but Hasan renounced his claim and Husayn was killed at the Battle of Kerbala in AD 680. This martyrdom is very important for Shi'ite Muslims, and is re-enacted annually. It means that Shi'is have some idea of the value of suffering, although they do not necessarily see it as redemptive. Because of their early history, they developed messianic hopes and expectations that a leader would emerge to establish justice.

There were Sunni caliphs from the seventh century until the end of the Abbassid caliphate in 1258. After this there were Fatimid caliphs in Egypt.

The Ottomans revived the caliphate in 1775; but it was finally abolished in 1924.

Found all over the Islamic world.

Rival imams led the Shi'ite community, but without exercising political power, until the twelfth, who disappeared in 874. It is believed that he has been in hiding ever since, waiting until the time for restoration. He has no successors.

They have their own secret books of the interpretation of the Qur'an, and their own collections of *hadith*.

Found mostly in Iran, Iraq and Lebanon. Subdivided into several smaller groups.

W. Montgomery Watt sums up the essential difference between Shi'i and Sunni Islam in the following way:

> The essence of Shi'ism is belief in the imam or charismatic leader, which includes the belief that salvation, or keeping to the straight path and avoiding error, comes from following the imam, in contrast to the Sunnite belief that it comes from being a member of the charismatic community. In keeping with the essential belief, the imam came to be regarded as a source of truth or guidance for his followers.[1]

Major sub-groups in Islam

The following summary is taken from Richard Tames, *Approaches to Islam*:[2]

	Origins	Distinctive Beliefs and Ritual	Historical Importance	Current Distribution
Kharijites	Discontented tribesmen dispute Ali's authority CE 656.	Militant puritan emphasis on jihad and asceticism. Egalitarian opposition to Arab aristocracy.	Assassinated Ali CE 661. Antagonised early Umayyads. Declined into antagonistic factions.	Scattered small communities in Algeria, Tunisia (especially Berber areas), Tanzania and Oman.

	Origins	Distinctive Beliefs and Ritual	Historical Importance	Current Distribution
Shi'a Twelvers (Imami)	Movement (Shi'a = faction) to restore caliphate to Ali and his line. Recognise twelve imams etc. to CE 873 when twelfth imam disappeared at Samarra – await return of 'hidden imam'.	Imam regarded as charismatic and infallible leader. First ten days of Muharram as major festival. Non-literal interpretation of Qur'an. Tombs of imams (especially Hussein) and Karbala as major shrines. Salvation through messianic return of Mahdi.	Attracted many non-Arab converts excluded from power. Anti-establishment revolts. State religion of Iran since 16th century.	Iran (majority of population), Iraq (c. 50%), Lebanon (c. 20%), India and Pakistan (c. 8%).
Seveners (Isma'ili)		Recognised imams ending with Isma'il. Mobilised social discontent. Evolved esoteric faith for initiates.	Established Fatimid caliphate in N. Africa 909–1171. Assassins flourished 12th & 13th centuries. Re-emerged under Aga Khan in 19th century.	India and East Africa.
Zaidi	Recognise only first four imams.	Apart from refusal to accept caliph's legitimacy, virtually Sunni.	Conquered Yemen in 9th century. Zaidi imams reigned until 1962.	

	Origins	Distinctive Beliefs and Ritual	Historical Importance	Current Distribution
Alawi	= 'worshippers of Ali' – offshoot of Isma'ili missionary activity.	Extreme syncreticism – include pagan and Christian elements.	Survive as withdrawn minority.	Syria (c. 10%).
Druze	Established by Darazi, 11th century Isma'ili missionary.	Fatimid Al-Hakim (d. 1021) as hidden imam. Monogamy. Transmigration of souls.	Evolved very distinctive doctrine and social structure.	Lebanon and Syria (c. ¼ million) (total).
Bahai	Established in 1844 by the Bab, a Persian teacher of religion, and developed by his disciple Bahaullah (1817–92).	Claims to be fulfilment of all previous religions. The Bahai faith should now be regarded as a separate world religion in its own right, representing a movement to find a common amalgam of faiths.	Persecuted – spread to Levant, USA and Europe.	Bahai communities in 139 countries (c. ½ million in Iran).
Ahmadiyya	Established in 1889 by Hazrat Mirza Ghulam Ahmad (1835–1908) to re-affirm Islam in the face of Western dominance.	Founder claimed to be Messiah mentioned in Biblical and Qur'anic prophecies.	Vigorous proselytising movement. Founder's claim to prophethood rejected by orthodox Muslims.	World-wide, but especially in Africa and Indonesia.

13

Sufism

Sufism has been defined as 'the pursuit of spiritual experience by bodily discipline and mystical intuition' (H. A. R. Gibb). It deserves a chapter on its own for the following reasons.

- It has been a major source of spiritual fervour, almost since the beginning of Islam, introducing an intense personal devotion into the daily life of believers, and producing famous saints who have inspired love and devotion.

- It was integrated into the mainstream of Islamic thought through the life and teaching of al-Ghazali (died 1111).

- It has influenced every level of Muslim society, and contributed significantly to the spread of Islam.

- It is very much alive in contemporary Islam, often influencing political and social action, and still proves to be one of the most attractive features of Islam to non-Muslims.

- It has profoundly influenced Christian mystics such as St John of the Cross and St Teresa of Avila.

The word *sufi* probably comes from the word *suf*, meaning 'undyed wool'. A *sufi* was someone who wore *suf*.

13.1 The origins of Sufism
1. Primitive Islamic asceticism

The main impulse [says H. A. R. Gibb] arose out of primitive Islamic asceticism, governed by the eschatology of the Koran and the fear of Hell, and passing into a positive search for God, then into the quest of the mystical experience of oneness with God.[1]

It is not hard to see how this kind of movement developed during the Umayyad period as a protest against the worldliness which had come into Islam. There were those who called for a simpler and more austere way of life, closer to that of the Prophet.

Similarly, whenever religion and worship seemed in danger of becoming a formality without any deep personal conviction, there were those who longed for a faith that had reality for the individual. This 'hunger of the heart' led many Sufis to seek to recover the intensity of the spiritual experiences of the Prophet. If Muhammad had had his 'journey into heaven' (the *mi'raj*), could the believer not enjoy something of the same kind of experience?

The Sufis appealed to verses in the Qur'an such as the following:

> We verily created a man and We know what his soul whispereth to him, and We are nearer to him than his jugular vein (50:16).

> O ye who believe! Whoso of you becometh a renegade from his religion, (know that in his stead) Allah will bring a people whom He loveth and who love Him, humble toward believers, stern toward disbelievers, striving in the way of Allah, and fearing not the blame of any blamer (5:54).

> Allah is the Light of the heavens and the earth ... Light upon light, Allah guideth unto His light whom He will. And Allah speaketh to mankind in allegories, for Allah is Knower of all things (24:35).

'What they looked for', says H. A. R. Gibb, 'was primarily intensity of religious devotion and intuitive understanding, and help in the problems and difficulties of daily life.'[2]

2. Christian influences

Muhammad and his followers had been in contact from the beginning with Christian monks and hermits. They must have learned something from their ascetic lifestyle and their regular patterns of devotion. Later mystics were influenced by Christian ideas of different kinds, such as the speculation about the *logos*, the eternal Word of God, and applied similar ideas to Muhammad.

3. *Eastern influences*

The emphases on asceticism, seeing the self as illusory, and the quest for inner enlightenment and union with God all have a very eastern flavour. If they did not actually come from the East, they would certainly have been strengthened through the considerable interaction with Indian thought that took place at various stages in Islamic history.

13.2 Basic practices and emphases in Sufism
1. 'Recollecting' or 'remembering' the name of God in prayer (dhikr)

This has been one of the most fundamental features of Sufi practice since the beginning, carried out either by the individual in private or by a group when they meet together for spiritual exercises. It is sometimes accompanied by music (*e.g.* the flute) and/or dancing, and occasionally by the use of drugs.

The following directions regarding the practice of *dhikr* come from an Algerian Sufi, Shaykh al-'Alawi (1869–1934):

> Any reasonably sensitive man will be conscious of the influence on him of the name he mentions. If we admit this we are bound to believe that the Name of God also produces an influence on the soul, as other names do, each one leaving the particular imprint that belongs with it and corresponds to it. I think you are aware that a name is ennobled with the nobility of him who is named, inasmuch as it carries his imprint in the hidden fold of its secret essence and meaning. Al-Ghazzali writes in his commentary on the Name *Allah*: 'That which the slave gets from this Name is *Ta'alluh*, or deification', by which is meant that his 'heart and his purpose are drowned in God, so that he sees naught but Him'.
>
> He also wrote: 'My son, rid thy heart of all attachment save unto God. Go apart by thyself and say with all thy

powers of concentration: *Allah, Allah, Allah.* When thy thoughts are muddied with other than God, thou hast need of negation: *La ilaha* ('There is no god but . . .'). But once thou hast withdrawn from all things in contemplation of Him Who is Lord of all, thou takest rest in the bidding: Say: *Allah . . .*

Open the door of your heart with the key of saying: *La ilaha illa Allah*: 'There is no god but God', and the door of thy spirit by saying: '*Allah*'.[3]

2. *Belonging to a group*

Meeting together with other Sufis in a group has always been important, and these groups – brotherhoods, communities or associations, as they are sometimes called – have something in common both with Christian orders such as the Franciscans, and also with the cell groups, house groups and base communities with which Christians are familiar. 'Sufi ecstasy', says Kenneth Cragg, ' . . . was essentially corporate in its nature.' This is how he describes the corporate action of the group in their 'remembering' of the name of God:

> *Dhikr*, for Sufis, meant a corporate action, a circle of rhythmic utterance, often accompanied by swaying (or whirling) of the body, controlled breathing, and accelerating tempo, until an ecstatic trance was reached. To say rhythmically and endlessly: *Allahu, Allahu, Allahu* or *Allahu akbar, Allahu akbar* ('God greater! God greater!') or the formula: *La ilaha illa Allah* ('There is no god but God . . .') with its limpid 'l's' and its 'a' vowels, served to induce that hypnotic state in which ecstasy was near at hand.[4]

All the Sufi orders were founded by holy men who trained others to follow the particular discipline of the brotherhood. People in the group would have their own spiritual director, guide or master, a *murshid, shaykh* or *pir* to guide them in their spiritual journey. Many of these saints were thought to have miraculous powers. 'It was ultimately the quality of their spiritual disciplines', says Kenneth Cragg, 'and the genius of their founders and saints which held them together.'[5] The brotherhoods also often brought together people of the same craft in special guilds.

3. The questioning of selfhood and the quest for union with God

Sufis have taught that although we all assume that we are self-contained individuals, distinct from other people and from God, we need to think again about our sense of individuality. Can we not strive until, instead of thinking of the relationship between ourselves and God in terms of 'I' and 'he', we reach the stage where we can speak of a single 'we', and are no longer aware of our own individual 'self'? In this way we may reach the state of *fana*, the passing away of the self, as either a momentary or a continuing experience.

This idea that union with God is possible and leads to identity with the Godhead was expressed in an extreme form by *al-Hallaj*, who was crucified for blasphemy in 992. When he said, 'I am the real, The Truth' (*ana-l-haqq*), he was understood to be claiming to be God. What he probably meant, however, was that when the truth of God enters the soul of the individual there is an inter-mingling of the divine spirit and the human spirit. This is there-fore a kind of incarnation of the divine spirit in individuals, who achieve deification. It is significant that for al-Hallaj Jesus was more of a model than Muhammad.

4. Walking the mystic 'way' (tariqa)

Each Sufi taught his own understanding of the mystic path and his own spiritual discipline to a group of disciples, who would then teach others. In Sufi teaching there are certain key stages through which the believer who is seeking for union with God must go: (1) repentance and renunciation, combined with the fear of God; (2) contentment and tranquility, with patience and self-control; leading to (3) the final stage, which is variously described as the vision of God, union with God, spiritual illu-mination or knowledge, absorption into God, or the love of God.

5. Missionary zeal

Not only did the Sufi brotherhoods help to keep believers together; they were also among the most effective agents in spreading the message of Islam. In many parts of the world it was wandering Sufis who took the message alongside, or independent of, the soldiers and traders. By the thirteenth and fourteenth centuries a large number of Sufi orders had been established, with their own communities and with branches in other places. These orders spread widely, creating further subdivisions all over the Muslim world. These Sufis were generally open to the culture of their new converts, and were prepared to incorporate many of their practices (which could often be described as folk religion or 'superstitions') into their Islamic practice. This was particularly true in Africa, the Indian subcontinent and the Far East.

13.3 Sufism and orthodox Islam

During the early centuries, orthodox Muslims made criticisms such as these of Sufi teaching and practice:

- It encourages individualism.

- If the inner meaning of prayer and pilgrimage is more important than carrying them out, Muslims will come to believe that observance of the five pillars is not important.

- In its emphasis on the quest for union with God, it seems to blur the distinction between the Creator and the creature.

- It allows, if not encourages, esoteric speculation, popular superstition and magic, and the desire for supernatural demonstrations of power.

In the early tensions between Sufism and traditional Islam, the most significant theologian was al-Ghazali (died 1111). He had been trained in all the traditional disciplines of Qur'anic study, law and theology, and had made a thorough study of Greek philosophy. He surprised his contemporaries when he gave up his post as a theological professor in Baghdad in order to become a Sufi. His greatest concern was to reach certainty in faith, and he came to believe that this could be gained through neither philosophical thought nor theological enquiry, but only through immediate personal experience of God. Although he later returned to teaching, he never ceased to follow the Sufi way.

His contribution was particularly significant because he

brought the best of the Sufi tradition within the mainstream of orthodox Islam. 'Al-Ghazali tried', says Ninian Smart, 'to do justice to the actual experience of the Sufis and the requirements of orthodoxy and the religion of worship . . . [he] succeeded in welding together orthodox piety and the inner quest of the contemplative. Through this synthesis Sufism gained an honourable and recognized place in orthodoxy.'[6]

Later Sufism, however, tended to become less and less orthodox, and at times verged on pantheism, as for example in Ibn al-Arabi of Spain (1165–1240).

The teaching of *Wahhabism* in the eighteenth century can be seen as a strong protest from orthodox Muslims against ideas and practices that had come into Islam from one type of Sufism and from folk Islam.

13.4 For further study

Here are examples of sayings and poetry written by Sufis:

> Love of God hath so absorbed me that neither love nor hate of any other thing remains in my heart (Rabi'a al-Adawiya, died 801).[7]

> I love thee with two loves, love of my happiness,
> And perfect love, to love thee as is thy due.
> My selfish love is that I do naught
> But think on thee, excluding all beside;
> But that purest love, which is thy due,
> Is that the veils which hide thee fall, and I gaze on thee,
> No praise to me in either this or that,
> Nay, thine the praise for both that love and this.
>
> (Rabi'a)[8]

Kenneth Cragg suggests that the following description of a modern Algerian saint, Abu-l 'Abbas al-'Alawi (1869–1934), conveys 'the genius of Sufism at its finest':

> In his brown *jallabah* and white turban, with his silver-grey beard and his long hands which seemed when he moved them to be weighted with the flow of his *barakah* (blessing), he had something of the pure archaic

ambience of Sayyidna Ibrahim (Abraham), the friend of God. He spoke in a subdued, gentle voice . . . His eyes, which were like two sepulchral lamps, seemed to pierce through all objects, seeing in their outer shell merely one and the same nothingness, beyond which they saw always one and the same reality – the Infinite. Their look was very direct, almost hard in its enigmatic unwaveringness, and yet full of charity. Often their long ovals would grow suddenly round as if in amazement, or as if enthralled by some marvellous spectacle. The cadence of the singing, the dances and ritual incantations seemed to go on vibrating in him perpetually. His head would sometimes rock rhythmically to and fro while his soul was plunged in the unfathomable mysteries of the Divine Name hidden in the *dhikr*, or remembrance . . .

He gave out an impression of unreality, so remote was he, so inaccessible, so difficult to take in, on account of his altogether abstract simplicity . . . He was surrounded, at one and the same time, with all the veneration due to saints . . . Yet, as another observes, he belonged to that class of men often to be met with in North Africa, who can pass without transition from deep thought to action, from the mysteries of the next world to the life of this, from the vast sweep of ideas to the smallest details of native politics.[9]

'Folk Islam' or 'popular Islam'

We have already seen how the 'hunger of the heart' expressed itself in the ideas and practices of Sufism. But where does one draw the line between the 'purer' expressions of Sufism (which may or may not have been acceptable to the orthodox), and the popular superstitious and magical practices that have been, and still are, so widespread in the world of Islam?

Some want to draw a sharp distinction between two aspects of Sufism: on the one hand its strong personal disciplines and its highly developed teaching about the mystic way, and on the other its superstitious practices. Other observers find it hard to draw any distinction between Sufism and all the manifestations of popular Islam that they see.

Wherever we come down in this debate, what we are dealing with in this chapter is the difference that seems to exist between the 'purer' kinds of Islam described in the textbooks (as outlined in the previous pages) and the Islam that is actually practised by many Muslims all over the world. The one is usually called 'ideal', 'orthodox', 'Qur'anic' or 'normative' Islam. Over against this, there are a number of practices which seem at first sight to be inconsistent with this 'pure' form of Islam, and which are therefore often grouped together under the heading 'folk Islam' or 'popular Islam'.

Bill Musk introduces his book *The Unseen Face of Islam: Sharing the Gospel with Ordinary Muslims* with this explanation:

> This book is about weary and burdened human beings. They constitute the 'ordinary people' of the Muslim world. As with the Jewish 'crowds' of Jesus' time, to whom his familiar words of invitation were initially addressed, so the masses of Muslims today live at two levels. Beneath a veneer of conformity to a major

world faith, ordinary Muslims express deep needs in their daily living … The aim of these chapters is to explore and explain the beliefs and practices of ordinary Muslims. The objective in such a search beneath the surface of religious behaviour is to understand the particular weariness and burdens of contemporary Muslims.[1]

14.1 Examples of folk Islam or popular Islam
Magical practices, including:

- wearing an amulet (*ta'wiz*) as a lucky charm to ward off evil spirits;

- warding off the 'evil eye' through displaying a representation of the eye on a house or car;

- writing a verse from the Qur'an on a piece of paper, putting the paper in water and then drinking the water;

- using the names of God in a magical way;

- drinking water from a particular spring because it is regarded as having magical powers.

The veneration of saints

Shrines are built over the graves of specially holy people, and people visit or make pilgrimage to them to obtain blessing or to seek relief from any kind of trouble or evil. Sometimes they visit shrines as a substitute for going on pilgrimage to Mecca. Many of these saints are regarded not only as examples of holy living but also as intercessors between the individual and God.

The veneration of the Prophet Muhammad

Although the Qur'an teaches that Muhammad was an ordinary man who needed to seek forgiveness from God, popular piety has often tended to exalt the status of the Prophet and to attribute to him qualities that seem to be semi-divine or even divine. The veneration of the Prophet has become specially popular in recent years in Pakistan.

Miracles, signs and wonders

Many of the phenomena which Christians associate with charismatic gifts can be found in Islam – healings, visions, and miracles of different kinds.

Astrology and occult practices

Many of the ideas and practices that we are familiar with in western societies today can be found in Muslim societies.

It needs to be emphasized that whereas in some situations practices noted under these five headings are widespread and public, in others they are not so common and certainly not evident to the casual observer.

14.2 Questions of definition and terminology

No-one can deny the existence of the various practices and phenomena which are put together under the label of 'folk Islam'. But labels can sometimes be misleading, because they can either create false distinctions or link together things which should be put in different categories. For this reason it may be wise to put the expression 'folk Islam' in inverted commas, simply to draw attention to the problem that exists with the terminology.

So, for example, some Muslims regard many of the practices of 'folk Islam' as dangerous compromises with paganism, and believe they are inconsistent with the teaching and the spirit of the Qur'an. They have accused Muslims who practise them of being superstitious infidels. Others see no fundamental difference or conflict between the so-called 'high' and 'low' expressions of Islam.

There is a similar range of opinions among Christians, often depending on the kind of contact they have had with Muslims and in what part of the world they have lived. It may help us to understand the nature of the problem if we recognize that there are similar differences between Christians over 'folk religion'. Some, for example, would regard the veneration of the Virgin Mary and the saints, or pilgrimages to shrines, as practices which have developed out of tradition, but which have no clear support in the Bible. They would see them as part of a kind of 'folk Christianity'. Others regard them as natural developments within the Christian tradition and in no way inconsistent with the teaching of the Bible or the spirit of Christianity.

Western Christians in the past have had to rely on reports from missionaries who had lived and worked in the Muslim world. Samuel Zwemer (1867–1952), for example, was an American Presbyterian missionary who worked in the Middle East for many years and wrote several books on Islam, one of which had the title *Animism in Islam*. This is how he explained the reasons behind his research in these areas:

> The student of Islam will never understand the common people unless he knows the reasons for their curious beliefs and practices . . . all of which still blind and oppress mind and heart with constant fear of the unseen. Witchcraft, sorcery, spells, and charms are the background of the native Muslim psychology to an extent that is realized only by those who have penetrated most deeply into the life of the people.[2]

Detmar Schuenemann, a Dutch missionary who worked in Indonesia, makes the same point about the need to be aware of actual religious practices in certain Muslim communities:

> Working for many years in a Muslim country, I have come to the conclusion that the power of Islam does not lie in its dogma and practices, nor in the antithesis of the Trinity against the Lordship of Christ and his redeeming death, but in the occult practices of its leaders, thus holding sway over their people.[3]

Alongside these descriptions, however, we need to consider the more precise analysis of anthropologist Paul Hiebert, whose main experience was in India. This is his explanation of the difference between high religion and folk religion:

> One of the crucial differences between high and folk religions has to do with their purposes. High religion seeks truth. It provides people with their ultimate map and story of reality. Consequently it turns to revelation, insight and reason. While it deals with power, it does so in a framework of truth . . .
> Folk religion, on the other hand, focuses on power and problem-solving in everyday life. It is, therefore, basically pragmatic. Any method will do so long as it

works. Moreover, several methods may be used simultaneously. A father with a sick son will ask the *mullah* to pray to God for him, tie an amulet to his arm to drive off evil spirits and give him modern medicine to kill the germs, all at the same time . . .

Given this difference between high and folk religion, it should not surprise us that leaders in high religion are often displeased with common folk who turn to religion simply for an immediate, pragmatic solution to present-day problems . . .

Power is central to our understanding of folk Islam.[4]

Michael Nazir-Ali's comment on different kinds of *pirs* in the Indian subcontinent illustrates the fineness of the dividing line between Sufism at its best and more degenerate kinds found in 'folk Islam':

A friend said to me recently that as far as he could see there were five different kinds of *pirs* in Indo-Pakistan. There were, firstly, those who were so by hereditary succession; some of these were no longer practising but had a large following nevertheless. The second kind were religious and secular leaders of their local communities. They were usually hereditary, though occasionally there were charismatic figures among them. The third kind were wandering mendicants, the fourth were practising occultists and only the fifth were genuine contemplative mystics![5]

14.3 For further study

'Folk Islam' naturally cannot be studied through texts in the same way as other aspects of Islam. The following document, however, called 'Ode of the Shawl' or 'The Prophet's Mantle' (*Qasidatu-l-burda*), is an excellent example of one aspect of 'folk Islam', the veneration of the Prophet.

The author, al-Bushiri, was an Egyptian who lived in the thirteenth century. He wrote the poem in praise of the Prophet while paralysed following a stroke. After writing the poem, he claimed that the Prophet came to him in a dream, wrapped him in his mantle, and healed him completely.

The poem has had a strong hold on the popular imagination of Muslims, and is still recited all over the Arabic-speaking and the Muslim world on social and religious occasions. It is also used as an amulet for protection against disease and as a cure. The following is a selection of the verses which speak about the Prophet Muhammad, many of which express ideas which orthodox Muslims would never associate with the Prophet:

> Muhammad, Lord of both worlds and both races
>   and both peoples, Arab and non-Arab,
> Our Prophet, who commands and forbids,
>   there is none more just than he in saying 'No' or
>   'Yes'.
> He is the Friend whose intercession is to be hoped for
>   Assaulting every kind of fearful threat . . .
>
> He excelled the prophets in bodily form and character,
>   nor did they approach him in deed or in honour
>   [nobility] . . .
>
> For it is he whose inner meaning and outward form are
>   perfect;
>   wherefore the Creator of souls chose him a a friend.
> He is free from peer in his excellent qualities,
>   so that the essence of goodness is in him undivided.
> Leave aside what Christians claim for their Prophet,
>   and judge what you will in praise of him; and be
>   reasonable . . .
>
> For the excellence of the Apostle of God has no limit
>   which
>   may be expressed by word of mouth.[6]

15

The spread and development of Islam

It is impossible to begin to understand Islam today without some idea of how it has developed since the time of the Prophet. This is specially important for Christians, since for fourteen centuries Islam has developed alongside Christianity, and for much of this time has not enjoyed an easy relationship with Christendom.

This is how Kenneth Cragg sums up some of the difficulties that Christians are likely to feel in reflecting on this history:

> Among the factors contributing to the rise of Islam was the Christian failure of the Church. It was a failure in love, in purity, and in fervour, a failure of the spirit. Truth, as often before and after, was involved to its hurt in the spiritual fault of its trustees. Islam developed in an environment of imperfect Christianity and later by its own inner force gathered such strength as to become, and remain, essentially at odds with the pure faith beyond the imperfection.
>
> This is the inward tragedy, from the Christian angle, of the rise of Islam, the genesis and dissemination of a new belief which claimed to displace what it had never effectively known. The state of being a stranger to the Christian's Christ has been intensified by further failures of love and loyalty on the part of institutional Christianity in the long and often bitter external relations of the two faiths through the centuries.[1]

15.1 The early spread of Islam

These are the main dates and events which we need to note:

632	Death of Muhammad
632–661	First four caliphs ruling in Medina
660–750	The Umayyad Dynasty rules in Damascus
661	Split between Sunnis and Shi'ites
710	Muslim forces reach the Indus
711	Campaigns in the Sindh under Muhammad ibn Qasim
714	Muslim occupation of Spain
732	(100 years after Muhammad's death) Islamic Empire stretches from Spain to Persia
732	Charles Martel defeats the Muslim forces at Poitiers in France
750–1258	The Abbasid Dynasty rules in Baghdad: a 'Golden Age of Islam'
909–1171	The Fatimid Dynasty in Egypt
c. 1000	Mahmud of Ghazna invades the Punjab (NW India): Muslim governor set up in Lahore

In studying the spread of Islam in the first few centuries, we need to take special note of the position of Jews and Christians under Islamic rule, and comment on certain stereotypes in the minds of many about the use of force in the spread of Islam:

1. In several cases Christians *welcomed* the spread of Islamic rule. In Syria, for example, it brought relief from Byzantine rule, while in Egypt it helped the Copts to depose a puppet patriarch and recall their own exiled patriarch. The Copts joined forces with the Muslims to drive out the Byzantines.

2. All non-Muslims living under Islamic rule paid a land tax (*kharaj*). Jews and Christians were treated as *dhimmis*, members of a protected community, and paid in addition a poll tax (*jizya*). They were not allowed to do military service or pay the Muslims' alms tax.

3. In the Indian subcontinent, in the Far East, and in West and East Africa, Islam was spread by traders, many of whom came originally from Arabia. Sufis also played an important role in spreading Islam.

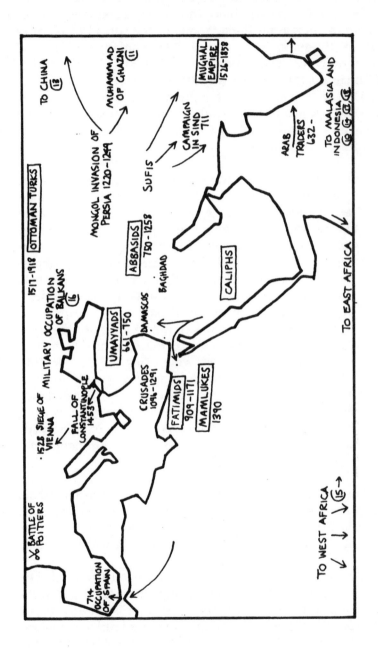

TO CHINA 18

MUHAMMAD OF GHAZNI 11

MUGHAL EMPIRE 1526-1858

OTTOMAN TURKS 1517-1918

MONGOL INVASION OF PERSIA 1220-1260

SUFIS

CAMPAIGN IN SIND 711

ARAB TRADERS 632-

TO MALASIA AND INDONESIA 19 19 19

ABBASIDS 750-1258

CALIPHS

BAGHDAD

MILITARY OCCUPATION OF BALKANS 16

UMAYYADS 661-750

DAMASCUS

CRUSADES 1096-1291

FATIMIDS 909-1171

MAMLUKES 1390

FALL OF CONSTANTINOPLE 1453

·1528 SIEGE OF VIENNA

TO EAST AFRICA

BATTLE OF POITIERS

711 OCCUPATION OF SPAIN

TO WEST AFRICA 15

4. It is a dangerous oversimplification to say that Islam was 'spread by the sword'. Since this is such a controversial issue, it is worth comparing the accounts of the spread of Islam in the first 400 years given by four writers who approach the subject from different perspectives, and are writing about the spread of Islam in a particular area at a particular time.

The first is an account written by a Muslim, Hammudah Abdalati, explaining the kinds of pressure that were brought to bear on those who refused to embrace Islam in Arabia in the earliest years of Islam:

> Those who rejected Islam and refused to pay tributes in collaboration with other sectors to support their state made it hard for themselves. They resorted to a hostile course from the beginning, and meant to create trouble, not so much for the new Muslim comers as for the new Muslim converts and their compatriots, the tribute-payers. In a national sense, that attitude was treacherous; in a human sense, mean; in a social sense, careless; and in a military sense, provocative. But in a practical sense it needed suppression, not so much for the comfort of the newcomers as for the sake of the state in which these very traitors were living. This is the only time force was applied to bring such people to their senses and make them realize their responsibilities: either as Muslims by accepting Islam freely, or as loyal citizens by being tribute-payers, capable of living with their Muslim compatriots and sharing with them equal rights and duties.[2]

The second is an account written by a Christian Islamicist, Michael Nazir-Ali, describing some of the campaigns within Arabia itself that were led by Khalid, the great military leader during the years immediately after the death of Muhammad:

> Much of the credit for this expansion must go to Khalid, who contributed more than any other man, apart from Muhammad, towards the creation of Islam as a world power. However, although we can admire his military prowess, the same, unfortunately, cannot be said of his

morality. His perfidious treatment of Malik Ibn Noweira is a case in point. Malik's tribe had surrendered to Khalid, and Malik had professed Islam. He was, nevertheless, taken prisoner along with his wife and family and, in the middle of the night, was treacherously murdered. Khalid forcibly married his widow on the spot. This caused a rebellion in the Muslim ranks and a formal complaint against Khalid was laid before Abu Bakr. Khalid was only slightly rebuked although Umar, later the second caliph, had advocated harsher punishment. When Umar became caliph, he relieved Khalid first of his command in the east and ultimately of all command. Khalid, so far as we know, spent his last days in great poverty and in obscurity.[3]

The third is an account of the main conquests in the Middle East, also written by a Christian Islamicist, John Taylor:

When Islam spread rapidly over much of the civilized world it spread first as a military and political success story; yet it was sometimes centuries before the inhabitants of the conquered lands voluntarily became Muslims. On the other hand, the motive in the minds of the caliphs behind the military and political expansion was that ultimately there should be those conversions to Islam; in the minds of the soldiers, as in every other generation, there was the desire for the spoils of war; but the Muslim conquests were remarkable for their discipline and lack of wanton destruction.[4]

The fourth is an account of the conquests in North India in the tenth century, written by Trevor Ling, a professor of comparative religion:

The purpose of Mahmud, the ruler of Ghazni, in carrying out these raids was to seize the treasure that was known to be available in the form of gold and jewels in the Hindu temples of the Punjab. It so happened that the Islamic concept of jihad, now interpreted as 'holy war', provided a religious motivation for the raids; for

131

as Mahmud's own account of his activities makes clear, he regarded himself as engaged in a war against infidels and idolaters. The nature of his operations has earned him the title of 'Mahmud the idol-smasher'. He is said also to have ordered the slaughter of many brahmin priests. The part which he played in the coming of the Muslim Turks to north India is of the kind which has too often been taken to be typical of the advance of Islam everywhere – by the sword. It was against this view that T. W. Arnold's account of the expansion of Islam (*The Preaching of Islam*, 1913) provided so valuable a corrective.[5]

15.2 The Crusades and medieval Muslim–Christian relations

It should not take Christians long to discover that the Crusades have left a deep scar on the minds of Muslims all over the world. Although they ended more than 700 years ago, for many Muslims it is as if they happened only yesterday. And recent events such as the Rushdie affair, the Gulf War and the Bosnian conflict have made many feel that the Crusades have never ended. These are some of the key dates and events:

1096–1291	The Crusades
1060	Beginning of campaigns to drive the Moors out of Spain
1169	Jerusalem captured from Christians by Salah-al-Din (Saladin)
1206	Invasion of Muslim Turks into North India; sultanate of Delhi set up
1220–1249	Mongol invasion of Persia under Genghiz Khan; Baghdad destroyed
1291	Fall of Acre
1396	The Turks enter Eastern Europe
1390	The Mamluke Dynasty in Egypt; Cairo becomes centre of Muslim world
1453	Fall of Constantinople to Ottoman Turks
1503–1722	Safavid Empire in Persia
1512–1918	Ottoman Empire, centre in Turkey
1526–1858	The Mughal Empire in North India
1565	Turkish attack on Malta repulsed
1683	Turkish attack on Vienna repulsed

The legacy of the Crusades is accurately summed up in a single sentence by Ling:

> An enduring result of the Crusades was the embittering of relations between Christians and Muslims for many generations and a vast amount of misrepresentation and misunderstanding on both sides.[6]

Albert Hourani similarly speaks about the legacy of suspicion and enmity that has been left by the struggle between the Christian world and Islam over many centuries:

> It is easy to see the historical relationship of Christians and Muslims in terms of holy war, of Crusade and *jihad*, and there is some historical justification for this. The first great Muslim expansion in Christian lands, Syria, Egypt and North Africa, Spain and Sicily; the first Christian reconquests, in Spain, Sicily and the Holy Land; the spread of Ottoman power in Asia Minor and the Balkans; and then the spread of European power in the last two centuries: all these processes have created and maintained an attitude of suspicion and hostility on both sides and still provide, if not a reason for enmity, at least a language in which it can express itself.[7]

He goes on to explain, however, that the relationship between the two faiths in western Europe has been more complex than this:

> But Crusade and *jihad* do not cover the whole reality of political relations between Christendom and the world of Islam, and still less do they explain the attitude of Christians to Islam and of Muslims to Christianity. The communities which profess the two religions have faced each other across the Mediterranean for more than a thousand years; with hostility, it is true, but with a look of uneasy recognition in their eyes.
>
> When western Europe first faced the challenge of Muslim power, it did so without any real knowledge of what it was fighting, and the combination of fear and

ignorance produced a body of legends, some absurd and all unfair.[8]

15.3 European colonialism and the missionary movement

Some will no doubt object to the idea of linking western colonialism with Christian mission. They probably feel uncomfortable about some of the links between the missionaries on the one hand, and the soldiers, the traders and the administrators on the other. The perception of the Muslim world, however, is that these two movements came basically from the same source – the desire of the Christian West to dominate the world.

1757	Start of British expansion in India
1792	William Carey begins his work in India
1798	Napoleon arrives in Egypt
1800–1812	Henry Martyn's work in India and Persia
1857	The Indian Mutiny/War of Independence
1910	Edinburgh Missionary Conference
1917	Allenby enters Jerusalem
	Defeat of the Ottoman Turks and end of the Ottoman Empire
1922	The caliphate abolished by Ataturk
1948	State of Israel established

Coming after centuries of uneasy relationships between Muslims and Christians in Europe and the Mediterranean, the colonial era, beginning in the middle of the eighteenth century, created a further crisis for the Muslim world. This is how Kenneth Cragg explains what over two centuries of 'Christian' imperialism meant to the Muslim world:

> Islam was largely under non-Muslim government in wide areas of its dispersion. Western imperial control did not, by and large, affect the practice of religion. It did not close mosques, forbid Ramadan, pilgrimage, or proscribe belief. By all these 'religious' tests (as a westerner might see them), Islam was altogether free. But, politically, in many areas, Muslims did not rule themselves. Recall the basic conviction, arising from its origins, that Islam must rule. Recall the long caliphal history when

Islam did rule. From the Hijrah on, Islam had bound religion and rule into one.

Not, then, to have Muslim rule, however free the rituals, is not to be Islam in a full sense. It is a state of exile, the puzzle and pain of which caused much debate in the nineteenth century. In India, for example, . . . Islam was bewildered and dismayed.[9]

15.4 Movements of revival and reform within Islam

Against this background of despair and defeat, we can begin to understand the significance of the following nine people who led movements for the reform and renewal of Islam. It is not always easy to determine the extent to which the impulses towards revival have come from outside influences and to what extent they have come from within.

Wali Allah (1702–62) of Delhi worked for the renewal of Islam in India. For him this meant getting rid of Hindu elements which had crept into Islam, and encouraging the hope that Muslim government would once again be restored. In Wali Allah's view of Islam 'a broad, humanistic sociological basis is overlain by a doctrine of social and economic justice in Islamic terms and crowned by a Sufi world-view' (Fazlur Rahman). According to S. M. Ikram, a Pakistani historian, 'more than anyone else he is responsible for the religious regeneration of Indian Islam'.

Muhammad ibn 'Abd al-Wahhab (1703–92) was an Arab sheikh who, after years of travel in Iraq and Persia, returned to Arabia at the age of forty and began a movement for the purification of Islam. The main targets of his attack were: (1) aspects of popular Islam, such as the veneration of saints, visiting the tombs of saints, belief in the intercession of the Prophet and saints, and other forms of what he regarded as 'superstition'; (2) the lowering of moral standards among Muslims; and (3) additions to basic Islamic beliefs and practices from the Sufis, philosophers and theologians. He appealed to the Qur'an and the *sunna* as the only sources of authority and rejected all other later Muslim authorities. The legacy of the movement which he began is summed up by Trevor Ling as follows:

The challenge of the Wahhabi movement to moral corruption within Islam, and its emphasis upon the importance of the moral element in Muslim life and thought, had a lasting effect, in that this became an almost universal feature of subsequent reform movements, both in Arabia and elsewhere in the Muslim world.[10]

Sayyid Ahmad Khan (1817–98) of Delhi was much more positive than many other Muslims towards modern scientific knowledge, and argued that it was fully compatible with Islam. He also tried to convince fellow Muslims that Islam and Christianity have much in common. 'It is to him', says Trevor Ling, 'that a great deal of credit must be given for the awakening of the Muslims of India to a new understanding of the possible place of Islamic religion in the modern world.'[11]

Jamal al-Din al-Afghani (1839–97) was more concerned with the social and political issues facing Muslims, and protested against the intrusion of alien elements in the areas of politics, culture and religion. In his concern to unite the Muslim world, he became the leader of the Pan-Islam movement, which called for the creation of an Islamic world state.

Muhammad 'Abduh (1849–1905), an Egyptian theologian who taught at the Al-Azhar University in Cairo, was critical of the rigidity and conservatism of many orthodox theologians whose minds seemed closed to everything in the modern world. He stood for a liberal and open kind of Islam, arguing that faith and reason were compatible, and that there need be no contradiction between faith and modern knowledge. He wanted to see greater flexibility in the formulation of Islamic law, believing that traditional laws should in certain cases be replaced by new laws that were more appropriate to the social context. He was not, however, prepared to apply modern critical methods to the study of the Qur'an. As a result of his teaching, a new kind of secular modernism grew up in the Middle East, some of whose adherents called for the separation of religion and state. At the same time there was opposition from fundamentalist groups which wanted to return to the Qur'an and *sunna*.

Muhammad Iqbal (1873–1938) was for many years the leader of the Muslim League, a movement which was founded in 1906 to focus the political aspirations of Muslims in India. From 1930 he began to argue for a separate Muslim state in India, and because of his widespread influence he is generally regarded as 'the spiritual founder of the state of Pakistan' (Trevor Ling).[12] In discussions about Islamic law, he believed that the interpretation of the law needed to be opened up in a radical way. He is also well known for his writings as a poet and philosopher.

Mawlana Abul A'la Mawdudi (1903–79) was a journalist and a self-taught Islamic scholar who founded the organization called *Jama'at-i-Islami* (Community of Islam) in 1941. Although at first he opposed the idea of establishing a separate Muslim state, when the state of Pakistan came into existence in 1947, his main aim became 'the thorough Islamization of the government of Pakistan and its purging from all Western moral, spiritual and political values and practices' (Trevor Ling).[13]

Hasan al-Banna (1906–79) was brought up in a small village in the Nile Delta in Egypt, and learned much of his Islam from his father who was a graduate of the Al-Azhar University in Cairo. While working as a teacher in Ismailiyya on the Suez Canal, he became acutely aware of the depressed state of the Muslim world – politically, culturally and economically. He and some friends bound themselves together by an oath and called themselves the Muslim Brothers (*Ikhwan al-Muslimun*).

During the 1930s and 1940s the movement grew rapidly, in spite of being officially banned at times by the government for demanding that the *shari'a* should be established as the law of the country. After a member of the Brotherhood assassinated the Prime Minister who had banned the movement, Banna himself was assassinated by the secret police. The Brotherhood, although officially suppressed in some Arab countries, is still very active, and continues to call for the restoration of *shari'a* law, sometimes by peaceful means and sometimes through revolution and violence.

Ayatollah Khomeini (1900–89) was born into a family in which both his father and grandfather had been religious scholars. At the age of nineteen he began his studies in the religious sciences under Shi'ite scholars, mostly at the holy city of Qom to the south of Tehran. He soon attracted the attention of his teachers and colleagues because of the way he combined a deep spirituality and mysticism with a passionate concern for social and political issues.

He found himself in opposition to the Iranian monarchy, which he saw as a totalitarian dictatorship determined to eliminate Islam as a cultural, social and political force. After his first public statement against the government in 1943, he became a popular leader who expressed the aspirations of his people. He was arrested in 1963 after protesting against a series of measures which he believed would bring the country further under foreign influence, and was later released.

During periods of exile in Turkey, Iraq and France (1964–79), his sermons and lectures were distributed widely through the network of mosques within Iran both in print and on cassette, and he received a rapturous welcome when he returned to Tehran in 1979 after the Shah had left the country. In a special ruling (*fatwa*) some months after the publication of the book *The Satanic Verses* in 1988, he pronounced the death sentence on its author, Salman Rushdie. He remained the leader of the Islamic revolution in Iran until his death in 1989.

With this summary of movements of revival and reform within Islam, we should be in a position to appreciate some of the issues facing the Muslim world today.

16

Islam and Muslims in the world today

Instead of attempting the impossible task of describing the state of the Muslim world at the present time, this chapter seeks to spell out some of the basic issues faced by Islam and Muslims in the world in the 1990s – or the 1410s of the Muslim era. As in all the previous chapters in part 2, we do this not in order to criticize, to score debating points, or to supply 'Christian answers'. Our aim is still to *understand*, to sit where Muslims sit, and to seek to enter into the dilemmas that they face.

1. The unity of the Muslim world: pan-Islamic or the nation state?
The radical changes brought about by the end of the colonial era and the coming of independence are summed up by Kenneth Cragg:

> The chief external fact about twentieth-century Islam is that almost everywhere it has recovered its political self . . . Political power is almost everywhere back in Muslim hands where there are Muslim people. The years since the Second World War, and even before it, have recorded the recession of western empire and the emergence, in Asia and Africa, of Muslim states, independent and autonomous. Islamic ideology is not now an academic matter, as it may have been under Queen Victoria or the Dutch. Islam is back where it belongs – with Muslims. True, political self-responsibility does not mean economic autonomy. But at least the exile from the political self of Islam is at an end.[1]

This new independence, however, created new questions, one of which concerned the nature of the unity of the Muslim world. For many centuries the caliphate, located in the capital of the

Ottoman Empire in Istanbul, represented an important focus of unity for the Sunni Muslim world. When it was abolished by Kemal Ataturk in 1924, Muslims were faced with the question of how the unity of the *umma*, the 'people' of Islam, should be expressed. Should it be through a single federation that links together all the Muslim countries in the world? Or should Islam accept the existence of independent nation states as inevitable and as the only realistic way of surviving in the modern world?

Various organizations have been created to develop closer links between Muslim countries – such as the Organization of the Islamic Conference (OIC, referred to in the case study on Nigeria, pp. 53–55) – and the heads of Muslim states meet from time to time. Those who go on pilgrimage to Mecca have a powerful sense of the unity of the Muslim world. But the dilemma of how to express the unity of Muslim peoples *in political terms* still remains.

2. *Statehood and law:* what is the most appropriate form of government for Muslims?

There are at present approximately forty-nine Muslim majority states, which together account for nearly 70% of the total number of Muslims in the world. Some of these (such as Egypt and Malaysia) are Muslim states in the sense that while the majority are Muslims, the law of the country is based on a combination of Islamic law and western law of some kind. Others (such as Saudi Arabia, Pakistan and the Sudan) are Islamic states in the sense that they attempt to base their law on Islamic law *alone*. One of the basic demands of the so-called 'fundamentalists' is that Muslim states should reject western models entirely and be much more consistent in returning to *shari'a* law.

The question at stake, therefore, is: what form should a Muslim or Islamic state take, and on what basis should it formulate its laws? Who is to determine how the principles of Islam should be put into practice in political and social terms? Should it be the religious teachers, the experts in Islamic jurisprudence, the democratically elected political leaders, or the army?

The remaining 30% of Muslims in the world find themselves living as minorities in non-Muslim countries (as in India, Europe and North America). They often make requests or demands for greater freedom to follow Islamic law in certain areas, for instance in family law and in education. The basic dilemma faced by Muslims living in this kind of secular state is summed up by Zaki Badawi:

> As we know, the history of Islam as a faith is also the history of a state and a community of believers living by Divine law. The Muslims, jurists and theologians, have always expounded Islam as both a Government and a faith. This reflects the historical fact that Muslims, from the start, lived under their own law. Muslim theologians naturally produced a theology with this in view – it is a theology of the majority. Being a minority was not seriously considered or even contemplated. The theologians were divided in their attitude to the question of minority status. Some declared that it should not take place; that is to say that a Muslim is forbidden to live for any lengthy period under non-Muslim rule. Others suggested that a Muslim living under non-Muslim rule is under no obligation to follow the law of Islam in matters of public law. Neither of these two extremes is satisfactory. Throughout the history of Islam some pockets of Muslims lived under the sway of non-Muslim rulers, often without an alternative. They nonetheless felt sufficiently committed to their faith to attempt to regulate their lives in accordance with its rules and regulations in so far as their circumstances permitted. In other words, the practice of the community rather than the theories of the theologians provided a solution. Nevertheless Muslim theology offers, up to the present, no systematic formulation of the status of being a minority. The question is being examined. It is hoped that the matter will be brought into focus and that Muslim theologians from all over the Muslim world will delve into this thorny subject to allay the conscience of the many Muslims living in the West and also to chart a course for Islamic survival, even revival, in a secular society.[2]

The political nature of Islam ensures that Muslims have to face up to these questions, which are both political and theological at the same time.

3. *Economics:* is there a uniquely Islamic approach to economics, and questions of wealth and poverty?

Muslims have been debating for decades whether capitalism or socialism is closer to the spirit of Islam, and Muslims have often said that Islam offers a *via media* between the extremes of both. Although Communism is no longer a valid option, certain aspects of Communism (such as the one-party state) have some attraction for Muslims in certain countries. The philosophy of the Ba'ath Socialist Parties in Syria and Iraq, for example, was once described to me as 'the largest dose of Marxism that the Muslim mind can take'.

One particular area in which Muslims have tried to be consistent in following Islamic teaching is that of banking. The Qur'an explicitly forbids the taking of usury (*riba*) in verses such as these:

> Allah hath blighted usury and made almsgiving fruitful. Allah loveth not the impious and guilty . . . O ye who believe! Observe your duty to Allah, and give up what remaineth (due to you) from usury, if ye are (in truth) believers. And if ye do not, then be warned of war (against you) from Allah and His messenger. And if ye repent, then ye have your principal (without interest). Wrong not, and ye shall not be wronged (2:276–279; *cf.* 3:130; 4:161; 30:39).

If the Qur'an forbids the charging or receiving of interest, how is a modern bank to function? How are farmers and traders to raise the capital needed to start a business? Some see the development of Islamic banks in many countries as a bold attempt to obey Qur'anic commands in the modern world. Others suspect that no economy can survive in the modern world without capital generating interest, and that Islamic banks in practice charge interest of a kind but simply call it by another name.

Some of these questions are particularly acute when we recognize the irony in the uneven distribution of resources in the Muslim world. The wealthiest countries (such as Saudi Arabia) have the fewest people, while the poorest countries (such as Bangladesh) have the largest populations and the least resources. Amir Taheri, an Iranian writer living in Paris, points out the connection between economics and terrorism when he says, 'The Middle East's serious problem of terrorism in the 1970s and 1980s is directly, though not exclusively, linked with the climate of social tension provoked by the rich–poor divide.'[3] It is understandable, therefore, that it is in the context of economic issues that Kenneth Cragg has to say, 'Never before since the rise of their faith have Muslims had to reckon on so many fronts with so vigorous a challenge to both creed and will.'[4]

4. Intellectual challenges: how does Islam respond to the questions of truth?

Some of the most fundamental questions raised by western philosophy have been in the area of the theory of knowledge (epistemology). The basic questions, 'How can we know anything?' 'How can we know that anything is true?' have led on to further questions about the truth of the Bible and the whole Christian revelation. The difficulty that Muslims have in responding to questions of this kind, however, is summed up by Wilfred Cantwell Smith:

> Muslims do not read the Qur'an and conclude that it is divine; rather, they believe that it is divine, and then they read it . . .
> The Muslim world, also, is moving into what may possibly become a profound crisis, too; in that it also is just beginning to ask this question, instead of being content only with answering it. Young people in Lahore and Cairo, labour leaders in Jakarta and Istanbul, are beginning to ask their religious thinkers, and beginning to ask themselves, 'Is the Qur'an the word of God?' Answering this question has been the business of the Muslim world for over thirteen centuries. Asking it is a different matter altogether, haunting and ominous.[5]

One particularly provocative way in which questions about truth have been raised in recent years was in Salman Rushdie's *The Satanic Verses*. Muslim criticism of the book focused largely on the mocking way in which the Prophet is portrayed by a writer who was born and bred a Muslim. Another major challenge of the book, however, is that it questions the very idea of divine revelation. How, it asks, are we to know whether the revelations that came to Muhammad were from God or from Satan? How can we know whether there is a God anyway? Perhaps there was something prophetic about Cantwell Smith's words, since the Rushdie affair has demonstrated that there *is* something 'haunting and ominous' about asking this kind of question in the Muslim world.

5. *Israel:* Can Islam tolerate the Zionist state?

'A dagger in the heart' is how an Indian Muslim, Rafiq Zakaria, sums up the feelings of Muslims all over the world and of Arabs in particular over the existence of Israel.[6] 'It has involved thousands of ordinary Muslims', says Kenneth Cragg, 'in the sharpest of personal distresses.'[7]

But why is it that the existence of a small state near the heart of the Arab and Muslim world causes Muslims such pain, and leads some Middle Eastern leaders to describe their opposition to Israel in terms of *jihad*? Ronald Nettler explains how the establishment of Israel, coming so soon after western colonial intrusion in the Middle East, was seen as 'the ultimate affront' to the Arab world:

> The Arabs reacted to Jewish aspirations and activities here with a sense of bewilderment, outrage, shock and embitterment, because they regarded Zionism from the beginning first as another manifestation of Western domination and secondly, but even more importantly, as an attempt by Jews to do something that was not legitimate: to seek political independence and that in the midst of what the Arabs regard as their own territory. This was for Islam and the Arabs the ultimate affront. How could the despised Jews, who had for centuries under Muslim rule been *dhimmis* and thus living in their proper place, have had the nerve and the ability to do something like this? This was to the Arab mind even more of a shock than the earlier Christian influence in the area.
>
> For the Arabs had hardly begun to come to terms with

144

the initial shock of the Christian displacement of Islam when they were dealt another blow, by another minority which had no legitimate right to seek independence for itself – a minority which, unlike the Christians, had not during Islamic times expressed itself in a politically independent way. The Christians, after all, had possessed their empires for centuries – a distasteful fact which Islam had been forced to swallow, sometimes after a bitter struggle – while the Jews had all the time kept their proper status as *dhimmis*, a people without power under both Christianity and Islam.[8]

It needs to be said that not all Muslims feel in the same way about Israel, and there is always a danger of creating stereotypes. But quite apart from all the questions about human rights involved in the Arab–Israeli conflict, one cannot escape the fact that there is an Islamic dimension to the conflict which deeply affects the way Muslims all over the world feel about the state of Israel.

6. Human rights: to what extent do Muslim countries accept and adhere to concepts of human rights as widely understood today?

Most Muslim states, if not all, have signed the different international agreements on human rights, such as the UN Declaration of Human Rights. But several of these countries, especially in the Middle East, have been challenged both by outside observers and by their own nationals over their record on human rights. It may be argued that the policies of governments have more to do with the social and economic factors than with Islam. But, as Amir Taheri points out, there is often a close connection between religion and politics:

> Overall, the human rights situation in the Middle East showed a marked deterioration in the 1980s compared with the preceding decade. Part of this was due to the Islamic Revolution in Iran and the Gulf War [*i.e.* Iran–Iraq War], events that frightened many states of the region and wrongly persuaded them that concessions on human rights could lead to revolution. Nevertheless, a growing constituency for western-style human rights

had, by 1988, become a fact of life in most countries of the region. Scores of private groups, large and small, campaigned for human rights in Iran, Iraq, Turkey, Egypt, Israel, Lebanon, Syria and the Gulf Emirates. These groups carried little political weight in 1988 and many of their leaders were either in exile or frequently imprisoned. And yet they represented a potentially serious political force which few governments could afford to ignore.

The argument most often used by governments in their attempt to justify the slow progress achieved on human rights is that the Middle East must consider economic development as its top priority at least for the foreseeable future. The assumption that respect for human rights might somehow compromise a nation's economic development is general among the governing élites in the region.[9]

We need to be careful not to get into the game of comparing the record of countries whose situations are totally different. But when changes are made in the constitution or the law codes of a particular country in the cause of Islamization, the world is likely to take particular note of its record on human rights.

7. The struggle between the fundamentalists and the modernists: which represents the true spirit of Islam and which is likely to have the upper hand?

Fundamentalism in Islam is an extremely complex phenomenon, and the very term itself (which comes out of a western, Christian context) needs to be used with caution. Some would argue that the religion of Islam is likely to be fundamentalist by its very nature, since it is based on a revelation given in the form of scripture. In attempting to define and analyse Islamic fundamentalism, it may be helpful to distinguish three elements which are quite distinct, even though they come together in many different contexts today:

■ There is the demand to return to the *shari'a*, and to make Islamic law the basis for the law of the country.

■ There is resistance to western imperialism in all its forms –

146

political, cultural, economic, religious and ideological.

■ There is the strong call for a more just society in which there is a fairer distribution of wealth.

The combination of these three elements in situations where there is poverty, injustice and a desire to resist all foreign pressures is producing a new generation of younger Muslims. They are disillusioned with traditional Islamic teaching (which appears to them too spiritual and other-worldly), with secularism, and with what they regard as corrupt and ineffective government.

If the fundamentalists are calling their countries back to the *shari'a*, however, the liberals are pleading for adaptation and flexibility in the practice of Islam in the modern world. Rafiq Zakaria's book *The Struggle within Islam: The Conflict between Religion and Politics* argues strongly against fundamentalism of different kinds in contemporary Islam, and in favour of a more liberal interpretation of the ideals of Islam. The struggle discussed in the book is defined as 'the continuous fight between the holders of power and theologians of all shades of opinion', and is seen as a struggle that has been going on throughout every stage in the history of Islam:

> Islam is a simple religion: it requires of its followers only two things – one, a belief in the unity of God and two, a belief in the prophethood of Muhammad. Despite the pure and homogenous nature of the faith, the history of Islam has been one of conflict. The first problem Islam faced was the issue of the succession to the Prophet. From then on, Islam has been riven by dissent – a result of the almost uninterrupted face-off between Islamic rulers, who were usually secular and flexible in their interpretation of the rules and practices of Islam, and fundamentalist theologians, jurists and their followers, who insisted on a rigid adherence to the Qur'an and the Sunna.[10]

Both sides are responding to the pressures of the non-Muslim world in different ways: the fundamentalists want to resist all non-Islamic influences as forcefully as they can, while the liberals want to be more selective in what they accept and what they reject. Only time will tell which of the two tendencies will prove to be the more powerful.

8. *The struggle with the West:* is conflict inevitable?

We have seen that while some reformers (such as Sayyid Ahmad Khan) could not see any basic conflict between Islam and the West, others (such as Hasan al-Banna) have called on Muslims to resist and renounce all western influences that have permeated the political, social and economic life of their countries. The potential for conflict between Islam and the West, and the nature of this conflict, are explained by Khurshid Ahmad:

> Muslims constitute one-fifth of the human race, around 900–1000 million in all parts of the world . . . If they want to reconstruct their socio-economic order according to the values of Islam, it is bound to come into conflict with the international *status quo*. So conflict is there. And to that extent, I would like to invite my Western colleagues to understand that Muslim criticism of Western civilization is not primarily an exercise in political confrontation. The real competition would be at the level of two cultures and civilizations, one based on Islamic values and the other on the values of materialism and nationalism. Had Western culture been based on Christianity, on morality, on faith, the language and *modus operandi* of the contact and conflict would have been different. But this is not the case. The choice is between the Divine Principle and a secular materialist culture. And there is no reason to believe that this competition should be seen by all well-meaning human beings merely in terms of the geo-political boundaries of the West and the East. In fact all those human beings who are concerned over the spiritual and moral crisis of our times should heave a sigh of relief over Islamic resurgence, and not be put off or scared by it.[11]

He has some pointed things to say about the way the West responds to Islamic resurgence:

Once the nature of the conflict as taking place on the level of values and culture is clarified, I want to underscore that there is a political dimension to the situation that we must not ignore. There is nothing pathologically anti-Western in the Muslim resurgence. It is neither pro- nor anti-West regarding the political relationship between Western countries and the Muslim world, despite the loathsome legacy of colonialism which has the potential to mar these relationships . . . *Much depends upon how the West looks upon this phenomenon of Islamic resurgence and wants to come to terms with it.* If in the Muslim mind and the Muslim viewpoint, Western powers remain associated with efforts to perpetuate the Western model in Muslim society, keeping Muslims tied to the system of Western domination at national and international levels and thus destabilizing Muslim culture and society directly or indirectly, then, of course, the tension will increase. Differences are bound to multiply. And if things are not resolved peacefully through dialogue and understanding, through respect for each other's rights and genuine concerns, they are destined to be resolved otherwise. But if, on the other hand, we can acknowledge and accept that this world is a pluralist world, that Western culture can co-exist with other cultures and civilizations without expecting to dominate over them, that others need not necessarily be looked upon as enemies or foes but as potential friends, then there is a genuine possibility that we can learn to live with our differences. If we are prepared to follow this approach, then we would be able to discover many a common ground and many a common challenge. Otherwise, I am afraid we are heading for hard times.[12]

9. *The mission of Islam:* is Islam still a missionary faith?

Zaki Badawi states without compromise the universal claims of a religion that seeks to win the world:

Islam is a universal religion. It aims at bringing its message to all corners of the earth. It hopes that one day the whole of humanity will be one Muslim community, the 'Umma.[13]

Is Islam, therefore, poised to fill the vacuum created by the decline of Christianity and the demise of Communism? Can Islam hope to capture the hearts and minds of secular-minded westerners in large numbers? And if so, what differences will they want to see in the way society is organized? Does the religion of Christianity need to find political expression in the same way that Islam has?

At this point we are inevitably reminded of all that is involved in the meeting of cross and crescent, since we are talking here about two religions that are both missionary by nature. What happens then in the meeting of cross and crescent? Are we to expect nothing but competition, confrontation and conflict?

Part 3 will open up some of the major issues which Muslims and Christians have been debating for centuries, and suggest ways of breaking through the conflicts. First, however, we must examine the controversial topic of the position of women in Islam.

17

Women in Islam

Muslims often argue that Islam has liberated women, giving them a dignity that no other religion has given them. Christians, on the other hand, have often been critical of the treatment of women in Islam. If one side has used this issue to commend Islam and the other to attack it, might it not seem wiser to leave such a sensitive and controversial issue completely alone?

There are three reasons why it may be appropriate at least to open up the subject:

1. The family plays such an important role in Islam that it is impossible to understand Muslim culture without understanding something of the place of women in Islam.

2. A study of the role of women in Islam leads us straight into several subjects which are crucial for our understanding of the nature of Islam, such as the place of the Qur'an, the traditions about the Prophet, and Islamic law (*shari'a*). If we can understand how Muslims think about this crucial subject, we should be able to appreciate more of their total worldview.

3. Tackling this subject should make us aware of some of the pitfalls in any comparison of Christianity and Islam. There are three in particular which we need to avoid: (1) comparing what we think is the worst in Islam with the best in Christianity; (2) criticizing Islam for the faults and weaknesses in individual Muslims, without recognizing that Christians have often been guilty of exactly the same things; (3) judging Muslims in the past by our own moral standards, which for many of us are simply those of the western world in the late twentieth century.

The material in this chapter, therefore, is not intended to be used as ammunition for scoring points against an adversary. Our task is to try to *understand* rather than to be judgmental, and to enter with as much sympathy or empathy as possible into a culture which is very different from our own.

17.1 The teaching of the Qur'an about women and marriage

The following are the main points in the teaching of the Qur'an, with references in brackets to some of the relevant verses:

- Men and women were created 'from a single soul' (4:1).

- God has created all living beings in pairs, male and female, and marriage is ordained by God (51:49; 30:20–21; 42:11).

- God will reward both men and women in Paradise (3:195; 16:97).

- Men are commanded to treat women kindly (4:19).

- Passages which appear to teach that women are inferior to men because 'men are a degree above them' are generally interpreted to mean that husbands are responsible for leadership of the family and for maintaining their wives; wives are to be obedient and chaste, and can be beaten if they are disobedient (4:34; 2:228).

- Women should dress modestly and draw their cloak or veil round them when they go outside; but there is no suggestion that they should be completely veiled (33:59; 24:30–31).

- Men may marry up to four wives, provided they treat them all fairly and equally (4:3). This permission was given after the Battle of Uhud, when seventy Muslim men were killed, and is therefore seen as a way of caring for widows and unmarried women in any community where there are not enough men. Some interpreters today believe that since it is virtually impossible for a husband to deal absolutely fairly with more than one wife, the passage should be interpreted to mean that polygamy is not encouraged, if not actually proscribed.

- This same verse which allows up to four wives also teaches that a Muslim may have any number of slave-concubines in addition to the four legal wives (4:3).

- Muslim men may marry Jewish or Christian wives (5:5), but may not marry pagan women who are from any other religion (2:221).

- Intercourse is not allowed during menstruation (2:222); women are to be regarded as 'tilth for you (to cultivate)' or 'a field of tillage' (2:223).

- Adultery is to be punished severely (4:15–18; 17:32; 24:2–5).

- Divorce is permitted (226: 242; 60:1–2; 65:1–2), but only after an attempt has been made at reconciliation (4:35). It would seem that no provision is made in these verses for a wife to divorce her husband.

- A person's estate is to be divided among his or her relatives after death (2:180). A husband is to receive a half of his wife's estate, while a wife should receive a quarter of her husband's estate (4:7–12).

17.2 The teaching and example of Muhammad

These are some of the relevant sayings of the Prophet which have been recorded in Muslim tradition, and which are therefore given considerable authority by Muslims:

> Paradise lies at the feet of your mothers.

> The best among you is the one who is the best towards his wife.

> O people, your wives have certain rights over you and you have certain rights over them. Treat them well and be kind to them, for they are your partners and committed helpers.

The following basic facts about the wives of Muhammad are based on authoritative traditions and are accepted by all Muslims:

At the age of twenty-five, Muhammad married Khadija, who was forty years old at the time, and had been widowed twice. She was his only wife for twenty-five years, and bore all Muhammad's children except one. She died at the age of sixty-five.

At the age of fifty, Muhammad married Sawda, whose husband had emigrated to Abyssinia to escape persecution and then died there.

In the same year there was a proposal of marriage to 'A'isha, who was seven years old, the daughter of his companion Abu Bakr. The marriage was not consummated until after the Hijra in 622, and she became his favourite wife. For six years, until he reached the age of fifty-six, Muhammad had only these two wives, Sawda and 'A'isha.

Between the ages of fifty-six and sixty Muhammad contracted marriages with nine women, including Hafsa and Juwayria, both widows whose husbands had been killed in battle; Zaynab bint Jahsh, a cousin of Muhammad, who had been the wife of his adopted son Zaid, and became Muhammad's wife after he claimed he had received a special revelation permitting him to marry her (recorded in the Qur'an, 33:37); and Mariya, a Coptic (Egyptian) slave girl, who bore Muhammad's only son, Ibrahim. He died at eighteen months.

If these are the basic facts, how are they to be interpreted? Here are four different interpretations:

The orientalist Alfred Guillaume, in his book *Islam*, echoes views that have often been expressed by western orientalists:

> The Qur'an has more to say on the position of women than on any other social question. The guiding note is sounded in the words, 'Women are your tillage', and the word for marriage is that used for the sexual act. The primary object of marriage is the propagation of children, and partly for this and partly for other reasons a man is allowed four wives at a time and an unlimited number of concubines. However, it is laid down that wives are to be treated with kindness and strict impartiality; if a man cannot treat all alike he should keep to one. The husband pays the woman a dowry at the time of marriage, and the money or property so allotted remains her own. The husband may divorce his wife at any time, but he cannot take her back until she has remarried and been divorced by a second husband. A woman cannot sue for divorce on any grounds, and her husband may beat her. In this matter of the status of

women lies the greatest difference between the Muslim and the Christian world . . . To a Muslim who takes his stand on the law of Islam, the gulf is unbridgeable, but in actual practice in the civilized communities of the Muslim world a more liberal view of women's place in society is gradually coming to the fore.[1]

W. Montgomery Watt, another orientalist, writes about the accusation that Muhammad's marriage to Zaynab bint Jahsh was to satisfy his own lust, and that it was an incestuous marriage because she had been married to Muhammad's adopted son:

> The marriage with Zaynab seemed incestuous, but this conception of incest was bound up with the old practices belonging to a lower, communalistic level of familial institutions where a child's paternity was not definitely known; and this lower level was in process of being eliminated by Islam.
>
> From the standpoint of Muhammad's time, then, the allegations of treachery and sensuality cannot be maintained. His contemporaries did not find him morally defective in any way. On the contrary, some of the acts criticized by the modern Westerner show that Muhammad's standards were higher than those of his time. In his day and generation he was a social reformer, even a reformer in the sphere of morals. He created a new system of social security and a new family structure, both of which were a vast improvement on what went before. By taking what was best in the morality of the nomad and adapting it for settled communities, he established a religious and social framework for the life of many races of men. That is not the work of a traitor or 'an old lecher'.[2]

The contemporary Christian apologist John Gilchrist comments on the fact that 'A'isha, Muhammad's favourite wife, is known from authoritative traditions to have been jealous of Muhammad's other wives:

> Ayishah's frustrations and jealousies are the best proof that Muhammad could not treat his wives equally – if for

155

no other reason than that he did not regard her with the same total, undivided affection that she regarded him. She may have been his favourite wife but her grievances clearly were motivated, perhaps only subconsciously, by the fact that she was not his *only* wife. Paradoxically, the fact that Muhammad singled her out as his favourite wife is further proof that he did not treat his wives equally. There is more than enough evidence in Muhammad's own marital affairs to prove that polygamy cannot ultimately be reconciled with God's perfect purpose for human marriage. It is no wonder that the perfect revelation of his will through the Gospel of his Son simultaneously outlawed polygamy. Muhammad enjoyed a twenty-five-year marriage with Khadijah which was, in all respects, unimpeachable. Unfortunately the same cannot be said for his many marriages at Medina and one can only sympathise with the young Ayishah who obviously regretted that she could not enjoy the same undivided devotion from her husband that she willingly offered to him.[3]

Gai Eaton explains how Muslims understand polygamy today and the traditions concerning Muhammad's married life:

In accordance with the Quranic injunction, he treated his wives equally in all material matters and in matters of justice. He divided his nights fairly between them and he drew lots to determine who should accompany him on his campaigns; but, as he himself said, a man's affections are outside his control and his particular fondness for A'isha was common knowledge. Jealousy was inevitable, and he tended to make light of it. Once he came into a room where his wives and other members of the family were assembled bearing in his hand an onyx necklace, which had just been presented to him. Holding it up, he said: 'I shall give this to her whom I love best of all!' He allowed a pause while they whispered together, sure that he would give it to 'the daughter of Abu Bakr'. When he had left them long enough in suspense, he called his little granddaughter to him and clasped it round her neck.

'If the revelation comes to me when I am under the coverlet of a woman', he said once, 'it is only when I am with A'isha.' She herself, as was mentioned previously, was not without a streak of jealousy. He asked her once, half-teasing, if she would not like to die before him so that he could bury her and pray at her funeral. 'I should like that well enough,' she said, 'if I did not think that on returning from my funeral you would console yourself with another woman' . . .

The tense and delicate balance between the glory of Muhammad's prophethood, his closeness to God and his visionary gifts, the Herculean tasks he undertook and accomplished in the world, and the warmth and liveliness of his household is at the heart of the Muslim view of life; if this is understood, Islam is understood.[4]

17.3 Islamic law

Since the Qur'an does not contain a complete system of law, the Muslim community had to develop its laws gradually after the death of Muhammad, using the Qur'an and the traditions about the Prophet as their starting-point. It was in the period between about 850 to 950 that the *shari'a* came to be codified and developed into a complete and all-embracing system of law. During this time the four main schools of law emerged, each of them placing different emphasis on the four main Islamic sources of authority (see chapter 12).

These were some of the basic provisions concerning women and marriage contained in the *shari'a*:

■ A man may marry up to four wives.

■ The husband has to pay a dowry to his wife at the time of the wedding. The first part of the dowry consists of jewellery and/or cash which is spent on the bride's trousseau or on household furnishings. The second part is payable in cash or in kind in case of divorce.

■ The testimony of two women is equivalent to the testimony of one man.

■ Temporary marriage (*mut'a*) was marriage for a limited period

157

(varying from a few days to many years), which involved the payment of a dowry, however small. The custom had probably been a pre-Islamic custom in Arabia which was given legal sanction by the Qur'an (4:24) and the traditions of the Prophet. It became a common practice in Shi'i Islam, mainly in Persia. Later opinion was divided, with some regarding it as little more than legalized prostitution.

■ Women can own property. Wives have a right to their own earnings, and they can give away their property and earnings as they wish. A woman has a right to a proportion of the inheritance of her dead father, husband or childless brother, but only half of the share of other male relatives, since men have greater financial responsibilities.

■ A Muslim man should marry a Muslim woman. A Muslim man may in some cases marry a Jewish or Christian woman. A Muslim woman, however, is not allowed to marry a non-Muslim man.

■ Divorce (*talaq*) is allowed on the grounds of incompatibility, cruelty, injustice, prolonged absence, adultery, insanity, and incurable or contagious diseases. Although in the past Muslim women have not generally been allowed to divorce their husbands, it is now allowed in many Muslim countries. There are strict rules to ascertain the paternity of a child in cases where a divorced wife is pregnant.

■ Abortion is strictly forbidden, although in Tunisia today it is legally possible, and in many other countries it is practised clandestinely.

17.4 The role of women in the history of Islam

Many examples can be given of women who have played a significant role in the history of Islam. 'A'isha is the source of a large number of traditions about the life of the Prophet. During the Battle of the Camel she took up arms against Ali. One of the Prophet's granddaughters, Sayyida Zainab (died 684), has been venerated as a saint for many centuries, and her tomb in Cairo is still an important shrine today.

Rabi'a of Basra (died 802) was one of the earliest and best known of the Sufi saints. She is specially remembered for her prayer: 'O my Lord, if I worship Thee from hope of Paradise, exclude me thence, but if I worship Thee for Thine own sake then withhold not from me Thine eternal Beauty.' Many women after her played an important part in the Sufi movement, and women have been as deeply influenced by the movement as men. Princess Radiya, for instance, ruled in Delhi for four years from 1236 until she was supplanted by one of her brothers.

In this century women have played prominent roles in many Muslim countries. Halide Edib Adivar, for example, was active in public life in Turkey as a teacher, journalist and author from the early 1900s until her death in 1964. Begum Ra'ana, the wife of the first Prime Minister of Pakistan, was ambassador to the United Nations, and in 1979 gained a human rights award from the UN. Benazir Bhutto in 1988 became the first woman to be Prime Minister of a Muslim country, and was elected again in 1993. Several Muslim women from France and North Africa have competed for their countries in the Olympic Games.

17.5 Muslim expectations concerning women and marriage

We need here to attempt to distinguish between those expectations which are clearly linked with Islamic teaching, those which have more to do with the cultural context of particular countries, and those which arise out of developments in the modern world.

Expectations which are influenced largely by Islamic beliefs

Muslims place a strong emphasis on the role of women in the home, and especially in caring for children. Women are very much involved in all the festivals, for example, in preparing special meals to be eaten during the night in Ramadan, cooking special dishes for 'Idul Fitr, buying new clothes and gifts, and so on.

There is a strong feeling among Muslims that men are expected to get married. There is a popular saying that 'marriage is "half of religion"' (*i.e.* the religion of Islam). Muslim men find it hard to understand the idea of life-long celibacy.

Marriages are generally arranged by the parents. It is becoming more and more common, however, for young people to accept or reject their parents' choice.

Muslims, even those living in the West, tend to disapprove of the mixing of the sexes after puberty. They prefer their children to go to single-sex schools, and disapprove of them having boyfriends or girlfriends.

If Muslim women go to the mosque to say their prayers, they must pray in the special room or gallery provided for them, since their voice must not be heard above men's voices. In many cases, however, women are encouraged to pray at home. Friday prayers are optional for women. Since it is thought that menstruation makes women unclean, they are not allowed to go to the mosque during their monthly period.

The concept of *izzat*, meaning 'honour' (from the Arabic word *izza*, meaning honour, self-respect or reputation) is very strong, particularly in India and Pakistan. This means, for example, that if a girl is known to have had any sexual relationships before marriage, the family are bound to punish her severely in order to maintain the honour of the family. Every member of the family is obliged to defend the honour and reputation of the whole family.

Many Muslim women wear the veil. In Arabic it is known as *hijab*; in Iran as *chador* (a veil which covers the head, but not the face); and in India and Pakistan it is known as *burqa* (a garment which covers the whole body). Since the Qur'an does not demand that women should be completely covered in public, it seems that the complete veiling of women practised in many countries reflects traditions in very conservative societies rather than the teaching of Islam. Some Muslim women today may therefore be more restricted than Muslim women were at the time of Muhammad.

Purdah (a Persian word meaning curtain or veil) is the word used (mainly on the Indian subcontinent) to refer to the seclusion of women. When Muslim women observe the custom, it means that from the age of puberty they mix only with near relatives and women friends, and must wear the veil or the *burqa* in public.

Expectations concerning women which are influenced more by local cultural factors and by 'folk Islam' or 'village Islam'

In some Muslim communities there may be a low view of women which has more to do with local culture and tradition than with

160

Islam. In Pakistan, for example, there is a popular saying among women, 'Whereas out of every thousand men only one will go to hell, yet out of every thousand women, only one will be found in heaven.' It should be recognized, however, that this kind of sentiment is not based on the Qur'an or on genuine Muslim tradition.

Although family planning has been supported by the governments of a number of Muslim countries, there is still considerable resistance to the practice among many Muslims. Their feeling is that since children are a gift from God, God must be able and willing to provide for them. Vivienne Stacey explains popular thinking in countries such as Pakistan:

> Ignorance and fear make some slow to adopt family planning techniques. Sometimes one spouse is willing and the other is not. Religious advisors – *pirs* and *marabouts* – are often against such devices which would reduce the number of Muslims ... Reinforcing these hindrances to family planning is the great fear of Muslim parents that they will not have enough sons. How often a wife is in distress because she has not produced a child! The wife who produces only girls will also seek religious help as well as perhaps medical help. If she has a son she will want more sons in case the child dies as it may easily do. So a woman's importance in society in general is estimated by her ability to produce sons. This is an inequality between the sexes which the laws of a country and the efforts of family planning associations can do little about.[5]

On the expectations of a young bride, Vivienne Stacey quotes the following account written by a midwife working in a rural area in Afghanistan. Although some aspects of this description do not apply outside this situation, some of them do apply in similar situations in other parts of the Muslim world.

> As the bride settles into life with her husband's family, she will be guarded from evil influences from the day of her marriage – by charms on her person or pinned up in the house. The Qur'an, wrapped carefully and put on a

161

special shelf just above the door, is a guard against any evil influence entering their new home . . . If as the months pass no sign of pregnancy appears, she will be taken to the local 'midwife' who may give advice on special herbal potions to drink. If this is not effective, she will visit the local 'holy man'. Some verses of the Qur'an will be chanted and blown on her, or a charm given her to be worn on her person – a small metal box sewn into cloth, holding pieces of paper on which verses from the Qur'an have been written. As a last resort she will visit a local shrine, walking round it a certain number of times, picking up stones and putting them on her forehead, or even kissing the shrine. After-wards a piece of cloth is tied near the shrine or a nail hammered into a nearby tree . . . The childless wife is a sad person who constantly fears the threat of another wife coming into the home. The stigma of having no children is strong. Other women may feel she is judged of God, or has the 'evil eye' . . . Fear surrounds her; she is thought to be more vulnerable to evil influences and therefore is protected from certain situations – meeting strangers, walking near graveyards, and having contact with anyone who might have the 'evil eye'. Because they believe that *jinn* (evil spirits) can listen to conversa-tions, very little is said about the pregnancy, and very little preparation is made for the baby; a small bundle of clothes may be laid ready for the delivery, but that is all.

Very soon after the birth the *mullah* [local religious leader from the mosque] will come to the house to shout the creed of Islam in the baby's ear. The baby's name is chosen either by the male members of the household, or by the *mullah*. Nobody compliments the baby in case evil spirits are listening, and if someone does say any-thing positive it is prefixed by 'in the name of God' (*bismillah*) as a protection . . . At the end of forty days the new mother may celebrate with her women friends.[6]

Expectations which are influenced by life in the modern world, including urbanization and the media

Tunisia is an example of a country which has for some years had a vigorous programme of public teaching on the value of family planning. As a result, the practice has become more widely accepted. In many Muslim countries, especially in North Africa, more women have been going out to work than formerly. They therefore acquire greater independence and come less under the control of their mothers-in-law.

17.6 Law reform in the twentieth century
Modern law codes

Vivienne Stacey describes the problems Muslims have had to face in making the traditional *shari'a* law relevant and applicable in different situations in modern times:

> Traditionalists and modernists in Islam are never so divided as on the question of the position and rights of women. New laws relating to the position of women have been introduced in many Muslim lands. Reform laws have often been linked to a new way of interpreting the Qur'an. How can a divine law be amended? In adapting and interpreting Qur'anic teaching for the modern world four principles can be observed. First, a procedural device by which the reformers did not change the divine law but gave orders that it was not to be applied. The courts in certain circumstances were not to hear a case. Secondly, laws were formulated partly from one school of law and partly from another or from several. Thirdly, a new use of consensus (*ijma'*) has developed which involves a going back to the original sources and making fresh deductions . . . Finally, administrative orders based on one of the three principles described above, sometimes with something added which is not contrary or repugnant to Islam, has made possible the adoption of reforms even in Islamic states.[7]

Turkey was the first Muslim country to bring in a family law in 1917. In Egypt a series of laws was passed between 1920 and

1929, and in 1943 a new law of inheritance was passed. Similar laws were passed in Jordan in 1951, and in Syria in 1953. In 1979 amendments to the 1929 personal status law were passed, giving women better rights in divorce and for alimony and child custody. Tunisia made polygamy illegal in 1956, and in 1959 made all sex discrimination illegal.

Amir Taheri describes some of the obstacles to the reform of laws relating to the status of women in countries of the Middle East:

> The 1980s could be described as a period of retreat for those who supported the cause of legal equality and more individual liberties for women. Under pressure from Islamic fundamentalists most Middle Eastern governments have either postponed or cancelled earlier policies in favour of more rights for women.[8]

The feminist movement in Islam

Abdur Rahman I. Doi, an Indian Muslim now teaching in Malaysia after many years' experience in Nigeria, traces the feminist movement in the Muslim world back to the nineteenth century, when 'the Christian West had almost dominated the Muslim world'.[9] Reforms initiated by such rulers as Muhammad 'Ali and Isma'il Pasha were intended to enable Egyptians to attain the same cultural level as Europeans, and therefore forced Egyptians to abandon their traditional Islamic way of life. Reformers such as Jamal al-Din al-Afghani, Muhammad 'Abduh and Qasim Amin pressed, for example, for better education for girls and women, and spoke against the practice of polygamy.

In 1919 the leadership of the movement passed to Huda Sha'rawi (1879–1947), the chairperson of the Women's Executive of a major political party in Egypt. In that year she led a demonstration of veiled women to support Egyptian nationalism. In 1923, after leading an Egyptian delegation to the meeting of an International Alliance for Women in Rome, she threw her veil into the sea as she disembarked on her return to Egypt. Through the growing influence of the movement a new marriage and divorce law was passed in 1928.

The feminist case, however, has been argued strongly in recent years by a growing number of Muslim women who have

164

tried to understand the culture of both the Muslim world and the Western world. Fatna Sabah, for example, a North African sociologist, is critical of the record of traditional Islam over its attitudes to women. This is how she explains 'the ideal of female beauty in Islam':

> The ideal of female beauty in Islam is obedience, silence and immobility, that is inertia and passivity. These are far from being trivial characteristics, nor are they limited to women. In fact, these three attributes of female beauty are the three qualities of the believer vis-à-vis his God. The believer must dedicate his life to obeying and worshipping God and abiding by his will . . .
>
> In the sacred universe, the believer is fashioned in the image of woman, deprived of speech and will and committed to obedience to another [God]. The female condition and the male condition are not different in the end to which they are directed, but in the pole around which they orbit. The lives of beings of the female sex revolve around the will of believers of the male sex.[10]

Using Sabah's analysis, Fatima Mernissi, a sociologist working at the Research Institute of the University of Rabat in Morocco, tries to explain why some recent feminist thinking represents such a threat to traditional ways of thinking in Islam:

> What happens when a woman disobeys her husband, who is the representative and embodiment of sacred authority, and of the Islamic hierarchy? A danger bell rings in the mind, for when one element of the whole structure of polarities is threatened, the entire system is threatened. A woman who rebels against her husband, for instance, is also rebelling against the *umma*, against reason, order and, indeed, God. The rebellion of woman is linked to individualism, not community (*umma*); passion, not reason; disorder, not order; lawlessness (*fitna*), not law.[11]

This is how she explains the dilemma facing many Muslim women in the modern world:

> In the struggle for survival in the Muslim world today, the Muslim community finds itself squeezed between individualistic, innovative western capitalism on the one hand, and individualistic, rebellious political oppositions within, among which the most symbolically 'loaded' is that of rebellious women. The common denominator between capitalism and new models of femininity is individualism and self-affirmation. Initiative is power. Women are claiming power – corroding and ultimately destroying the foundation of Muslim hierarchy; whence the violence of the reaction and the rigidity of the response. Femininity as a symbol of surrender has to be resisted violently if women intend to change its meaning into energy, initiative and creative criticism.[12]

Christian readers will recognize the uncanny parallel with the tensions among Christians over traditional responses to feminism.

Islamization and the demand for a return to the shari'a

In several countries groups of Muslims are calling for their governments to adopt a new legal code which is based on the *shari'a* rather than on any western law codes. Abdur Rahman I. Doi expresses the feeling of many that Muslims have absorbed too much from the West in their attitudes to women, and need to recover a more traditionally Islamic approach:

> During the days of European colonialism and the scramble to take over the Muslim world, the influence of feminism spread into Muslim countries. The first victims of the glittering Western way of life were the Muslim rulers of various Muslim countries. In the days of the political decline of Islam, they were made to believe that the Muslim world was lagging behind because of the 'maltreatment and slavery of women'.[13]

I would like to appeal to Muslim scholars the world over to re-examine the role they played in this most difficult period of Islamic history when the Christian West had almost dominated the Muslim world. I have a feeling that perhaps they went too far in proposing reforms in the Shari'ah. Perhaps with the best of intentions, they proposed so-called 'reforms' in the matter of the Shari'ah and galloped on the unbridled horse of reason and imagination, giving *fatawa* [juristic opinions] which did great damage which they did not live long enough to see.[14]

Many of my Egyptian friends will not be happy to read that not only did Egypt shelve, and to a great extent discard, the Islamic system of values as taught by the Qur'an and the Sunnah by adopting Western culture and the Western way of life, but it also exported it to other Arab and Muslim countries. Walking in the streets of many cities in Egypt, one feels that one is in Europe.[15]

It must not be thought, however, that a return to the requirements of *shari'a* necessarily means putting the clock back and keeping women isolated in the modern world. Muslim women who wear the veil can be highly educated, working women. In many countries there is nothing strange about seeing a professional woman wearing a veil and working at her computer. Hinde Taarji, a Moroccan journalist, wrote a book in 1991 entitled *Les Voilées de l'Islam*, in which she recorded the results of interviews with women throughout the Arab world who had decided to wear the veil (*hijab*). These are some of the reasons given for wearing the veil:

- It can liberate women by helping them to escape from masculine aggression in public and encouraging men to respect them. The veil will not necessarily destroy the emancipation of Muslim women.

- It is a sign of total commitment to Islam, and provides the security and stability of a familiar code in a changing society.

- It has little or nothing to do with a desire to remain secluded in the home, since many who wear the veil want to go out to work.

■ It indicates to men that Muslim women can have their own interpretation of Islam, in spite of the fact that men have traditionally been the guardians of orthodox Islamic teaching. These veiled women are 'entering the centre of Islam' – with the approval of men.

Throughout this chapter Christian readers will inevitably have been making comparisons with the place of women in Christianity. Are there any firm conclusions that can be drawn from such comparisons?

In the first place, we need to be careful when we speak about 'the teaching of the Bible' with regard to women and marriage. The early chapters of Genesis speak about origins, and describe the marriage of one man and one woman as something instituted by God since the beginning (Genesis 2:18–24). Sadly, however, there are many examples in the rest of the Old Testament of great characters, such as Abraham, David and Solomon, who did always live up to the ideal described in Genesis. Was it that they did not know that monogamy was God's ideal for the human race, or that God was allowing the Jewish people to learn the hard way, through experience?

When we come to the New Testament, Jesus bases his teaching about marriage squarely on the teaching of Genesis (Mark 10:1–12), whereas Paul sees the relationship of love between Christ and his church as the pattern of the relationship between husband and wife in marriage (Ephesians 5:22–33). While we may find it difficult to explain some of the behaviour described in the Bible, most of us would feel that when we take the whole of the Bible's teaching, there are significant differences between biblical and Qur'anic teaching about marriage.

We need to resist the temptation, however, to exaggerate these differences or to compare the best in our own tradition with the worst in the other. We also need to be extremely careful about our motives in making the comparisons or speaking about the differences with Muslims.

Although we may believe that the Christian faith provides a better basis for the dignity of women than any other faith, we need to admit that the Christian church has not always had a very good record over its attitudes to women. We may be able to explain this to ourselves by saying that at certain periods Christians cannot have been fully aware of the distinctive Christian teaching, or that they were more influenced by their culture than by the gospel. Our problem often is, however, that Muslims do not generally find it easy to distinguish between Christian teaching and Christian practice.

Does this seem a strangely inconclusive point at which to end a chapter on women in Islam and a whole section of the book which deals with understanding Islam? If so, at the very least we should have realized the complexity of the subject we are dealing with.

We have not, I trust, acquired a new armoury of weapons to use against Islam and Muslims. I hope rather that we have gained some insight into the role of women in Islam and developed some sympathy for the aspirations of women in different Muslim communities.

If we have also recognized the need for greater humility and deeper repentance over *Christian* failures to live up to the standards set before us in the Christian tradition, we may have added something to our reflection in Part 1 on meeting our Muslim neighbours, and be better prepared for the kind of discussion and dialogue we need to explore in Part 3, 'Entering into Discussion and Dialogue'.

Resources for further study

Hammudah Abdalati, *Islam in Focus* (World Assembly of Muslim Youth, 1980)

Akbar S. Ahmed, *Discovering Islam: Making Sense of Muslim History and Society* (Routledge, 1988)

Sir Norman Anderson, *Islam in the Modern World: A Christian Perspective* (Apollos, 1990)

Kenneth Cragg, *The Call of the Minaret* (Collins, 1986)

———, *Counsels in Contemporary Islam* (Edinburgh University Press, 1967)

———, *Islam and the Muslim* (Open University Press, 1978)

K. Cragg and M. Speight, *Islam from Within: Anthology of a Religion* (Wadsworth, 1980)

Norman Daniels, *Islam and the West: the Making of an Image* (Edinburgh University Press, 1960)

Abdur Rahman I. Doi, *Shari'ahd: The Islamic Law* (Ta Ha Publishers, 1984)

———, *Women in Shari'ah (Islamic Law)* (Ta Ha Publishers, 1989)

Gai Eaton, *Islam and the Destiny of Man* (George Allen and Unwin, 1985)

D. Eck and D. Jain, eds., *Speaking of Faith: Cross-Cultural Perspectives on Women, Religion and Social Change* (The Women's Press, 1986)

John L. Esposito, ed., *Voices of Resurgent Islam* (Oxford University Press, 1983)

Alfred Guillaume, *Islam* (Penguin, 1983)

John Hinnels, ed., *A Handbook of Living Religions* (Penguin, 1985)

Chris Horrie and Peter Chippendale, *What is Islam?* (Virgin, 1991)

Nabeel Jabbour, *The Rumbling Volcano: Islamic Fundamentalism in Egypt* (Mandate Press, 1993)

Jacques Jomier, *How to Understand Islam* (SCM, 1989)

Mervyn Kiskett, *Some to Mecca Turn to Pray: Islamic Values in the*

Modern World (Claridge Press, 1993)

M. S. Langley, *The World's Religions* (Lion, 1982)

Trevor Ling, *A History of Religion East and West* (Macmillan, 1982)

Abul A'la Mawdudi, *Towards Understanding Islam* (The Islamic Foundation, 1981)

Bill Musk, *The Unseen Face of Islam* (MARC Europe, 1989)

Seyyed Hossein Nasr, *Ideals and Realities of Islam* (Unwin Hyman, 1988)

Michael Nazir-Ali, *Islam: A Christian Perspective* (Paternoster, 1983)

Constance E. Padwick, *Muslim Devotions: A Study of Prayer Manuals in Common Use* (SPCK, 1961)

Phil Parshall, *Bridges to Islam: A Christian Perspective on Folk Islam* (Baker, 1983)

Fazlur Rahman, *Islam* (Chicago University Press, 1979)

L. Smith and L. Bodin, *The Islamic Tradition* (Argus, 1978)

Vivienne Stacey, *The Life of Muslim Women* (Fellowship of Faith, 1980)

W. Montgomery Watt, *Bell's Introduction to the Qur'an* (Edinburgh University Press, 1977)

——, *Muhammad: Prophet and Statesman* (Oxford University Press, 1975)

——, *What is Islam?* (Longmans, 1968)

Rafiq Zakaria, *The Struggle within Islam: The Conflict Between Religion and Politics* (Penguin, 1988)

Part 3

Entering into discussion and dialogue

The areas of conscious difference with Christians seem to act like a magnet which draws their mind in any conversation.

Roger Hooker[1]

It is hardly too much to say that the intellectual challenge to Christianity from Islam at the present time is greater than any challenge Christians have had to meet for fifteen centuries, not excluding that from natural sciences.

W. Montgomery Watt[2]

O that I could converse and reason, and plead, with power from on high. How powerless are the best-directed arguments, till the Holy Spirit renders them effectual.

Henry Martyn[3]

For far too long evangelical missions have been limping along without an effective apologetic to Islam. Since the demise of the nineteenth-century polemical method, known as 'The Moham- medan Controversy', no significant Christian apologetical work for Muslims has been written.

Sam Schlorff[4]

Having tried in Part 2 to gain a deeper understanding of Islam as a total way of life, we turn now to consider the main controversial issues that tend to arise in conver- sation between Muslims and Christians. In some cases these are issues over which Muslims and Christians have been talking and arguing for centuries.

18

Questions and objections concerning Christian practice

Each question or comment is followed by the outline of a possible answer. It should be emphasized that what is set out here is nothing more than suggestions for answers which can be given immediately. They are not intended to be exhaustive, and are no substitute for hard thought and study on our part.

1. *'Why do you eat pork, which is unclean?'*

The Jews were taught in the *tawrat* (the Torah) that pork was unclean. People today think that this was partly because of hygiene; but it was also a sign that they were God's special people. Jesus, however, taught that cleanness and uncleanness in God's eyes are more a matter of what goes on secretly in our hearts than of what we eat or don't eat. This is the teaching that he gave when he had a dispute with the Jewish teachers about keeping traditions concerning cleanliness:

> Nothing outside a man can make him 'unclean' by going into him. Rather, it is what comes out of a man that makes him 'unclean' . . . Don't you see that nothing that enters a man from the outside can make him 'unclean'? For it doesn't go into his heart but into his stomach, and then out of his body . . . What comes out of a man is what makes him 'unclean'. For from within, out of men's hearts, come evil thoughts, sexual immorality, theft, murder, adultery, greed, malice, deceit, lewdness, envy, slander, arrogance and folly. All these evils come from inside and make a man 'unclean' (Mark 7:15–23).

2. *'Why do you drink alcohol?'*

In the *tawrat* there is no command to refrain from drinking alcohol, although any individual could take a special vow not to drink alcohol, and call himself a 'Nazirite'. In the *injil* (gospel) we are taught that Jesus did drink wine, but that John the Baptist (Yahya in the Qur'an), his cousin, who prepared the way for him, did not drink. This means that since there is no law on the subject, we are free to follow the spirit of the teaching of Jesus, which is that we should practise self-control and be careful stewards of what God has given to us. All Christians believe that it is wrong to be drunk. Some choose voluntarily not to drink alcohol, but others feel free to drink in moderation.

3. *'Do you drink wine in church?'*

We do have a special service that Jesus commanded us to keep, which we call 'the Holy Communion' or 'the Lord's Supper' or 'the Eucharist'. It is a time when we remember the death and resurrection of Jesus. We have just a taste of wine and a small piece of bread, following the command that Jesus gave at the last meal before he died.

4. *'Christianity makes impossible and unrealistic moral demands (such as "turning the other cheek"). Islam doesn't demand more than is reasonable, or expect an unnatural degree of self-denial.'*

We agree that Christianity does set very high moral standards, but this is because God is holy and says many times in the Bible, 'Be holy, for I am holy' (*e.g.* Leviticus 11:44). When we read the teaching of Jesus, we try to understand the spirit of what he said rather than treat his words as a series of laws which have to be obeyed to the letter. 'Turning the other cheek', for example, means that when I am insulted, I don't reply with an insult.

Although we recognize that the standards set by Jesus are very high, we believe in God's forgiveness. When, therefore, we know we have fallen short of God's standards, and ask forgiveness, we can be sure that God has forgiven us. We also believe that the Holy Spirit of God lives within us when we trust Jesus. He works in our conscience, prompts us about how we should behave in particular situations, and gives us power beyond our own natural power to follow the way of Christ.

5. *'Islam has no priesthood, no special caste of people who are set aside to perform priestly functions which no-one else can perform.'*

In most churches there are certain services (such as Holy Communion or the Lord's Supper, baptism and marriage) which can be led only by a priest or an ordained minister, although in some churches there are no ordained ministers. Different churches give different reasons to explain the reasons for this, but all agree that these ceremonies are not a special kind of magic. They believe that, for the sake of good order in the church, the services should be led by a person who is authorized by the whole church to lead them. While there are significant differences between the main branches of the church (Orthodox, Catholic and Protestant), there is no suggestion that the priest is a kind of mediator without whom we cannot come into the presence of God.

19

Questions and objections concerning Christian beliefs

The following are some of the main objections which Muslims tend to put to Christians about their beliefs. All we are attempting to do here is to suggest the kind of short answers that we can give, which (we may hope) will lead into further discussion. Chapter 22 goes into some of these issues in greater depth.

1. *'Why do you believe in the Trinity? Do you believe in three gods?'*

We don't believe in three gods! We believe in one God as strongly as any Muslim. When we speak of God the Father, God the Son and God the Holy Spirit, we are not thinking of three separate and distinct gods. Christianity is a monotheistic religion, as much as Islam. The *word* 'Trinity' is not found in the Bible; but the *idea* is taught in the Bible.

2. *'Why do you say that Jesus is the "Son of God"?'*

Because Jesus called himself 'the Son' and spoke of God as 'the Father' and 'my Father'. We don't believe that Jesus was the son of God in any physical sense; this idea is as repugnant to us as it is to Muslims.

We believe that 'God is love' in his very nature, and that there has always been a relationship of love between God the Father, God the Son and God the Holy Spirit, even before the creation of the universe. Jesus of Nazareth is more than a prophet, since he was fully human *and* fully divine. When we say that Jesus is the Son of God, what we mean in the simplest possible language is that he was *like God* in a way that no other human being has ever been. When we look at Jesus, therefore, and see what he was like, we have some idea of what God is like.

3. *'Why do you believe that Jesus was crucified?'*

Because this is what our Scriptures teach. The New Testament explains that it wasn't out of weakness that God allowed Jesus to be crucified. It was his way of showing up the evil in human nature in its true colours. But it was also his way of showing how much he loves us and wants to forgive us for all our sins. Christians see the death of Jesus as a 'sacrifice for sins', as the one final and complete sacrifice which does away with the need for any other sacrifice offered to gain forgiveness of sins. God allowed Jesus to experience death because all human beings have to die. But by raising him from the dead, God not only vindicated Jesus and revealed his true identity, but also destroyed the power of death once and for all who trust in him.

4. *'Your Scriptures have been corrupted.'*

I know this is what you have been taught. But have you read them? According to the Holy Qur'an, the message which God revealed to the Prophet Muhammad confirmed the previous Scriptures: the *tawrat* revealed to Moses, the *zabur* revealed to David, and the *injil* to Jesus. If these Scriptures, which were in the hands of the Jews and the Christians at the time of the Prophet Muhammad, were *already* corrupt, how could the Qur'an confirm these Scriptures? Can you tell me who corrupted the Scriptures, and when it was done? Would you like to read the life of Jesus as it is recorded in our *injil*? How can you say that our Scriptures are corrupted if you haven't read them?

5. *'Your Scriptures are full of mistakes and contradictions.'*

Christians are aware of the so-called contradictions that you find in the Bible, because Christian scholars have been aware of them for a long time. But they have their own way of explaining these differences, and some of them can be explained very easily. Others raise harder questions of interpretation. Are you prepared to listen to the way we explain these difficulties?

Two can play the same game! Some Christians say that they find contradictions in the Qur'an. How would you feel if I were to criticize the Qur'an? But I don't want to do so, because I am not interested in criticizing the Qur'an. If Muslims don't like Christians criticizing the Qur'an, why do Muslims criticize the Bible?

The basic reason you have problems with the apparent contradictions in the Bible is that you are comparing the Bible with the Qur'an. You believe that the Qur'an is the very words revealed directly to Muhammad, and you assume that the Bible

was revealed in exactly the same way. Christians *do* believe that
the Bible is the Word of God, and that God through his Holy
Spirit inspired the different books of the Bible. But the Word of
God in the Bible has come through a large number of different
authors. The Bible is therefore for us *both* the Word of God *and*
the words of human beings. The fundamental problem between
us at this point is that we have different views of revelation.
Muslims believe that the supreme revelation God has given was
in the form of a *book*, the Qur'an. Christians, however, believe
that the supreme revelation was given in a *person*, Jesus (see
further chapter 28).

6. *'We recognize Jesus as a prophet. Why don't you recognize Muhammad as a prophet?'*

If we did recognize Muhammad as a prophet in the way that
you do, we would be Muslims. We are glad to accept the teaching of the Qur'an about the one true God which we also find in
our Scriptures. But we cannot believe the *whole* Qur'an, because
its teaching is different at many points from the teaching of our
Scriptures.

We believe that Jesus was the last of the prophets, God's final
word to the world. We see Jesus as the most complete revelation
of God in the form of a human being. We cannot believe that
there could be any more complete revelation of God *after* Jesus.

7. *'Why do you not recognize that the Bible foretells the coming of
Muhammad?'*

There are two verses which are often used to support this
argument. The first is the words from Deuteronomy about a new
prophet who was to come: 'The LORD your God will raise up for
you a prophet like me from among your own brothers'
(Deuteronomy 18:15). This could hardly refer to Muhammad,
since Moses says that this prophet is to be raised up 'from among
your own brothers', that is, from among the children of Israel.

The second verse gives us the words of Jesus about the coming
of the Paraclete: 'I will ask the Father, and he will give you
another Counsellor to be with you for ever – the Spirit of truth'
(John 14:16; *cf.* 14:26; 15:26; 16:7). Christians have always interpreted these as predictions about the coming of the Holy Spirit.
Jesus never spoke about another *prophet* who was to come after
him.

8. *'All religions are basically the same. Why worry about the differences?'*

(This attitude comes as a surprise to Christians who have been accustomed to questions which are highly critical of Christian beliefs. It is also often much harder to answer, simply because it seems to be so generous and tolerant towards Christians. This apparently charitable and tolerant view of other faiths springs in some cases from a genuine desire to avoid the painful controversies of the past. In other cases, however, it arises out of complacency and indifference, and may suggest that the person is not interested in the search for truth and wants to avoid discussion of differences between faiths.)

This is not how the Qur'an speaks about other faiths! Although it is generous towards Jews and Christians, because they are 'people of the Book', it is very critical of them in certain respects. Muhammad therefore openly invited them to reject some of their distinctive beliefs and to accept the religion of Islam. The Qur'an is much less generous, however, towards 'idolaters'; and during the first few centuries of the spread of Islam, those who were not Jews or Christians were offered the choice of accepting either Islam or death. This kind of tolerance towards other faiths which you are expressing, therefore, is quite different from the teaching of the Qur'an and of orthodox Islam in the past.

Do you actually know what we believe about Jesus? A detailed comparison between the Muslim's understanding of Muhammad and the Christian's understanding of Jesus should indicate that there are very significant differences between the two faiths. There are dangers in making such comparisons, since the role of Muhammad in Islam is quite different from the role of Jesus in Christianity (see p. 76). But if you know and understand what Christians believe about Jesus (even if you don't believe it), you can hardly say that the differences between the two religions are insignificant.

20

Social and political issues

1. *'Children don't obey their parents in the West as they do in Muslim countries.'*

We recognize that Islam emphasizes obedience to parents very strongly, and as Christians we agree with this teaching because one of the Ten Commandments says, 'Honour your father and your mother' (Exodus 20:12). So both Christianity and Islam have the same teaching at this point. This is an example, however, of how the Christian way of life is not being followed in the West. The methods of discipline that are used in some societies rely on the pressure of the extended family and the pressure of the community. But these pressures tend to become weaker in western societies, with the result that young people of *all* religious communities don't see the same need to obey and respect their parents.

As Christians living in a society that is not Christian, we try to teach our children the right way to live and behave; but when they reach a certain age we don't feel we can force them against their will to live in a certain way. We want to leave them free to choose the right way for themselves, because we believe that they may be stronger in the end if they follow this way without being forced to.

2. *'Look at how degenerate the West has become! If this is what Christianity has done for the West, it isn't a very good advertisement for Christianity.'*

For many centuries during the Middle Ages, it was assumed that almost everyone in western countries was a Christian, just as in Muslim countries today everyone is regarded as a Muslim, unless he or she belongs to another religion. The situation today, however, is very different: only a minority would call themselves committed or convinced Christians, while the majority would say that they are Christians only in name, that they believe in God but not in Jesus, or that they have no religious beliefs at all.

Christians would argue that violence and permissiveness in the West today are not the result of following Christian teaching, but of refusal to follow Christian teaching. If Muslims say that the West is in a bad state because of Christianity, it's all too easy for the Christian to reply that the Muslim world is in a bad state because of Islam. We need to get beyond this kind of accusation and try to understand that both Christians and Muslims face the same difficult problems and challenges in the modern world.

3. *'Why do Christians tend to support the state of Israel without question?'*

We have to admit that many Christians do give strong support to the Zionist state, partly because of their sympathy with the Jewish people, and partly because they have been taught that the establishment of the state of Israel is the fulfilment of promises and prophecies given by God in the Bible. A growing number of Christians, however, disagree with this way of interpreting the Bible. They are also becoming critical of the policies of Israel, and are questioning the idea of a Jewish state. Official statements from church leaders have encouraged Christians to have a more balanced view of the conflict. They are very aware of the injustices suffered by the Palestinian Arabs, and want to work for a just solution which allows Jews and Arabs to live side by side in peace.

21

Guidelines and aims in discussion with Muslims

This section outlines some basic do's and don'ts.

1. *Don't start an argument if you can possibly help it!* Whenever we see the warning signals in ourselves, we need to be reminded of Paul's words addressed to Timothy, the young and enthusiastic Christian worker: 'Don't have anything to do with foolish and stupid arguments, because you know they produce quarrels. And the Lord's servant must not quarrel; instead, he must be kind to everyone, able to teach, not resentful' (2 Timothy 2:23–24).

2. *Resist the temptation to criticize Islam.* The words of Jesus about standing in judgment on other people are surely relevant to our dealings with Muslims: 'Do not judge, or you too will be judged. For in the same way as you judge others, you will be judged, and with the measure you use, it will be measured to you' (Matthew 7:1–2). In other words, if we criticize Islam, its civilization, its beliefs and its whole way of life, we may be inviting Muslims to do the same to us and our faith.

The words that follow are also relevant: 'Why do you look at the speck of sawdust in your brother's eye and pay no attention to the plank in your own eye? . . . You hypocrite, first take the plank out of your own eye, and then you will see clearly to remove the speck from your brother's eye' (Matthew 7:3, 5).

3. *Do all you can to remove misunderstanding (e.g. about Christians worshipping three gods, about Jesus being the 'Son of God' in a physical sense, about the West being Christian, etc.).* Even if we don't feel we have achieved very much by doing so, we may at least be clearing the ground, making it easier for someone to see Jesus and understand the Christian way more clearly. Robert Bruce, a missionary in Persia in the nineteenth century, used to say: 'I

I am not reaping the harvest; I can scarcely claim to be sowing the seed . . . but I am gathering out the stones.'

4. *Try to distinguish between what is important and what is less important.* For example, don't spend all your time debating secondary issues (such as eating pork and drinking wine), if you then have no opportunity to deal with the more important issues such as the role of law, the diagnosis of the human condition, and forgiveness.

5. *Be prepared to admit the mistakes and crimes of Christians in the past and present.* We need to be willing to accept that Paul's words in Romans 2:24 about the Jews of his time can easily be paraphrased and made to apply to the Christian church throughout its history: 'Christ's name is blasphemed in the Muslim world because of you.'

We need to be willing to say with the psalmist: 'We have sinned, even as our fathers did; we have done wrong and acted wickedly' (Psalm 106:6). This means, for example, admitting our shame about the Crusades.

6. *Be positive.* Don't always be defending Christianity. Take every opportunity to say what you believe and why you believe it (1 Peter 3:15).

7. *Love is more persuasive than argument.* Even if you win an argument, you may lose the person. Even if you lose an argument, you may still win the person if you show that you really love him or her.

8. *Don't underestimate the power of personal testimony.* If you believe that you know God in a personal way, don't be afraid to say so, and to tell your friend why you believe that this kind of personal relationship is possible. If you believe your sins have been forgiven and that you have no fear of the day of judgment, explain the basis of your confidence in God's forgiveness.

9. *Be content to communicate one small aspect of the gospel at a time.* Don't feel you have failed if you haven't been able to explain 'the whole gospel' at one time. There is no single technique for communicating the gospel to a Muslim. We must resist the temptation to think that one simple technique is bound to produce results and save us from much heartache and agony. You can sometimes convey more of the gospel in an indirect way than in a direct way.

10. *Make it a priority to encourage your friends at the appropriate time to read one of the gospels.* If they say that the Bible has been corrupted, say that you are willing to discuss the question after they have read some of the Bible.

Luke is perhaps the best gospel to start with (see chapter 33, 'Using the Bible'). Matthew is also valuable, and the Sermon on the Mount is specially powerful for Muslims. But some Muslims find it difficult because it is so Jewish. Mark introduces a stumbling-block in the very first sentence by speaking of Jesus as 'the son of God'. John may be helpful as a second gospel to read, or for Muslims who have been influenced by Sufism.

A deeper look at the main Muslim objections

We want here to go deeper into some of the objections touched on in chapter 19. In each case we need first of all to listen carefully to what is behind the objection; only then can we reflect on how we can respond.

22.1 'The Bible has been corrupted.'

The Qur'an speaks of three Scriptures that were revealed before the Qur'an:

- the *tawrat* (Torah), revealed to Moses (*e.g.* 3:93)
- the *zabur* (Psalms), revealed to David (*e.g.* 4:163; 17:55; 21:105)
- the *injil* (gospel), revealed to Jesus (*e.g.* 5:46).

Jews and Christians are called 'people of the Book' or 'people of the Scriptures' (*e.g.* 2:105; 3:64), and Muslims are told that they must believe the previous Scriptures as well as the Qur'an:

> O ye who believe! Believe in Allah and His messenger and the Scripture which He hath revealed unto His messenger, and the Scripture which He revealed aforetime. Whoso disbelieveth in Allah and His angels and His scriptures and His messengers and the Last Day, he verily hath wandered far astray (4:136; *cf.* 5:66, 68).

Muslims are to believe the previous Scriptures because the Qur'an confirms the truth of them:

> As for that which We inspire in thee of the Scripture, it is the Truth confirming that which was (revealed) before it (35:31; *cf.* 2:97).

There are, however, four verses in the Qur'an which speak about the 'corruption' or 'falsification' (*tahrif*) of these previous Scriptures, using the word 'change':

> . . . a party of them used to listen to the Word of Allah, then used to change it, after they had understood it, knowingly (2:75).

> Some of those who are Jews change the words from their context [or 'pervert words from their meanings', Bell] . . . distorting with their tongues and slandering religion (4:46).

> They change words from their context and forget a part of that whereof they were admonished (5:13).

> . . . the Jews: listeners for the sake of falsehood, listeners on behalf of other folk who come not unto thee, changing words from their context . . . (5:41).

How should we attempt to answer this charge that the Scriptures have been corrupted?

1. *None of these verses suggests that the* text *of the Bible has been corrupted.* One of the accusations seems to be that certain Jews deliberately mispronounced words spoken by Muhammad, probably playing on the resemblance between certain Arabic and Hebrew words (see 3:78). They are also accused of taking words in their Scriptures out of context and changing the meaning of words.

In other verses the Jews are accused of 'hiding' or 'concealing' their Scriptures:

> A party of them knowingly conceal the truth (2:146; *cf.* 2:159, 174; 3:72).

> O people of the Scripture! Now hath Our messenger come unto you, expounding unto you much of that which ye used to hide in the Scripture (5:15; *cf.* 6:92).

186

This probably means that in discussion with Muslims, the Jews refused to quote verses which would support the teaching of Islam. This could have included predictions about prophets to come in the future, which might be interpreted as referring to the coming of Muhammad.

There are only two verses in which accusations of this kind are made explicitly against Christians. In one of these the Christians are accused of *hiding* or *concealing* parts of what God had revealed in their Scriptures (2:140). In the other they are blamed for *forgetting* part of God's revelation in Scripture (5:14).

2. *The accusation about the corruption of the* text *of the Bible was developed by later Muslim apologists.* Muslim writers from the time of Muhammad to the eleventh century consistently understood the Qur'anic verses about 'corruption' to mean that Jews and Christians had *misinterpreted* their Scriptures.

'Umar, for example, the second caliph, believed that Christian monks and teachers had distorted the teaching of the Bible by giving false interpretations, or simply by covering up clear teaching (*e.g.* about the coming of Muhammad). Similarly, al-Tabari (839–923), one of the earliest authoritative commentators on the Qur'an, records a saying of Muhammad in which he admits that the Torah is God's truth, but accuses the Jews of suppressing its teaching and altering its contents. A work attributed to al-Ghazali (died 1111), called *An Excellent Refutation of the Divinity of Jesus According to the Gospels*, quotes many passages from the Bible, and especially the New Testament, without ever questioning the trustworthiness of the text.

The accusation that Jews and Christians had tampered with the text of their Scriptures first appeared in the writings of Muslim apologists from the eleventh century onwards. It was probably developed to explain the many discrepancies between the Bible and the Qur'an. Al-Juwayni (died 1085), for example, wrote a treatise in which he argued that the Scriptures must have been corrupted because the Qur'an says that the coming of Muhammad *was* foretold in the previous Scriptures, but Christians say that the coming of Muhammad is *not* foretold in them. He based his argument also on the differences between the four gospels. Ibn Hazm (994–1064), a more polemical writer from Spain, lists contradictions within the Bible and discrepancies between the

Qur'an and the Bible to prove that the text has been corrupted.

Not all Muslim apologists, however, have adopted this argument about the corruption of the text. Muhammad 'Abduh (1849–1905), for example, an Egyptian reformer who worked for the renewal of Islam, wrote in his commentary on the Qur'an that, although he believed that the Jews had altered their Scriptures, he accepted the text of the gospels as authentic.

3. *In answering Muslims who say that our Scriptures have been corrupted, we can politely but firmly ask in reply, 'When do you believe they were corrupted and by whom?'*

If they say they were corrupted *before the time of Muhammad*, we can ask them to explain why the Qur'an says that the message revealed to Muhammad was a confirmation of previous Scriptures:

> He hath revealed unto thee [Muhammad] the Scripture with truth, confirming that which was (revealed) before it, even as He revealed the Torah and the Gospel (3.3; *cf.* 2:136; 4:136; 10:95; 41:43).

It is clear that the Scriptures referred to here must be those which the Jews and Christians had *in their hands at that time*:

> Believe in what We have revealed confirming *that which ye possess* (4:47, my italics; *cf.* 2:91).

> And unto thee have We revealed the Scripture with truth, confirming whatever Scripture was before it, and a watcher over it (5:48; *cf.* 6:116; 10:65; 18:28).

How, then, could Muhammad say, on the one hand, that the revelations contained in the Qur'an simply confirm the Scriptures of the Jews and Christians, and on the other hand claim that the Scriptures which the Jews and Christians have in their hands have been corrupted?

If they say that they were corrupted *after the time of Muhammad*, we can point out that the manuscripts on which our present Bible is based were written centuries *before* the time of Muhammad. For example, the Dead Sea Scrolls, which include manuscripts of every book of the Old Testament except one, were written before AD 68. One of the oldest Greek manuscripts of the whole of the New Testament, the Codex Alexandrinus, dates from the fifth century, and can be seen by anyone in the British Museum in London; and manuscripts of some parts of the New Testament can be dated to the second century.

4. There are verses in the Qur'an which speak about God 'watching over' Scripture:

> Lo! We, even We, reveal the Remainder, and lo! We verily are its Guardian (15:9).

This suggests that it is unthinkable that God could allow any of his Scriptures to be corrupted.

5. If Muslims claim that the gospel of Barnabas is the original injil *which was revealed to Jesus, it is not difficult to show from internal evidence that it cannot be an authentic gospel from the first century.*

- It contains historical anachronisms: *e.g.* the custom of a vassal owing his lord a portion of his cup; a notary recording a case in court; wine casks made of wood.

- It contains elementary errors in geography: *e.g.* it locates Nazareth on the shores of the Lake of Galilee.

- It contradicts the Qur'an at several points: *e.g.* it claims that Jesus said that he was not the Messiah, whereas in the Qur'an Jesus is frequently called the Messiah; it supports the doctrine of free will.

- Certain images seem to come from Dante, the fourteenth-century poet: *e.g.* the idea of 'circles of hell'.

From other internal evidence it is generally thought that the gospel of Barnabas was written in Italy in the sixteenth century. The author was probably a Spaniard of Jewish background who had recently converted to Islam. The Italian manuscript was discovered in Amsterdam in 1709, and there is no evidence of its existence before that time.

6. We need to recognize also that underlying the charge of corruption is the Muslim understanding of revelation and inspiration of Scripture, which is different from the Christian understanding. As long as Muslims approach the Bible with the idea that it must have been revealed directly to the minds of prophets in precisely the same way as they believe the Qur'an was revealed to Muhammad, they are bound to have problems, since the Bible does not read as if it were dictated by God (see further chapter 27, 1–2).

7. *Even if we can convince Muslims with these arguments, however, we have not solved the problem for them!* As far as they are concerned, since the New Testament speaks of Jesus as God, or as the Son of God, *it must by definition be corrupted* – regardless of what the Qur'an or Muslim apologists say. Our arguments, therefore, have limited value unless we can persuade our Muslim friends to read one of the gospels with a slightly more open mind. And we will then need to be able to tackle other fundamental issues, such as the divinity of Christ, the Trinity and the crucifixion.

22.2 'Jesus was not the Son of God.'

The Muslim denial of the divinity of Christ is based on such passages as the following:

> And they say: Allah hath taken unto Himself a Son. Be He glorified! Nay, but whatsoever is in the heaven and the earth is His. All are subservient unto Him (2:116).

> And the Jews say: Ezra is the son of Allah, and the Christians say: The Messiah is the son of Allah. That is their saying with their mouths. They imitate the saying of those who disbelieved of old. Allah (Himself) fighteth against them. How perverse are they!
> They have taken as lords beside Allah their rabbis and their monks and the Messiah son of Mary, when they were bidden to worship only One God. There is no god save Him. Be he glorified from all that they ascribe as partner (unto Him)! (9:30–31).

> Say: He is Allah, the One!
> Allah, the eternally Besought of all!

He begetteth not nor was begotten.
And there is none comparable unto Him (112:1–4).

They indeed have disbelieved who say: Lo! Allah is the Messiah, son of Mary. Say: Who then can do aught against Allah, if He had willed to destroy the Messiah son of Mary and his mother and everyone on earth? Allah's is the Sovereignty of the heavens and the earth and all that is between them. He createth what He will. And Allah is Able to do all things (5:17; cf. 5:72).

It befitteth not (the Majesty of) Allah that He should take unto Himself a son. Glory be to Him! When He decreeth a thing, He saith unto it only: Be! and it is (19:35; *cf.* 19:19–92).

We can make these points in working out our response:

1. *The original background to these denials of the divine sonship of Jesus seems to have been Muhammad's crusade against the gods and goddesses in Mecca who were thought to have sons and daughters.* Although Muhammad certainly had contact with some Christians during his early ministry in Mecca, his main conflict was with the pagan idolaters who worshipped, for example, Allat, al-Uzzah and Manat, the daughters of Allah.

Muhammad also certainly directed his protests at Christian beliefs about Jesus, which must have seemed to him to come into the same category as these pagan ideas. But his original protest was against the debased polytheism which he encountered at Mecca. This is clear from such passages as the following:

Yet they ascribe as partners unto Him the jinn, although He did create them, and impute falsely, without knowledge, sons and daughters unto Him. Glorified be He and high exalted above (all) that they ascribe (unto Him) (6:101).

We will want to say to Muslims that we reject the idea of Jesus being the son of God in any physical sense as strongly as they do. The idea of Jesus being born of a union between God and the

Virgin Mary is utterly abhorrent to us as Christians. If this is what Muhammad understood by this term, it is as blasphemous to us as it is to Muslims.

2. *There are good reasons for believing that the 'Trinity' rejected by Muhammad was not the Trinity of the Father, Son and Holy Spirit, as we understand it.* The following verse is attempting to correct the misunderstanding that Jesus and Mary had been made into gods by Christians:

> And when Allah saith: O Jesus, son of Mary! Didst thou say unto mankind: Take me and my mother for two gods beside Allah? he saith: Be glorified! It was not mine to utter that to which I had no right (5:116).

It is not hard to understand how the portrayal of Mary in Christian art at the time could have given any observer the idea that Mary was to be honoured and worshipped in the same way as Jesus.

3. *There is no need to make too much of the title 'Son of God' in discussion with Muslims, and there is good biblical precedent for avoiding names and titles that cause offence and create misunderstandings.* Although the word 'Messiah' (= Christ) came from the Old Testament, the idea had been distorted by the Jews in their speculation about the coming messianic age. Since Jesus never referred to himself as the Messiah, it must have been because he refused to conform to the popular conception of the Messiah as a political and military figure. He preferred to speak of himself as 'the Son of Man' (a title almost certainly taken from Daniel 7:13ff.) and alluded to himself as the Suffering Servant (from Isaiah 53, *etc.*; *cf.* Mark 10:45). Thus when Peter confessed that Jesus was the Christ, Jesus went on to say, *'The Son of Man* must suffer . . .' (Mark 8:29, 31).

Similarly, when the High Priest said, 'Tell us if you are the Christ,' Jesus answered: 'Yes, it is as you say. But I say to all of you: In the future you will see the *Son of Man* . . .' (Matthew 26:63–64). It was as if Jesus was saying, 'I am not the Messiah in the sense that *you* understand the word. And because the term is so open to misunderstandings, I prefer to speak of myself as the "Son of Man".'

When Pilot asked the similar question, 'Are you the King of the Jews?' Jesus answered: 'Yes, it is as you say' (Matthew 27:11). In John's version, Jesus went on to describe his ministry in terms of declaring the truth (John 18:33–37).

If Jesus avoided the term 'Messiah' so deliberately, we today have every justification for avoiding the title 'Son of God' as much as we can in speaking with Muslims. There is no dishonesty or compromise in trying to find other ways of speaking about Jesus.

4. *Our belief in Jesus as the Son of God is based on the words and actions of Jesus himself, and not only on the teaching of John, Paul and the other apostles.* When Muslims say it was Paul and the early Christians who corrupted the simple *injil* which Jesus proclaimed, we need to show that Paul's teaching was entirely consistent with the teaching of Jesus. According to the gospels, Jesus said and did things which amounted to a claim that he was equal with God.

■ He said he would one day judge all people (Matthew 25:31–46; John 5:22–23).

■ He said he could give people eternal life (John 5:19–21; 11:25–26).

■ He forgave sins (Mark 2:5–7).

■ He called God 'Father' or 'my Father' and, when speaking to his disciples, spoke of 'your Father'. He never spoke of 'our Father', except when giving his disciples words to use in prayer. He thus made a clear distinction between his own relationship with God and his disciples' relationship with God (Matthew 12:50; 6:6; John 20:17).

There are at least two important ideas implied in this Father–Son relationship: (1) Jesus was claiming to know God in a unique way (Matthew 11:25–27). (2) Jesus claimed to be completely obedient to the will of God (John 8:27–29, 55). When the Jews heard him speaking of God as his Father, they understood that he was claiming to be equal with God, and it was this claim which was one of the main reasons for the opposition which led to his death. There are about 150 verses in the gospels in which

Jesus speaks of God as 'Father'. They are an integral part of the teaching of Jesus, and cannot be cut out without changing the whole message.

5. *It may be helpful to speak from the point of view of the first disciples of Jesus.* They were not pagans who believed in many gods, but orthodox Jews who believed in the oneness of God. As orthodox Jews they would have been brought up to recite these words from the Shema daily: 'Hear, O Israel: The LORD our God, the LORD is one' (Deuteronomy 6:4). They were therefore as convinced and passionate monotheists as Muslims are.

At first they followed Jesus simply as a rabbi, a religious teacher. When they were impressed by his miraculous powers, they still thought of him as an ordinary man: 'Who is this? Even the winds and the waves obey him!' (Mark 4:41). But when he said and did things that only God can do, they had to find some way of saying that he was in a much closer relationship with God than a prophet or any other ordinary human being. Their belief in Jesus developed gradually, and it was a long time before they were able to formulate their convictions about him in precise theological language.

6. *The question of the sonship of Jesus is not a purely theological issue, but has profound implications for our understanding of who we are and the kind of relationship God wants to have with those who trust in him.* If the Qur'an teaches us to think of ourselves as slaves or servants of God, the New Testament offers us the possibility of becoming sons and daughters of God who know, love and obey God as Father. Jesus spoke of God as 'my Father' and shocked his contemporaries by addressing God as *Abba* (almost the familiar 'Father' or 'Daddy'). The wonder of the gospel is that Jesus also gave his disciples the right to address God as 'our Father' (Matthew 6:9). Paul shows the same familiarity in speaking of God as *Abba* (Romans 8:15). When we trust in Jesus, he gives us the right to *become* sons of God (John 1:12–13).

7. *There are possible starting-points for further discussion within the Qur'an itself.*

■ The Qur'an recognizes that the expression 'son of' can be used in a metaphorical sense. The expression 'son of the way' (2:215) is translated 'wayfarer'.

■ There are two verses which suggest a different idea of what it might mean for God to have a 'son':

> If Allah had willed to choose a son, he could have chosen what he would of that which He hath created. Be He glorified! He is Allah, the One, the Absolute (39:4).

In these words put into the mouth of Muhammad, the possibility of God having a son is not ruled out, although the idea of sonship assumes that the son is a creature and not of the same nature as God himself.

In the following verse, however, there is no such assumption about the kind of sonship implied:

> Say: 'If (God) Most Gracious
> had a son, I would
> be the first to worship' (43:81, A. Yusuf Ali's translation).

The implication of this verse seems hard for some Muslims to accept, and this must explain why Pickthall gives a completely different translation:

> Say (O Muhammad): The Beneficent One hath no son. I am first among the worshippers.

■ Although the Qur'an frequently says that God makes no difference between the prophets, there are many ways in which Jesus, son of Mary, is unique among the prophets: he was born of a virgin: he worked miracles; and he was given titles which no other apostle or prophet was given:

> exalted (above others) in degree . . . supported . . .
>   with the Holy Spirit (2:253)
> a messenger of Allah, and His word which he conveyed
>   unto Mary, and a spirit from Him (4:171)
> illustrious in the world and the Hereafter, and one of
>   those brought near (unto Allah) (3:45)

It can sometimes be helpful to ask Muslims to give their explanation of the uniqueness of Jesus, and then to offer our explanation from the *injil*.

■ Many Christians have found that one of the most useful bridges in the Qur'an is the following verse which speaks about Jesus:

> O People of the Scripture! Do not exaggerate in your religion nor utter aught concerning Allah save the truth. The Messiah, Jesus son of Mary, was only a messenger of Allah, and His Word which He conveyed until Mary, and a spirit from Him. So believe in Allah and His messengers, and say not 'Three' – Cease! (it is) better for you! – Allah is only One God. Far is it removed from His transcendent majesty that he should have a son. His is all that is in the heavens and all that is in the earth. And Allah is sufficient as Defender (4:171).

This verse accuses Christians of claiming too much for Jesus, although it seems to suggest that Christians believe in three gods rather than in one. In spite of this, however, if we are prepared to listen to Muslims' understanding of the titles 'Word' and 'spirit', they may be open to listen to what we mean when we speak of Jesus as 'the Word'. Our words are a part of us – they express our mind and our will. Similarly, if we cannot separate our words from ourselves, how can we separate Jesus from God?

Muslims believe that Jesus is a Word from God in the sense that he was created by divine *fiat*, by the word of God. Christians believe that he is the Word of God in the sense that he is the one who expresses the mind and will of God most fully to the human race. Through Jesus, God has spoken and acted in a unique way. (See further chapter 34.)

In using the Qur'an in this way, we are not trying to 'prove from the Qur'an' that Jesus is divine. Rather, we are using the Qur'an as a bridge, and trying to understand the differences between the Muslim and the Christian understanding of the same titles given to Jesus in the Qur'an and the Bible.

22.3 'Jesus was not crucified.'

The most important verses in the Qur'an about the crucifixion come in a passage which lists many of the sins of the Jews: they worshipped the calf (4:153); they broke the covenant made at Sinai; disbelieved the revelations of God; killed his prophets (4:155); and spoke against the Virgin Mary 'a tremendous calumny' (4:156). The passage continues:

> And because of their saying: We slew the Messiah Jesus son of Mary, Allah's messenger – They slew him not nor crucified, but it appeared so unto them; and lo! those who disagree concerning it are in doubt thereof; they have no knowledge thereof save pursuit of a conjecture; they slew him not for certain.
> But Allah took him up unto Himself. Allah was ever Mighty, Wise.
> There is not one of the People of the Scripture but will believe in him before his death, and on the Day of Resurrection he will be a witness against them . . . (4:157–159).

The traditional interpretation of this passage is that God raised Jesus up to heaven in a miraculous way before he was actually crucified, and that someone else who looked like him was crucified in his place. This interpretation has been linked with a saying of Muhammad about the return of Jesus to earth at the end of the world.

Many Muslims today, therefore, believe that when Jesus returns, he will establish Islam as the one true religion. Jews and Christians will believe in him in the same way that Muslims believe in him now. He will die and be buried. Finally, on the Last Day he will be raised along with all people, exposing the false beliefs about him held by Jews and Christians.

There are at least two ways of understanding and responding to this traditional interpretation of the text.

1. *It can be argued that the Qur'an does not actually deny the crucifixion; all it denies is that it was the Jews who carried out the crucifixion.* It is pointed out that a verse in another *sura* refers in similar terms to the victory of the Muslims over the forces of Mecca at the Battle of Badr:

> Ye (Muslims) slew them not, but Allah slew them. And

thou (Muhammad) threwest not when thou didst
throw, but Allah threw, that He might test the believers
by a fair test from Him (8:17).

David Brown offers the following suggestion as to how the
reference to the crucifixion in 4:156–158 can be explained in the
light of this verse:

> These verses are intended to be a rebuke to the Jews,
> and particularly to Muhammad's contemporaries in
> Medina, for various acts of unbelief, and they only refer
> in passing to the story of the crucifixion. Within this
> context of an attack on the Jews for their opposition
> towards Muhammad as well as for other acts of
> unbelief, the reference to the crucifixion does no more
> than dispute the claim made by the Jews that they had
> disposed of the Christian Messiah and repudiated his
> claims to be an apostle of God by crucifying him. In
> particular, the phrases 'they did not kill him, nor did
> they crucify him', do not necessarily mean that there
> was no crucifixion, but that, even if there was, it was
> God who was responsible for all that happened during
> the last hours of the Messiah's life and that the Jews had
> done whatever they did only by permission of God's
> will. A similar figure of speech occurs in 8:17 [quoted
> above] in which the Muslims' actions at the Battle of
> Badr are attributed to God and not to their own volition;
> they did in fact fight and kill, but only by God's permis-
> sion and direction.
> These verses, therefore, do not explicitly deny the
> Christian story of the crucifixion, for they refer prim-
> arily to Jewish claims against the Christians.[1]

This interpretation can perhaps be supported by three other
passages in the Qur'an which appear to speak about the death of
Jesus and imply that he died like every other human being.

■ In the account of the birth of Jesus, the infant Jesus speaks to
the people from the cradle: 'Peace on me the day I was born,
and the day I die, and the day I shall be raised alive!' (19:33).

Similar words are used in the same *sura* about John the Baptist (19:15), where they presumably refer to his death and to the general resurrection of all people.

■ In another passage God says to Jesus: 'O Jesus! Lo! *I am gathering thee* and causing thee to ascend unto Me, and am cleansing thee of those who disbelieve and am setting those who follow thee above those who disbelieve until the Day of Resurrection' (3:55, my italics).

■ In the third passage, Jesus is speaking to God: 'I spake unto them only that which Thou commandest me (saying): Worship Allah, my Lord and your Lord. I was a witness of them while I dwelt among them, and *when Thou tookest me* Thou was the Watcher over them' (5:117, my italics).

The italicized words in the last two passages are forms of the same Arabic word *tawaffa*. The first passage could also be translated 'Truly I am he who calls you to death' or 'It is I who am causing you to die'.

David Brown comments:

> Both these verses refer to the return of Jesus to God at the end of his life, and the most straightforward interpretation of them is to suppose that they refer to a natural death of Jesus at the end of his earthly life. *Tawaffa* is often used in the Qur'an in the sense of bringing a soul to God at death, both when the subject of the verb is God (e.g. 3:193; 10:46), and when the subject is the angels (e.g. 16:28, 32). The word *tawaffa*, however, was originally used of a person receiving the full payment of his due or his rights, and when used of God in the Qur'an refers to men being called to pay their account in his presence, either at death, or in sleep when the soul comes to God but is returned to the body for a further term of life on earth . . .
>
> Thus the use of the word *tawaffa* in these two passages, with reference to the Messiah, is ambiguous and its exact meaning must be determined by consideration of other verses in the Qur'an: it could mean that Jesus died

199

a natural death, but it can also mean that he was taken to heaven without undergoing the experience of physical death.[2]

If these verses, therefore, are interpreted as meaning that Jesus died a natural death on the cross, and if the crucial passage in 4:156–159 is taken to mean only that it was the Romans who crucified Jesus, not the Jews, it can perhaps be argued that the Qur'an does not in fact deny that Jesus died on the cross.

In support of this argument it is pointed out that the early commentators were not agreed about the interpretation of these verses. For several centuries there was considerable debate about the crucifixion, and many different answers were given by orthodox Muslims. Some Muslims today, who are more liberal in their approach but still consider themselves to be within orthodox Muslim tradition, reject all theories about a substitute being crucified in the place of Jesus. Kamel Hussein, for example, writes in the introduction to his book *City of Wrong*:

> The idea of a substitute for Christ is a very crude way of explaining the Qur'anic text. They had to explain a lot to the masses. No cultured Muslim believes this nowadays. The text is taken to mean that the Jews thought they killed Christ, but God raised him in a way we can leave unexplained among the several mysteries which we have taken for granted on faith alone.[3]

The main difficulty of this first approach is that however careful and convincing our exegesis of the Qur'an may be, it goes against the traditional teaching which most Muslims today accept about the crucifixion. It means therefore that we are putting ourselves in the position of correcting traditional Muslim teaching. Although some more open-minded and liberal Muslims are willing to accept this interpretation, the vast majority accept as dogma that Jesus was not crucified.

Another approach to the question of the crucifixion in the Qur'an is to proceed in the following stages.

■ We can start with the traditional Muslim interpretation that these verses deny that Jesus was crucified, and accept the possibility that the Qur'an may not be entirely consistent with itself. While some verses may suggest a natural death, others suggest a miraculous deliverance.

■ We take care to distinguish between what the Qur'an seems to deny and what it does *not* deny. Kenneth Cragg, for example, has drawn attention to the fact that the Qur'an does not deny that the Jews *wanted* to kill Jesus, or that Jesus was *willing* to be killed. All it seems to deny is that God could allow it to happen.[4]

■ We should note that before the time of Muhammad there were heretical sects which taught that Jesus was not crucified. Muhammad may therefore have heard the idea from sources of this kind. Geoffrey Parrinder describes some of these heretical ideas as follows:

> There early arose in some Christian circles a reluctance to believe that Jesus, as a divine being and Son of God, could really die. Ignatius, writing about AD 115, said that some believed that Jesus 'suffered in semblance'. The apocryphal Gospel of Peter in the second century said that on the cross Jesus was silent, since he 'felt no pain', and at the end 'the Lord cried out, saying, "My power, my power, you have left me." And when he spoke he was taken up ...' The apocryphal Acts of John, about the middle of the second century, said that Jesus appeared to John in a cave during the crucifixion and said, 'John, unto the multitude below in Jerusalem I am being crucified and pierced with lances and reeds, and gall and vinegar is given me to drink. But unto thee I speak.' And later it is said, 'Nothing, therefore, of the things which they will say of me have I suffered ... I was pierced, yet I was not smitten; hanged, and I was not hanged; that blood flowed from me, and it flowed not.'[5]

Some of these ideas were found in the teaching of the Docetists (from the Greek word meaning 'to appear') who taught that the suffering of Jesus was apparent, not real.

■ If this was the background to the denial of the crucifixion in the Qur'an, it might explain the difficult phrase *subbiha lahum* ('it appeared so to them', 4:157). Muhammad could have first heard the idea from heretical Christian circles, and accepted it – not because he believed the teaching of the Docetists, but because the idea of Jesus not being crucified fitted in with his understanding of the uniqueness of Jesus and of God's obligation to vindicate his apostles. Since Jesus was unique in that he was born of a virgin, worked miracles, and was the 'Word' of God and 'a Spirit from Him', it makes perfect sense to believe that God should rescue him from death through a clearly supernatural intervention.

The Qur'an recognizes that the Jews killed some of the *prophets* 'wrongfully' (4:155). Generally, however, the Qur'an teaches that God gives victory to his prophets and is bound to vindicate his servants. And there is no record of any *apostles* being killed. 'Verily Allah helpeth one who helpeth him' (22:40). 'It is incumbent upon Us to save believers' (10:104). Thus there are accounts of how God delivers Noah (21:76–77), Abraham and Lot (21:71), and Moses (28:18–28).

There is a compelling logic in this kind of thinking. A government has an obligation to protect its ambassador in a foreign country, because the honour of the whole country is vested in its ambassador, and it cannot stand idly by if he is insulted and humiliated in public. In the same way, thinks the Muslim, God cannot and will not stand idly by if his apostles and prophets are treated shamefully. He has an obligation to step in to vindicate them, for in vindicating their honour he is vindicating his own honour. (See further chapter 34.)

■ The greatest challenge for us is to find ways of helping Muslims to see the deeper logic which demands that the Messiah *must* suffer before entering his glory. We believe that God did vindicate Jesus, but not in the way that the disciples expected. God did vindicate and honour him, but not by rescuing him before death. He allowed him to go through death on our behalf, and only after that raised him from death.

Muslims believe that since forgiveness depends only on God's mercy and human repentance and belief, there is no need for any sacrifice or atonement. Christians believe that forgiveness somehow involves suffering. God cannot simply forgive, as it were by decree or a word, since forgiveness that is as easy as this must inevitably undermine the divine law. But by allowing Jesus to die on the cross, God demonstrated his judgment and condemnation of all that is evil, and at the same time showed his sacrificial and forgiving love to all who turn to him.

It may be helpful to remind ourselves that the first disciples had the greatest difficulty in understanding how God could have allowed Jesus to be crucified. Peter's reaction to Jesus' announcement of his cruel death (Mark 8:31–38) is very close to the reaction of the Muslim to the idea of an apostle of God being killed. After his resurrection Jesus had to explain the necessity of his sufferings and death to his disciples: 'Was it not necessary that the Christ should suffer these things and enter into his glory?' (Luke 24:26, RSV).

If Muslims can begin to see *why* God could allow Jesus to be crucified, they may be more willing to accept the *fact* that he was crucified. (See further chapters 35.3, 36.1 and 36.3.)

23

Learning from the controversies of the past

If Christians and Muslims have been locked in discussion and argument for 1,400 years, are we any nearer to understanding one another? And are there any lessons we can learn for today from the way these controversies have developed over so many years?

This chapter gives examples of people – some Christians, some Muslims – who have engaged in discussion and dialogue in different situations and with widely differing styles. It is important to notice in each case the context in which the Christians and Muslims were meeting: which was the majority community, and which the minority? Which side was in the position of power? It will also be helpful for us in several cases to try to evaluate the different approaches, noting their strengths and weaknesses.

23.1 Muhammad and the Christians of Najran
(*c.* 632 AD)

It comes as a surprise to many to find that Christian communities had existed in parts of Arabia centuries before the rise of Islam. One such community was based in Najran in the south west of the peninsula (in modern Yemen) from the fourth century, and had its own cathedral and bishop. Ibn Ishaq's *Life of the Apostle of God*, one of the first Muslim biographies of Muhammad, written around 750 (see chapter 9.6), describes a meeting between Muhammad and a delegation of sixty Christians who came from Najran.

This is a summary of the arguments put forward by each side at the meeting:

Christian arguments

Jesus is God because (1) he worked miracles. For instance, he raised the dead, healed the sick and declared the unseen; he also made clay birds and breathed into them so that they flew away. (2) He had no human father; he was born of a virgin; and he spoke while he was still a baby in the cradle to defend the honour of his mother Mary.

Jesus is 'the third out of three', because God says, 'We created, we commanded,' etc. (using the plural). If God were one in the strictly mathematical sense, he would have said, 'I have commanded,' etc.

Muslim arguments

Christians have not 'submitted to God' in the fullest sense, because they say God has a son; they worship the cross and eat pork.

God is eternal. If Jesus was God, how could he die? How could he leave his place in heaven? Christians are guilty of 'association': they 'associate' a created being (Jesus) with God, putting him on the same level as God. God's transcendence and unity must be protected, and they are called in question by the idea of Jesus being God.

Miracles do not prove the deity of Christ. And although Jesus did work miracles, his power was limited; for example, he did not have the power to change day into night. If he really was God, he could have done anything.

Jesus was born of a virgin, but he was created by divine *fiat*; he was created without a human father, like Adam.

Christian interpretations of the Bible are arbitrary. The Qur'an, by contrast, is one speech from God, and has one meaning that is plain to all.

Christians should recognize their error and accept Islam.

This account was no doubt coloured by the way Christian and Muslim apologetic developed after the time of Muhammad. Some of the Christian arguments clearly reflect Muslim beliefs which probably came originally from heretical Christian sources. The document is valuable, however, as an early Muslim account of Christian–Muslim dialogue.

23.2 St John of Damascus (675–753)

John was born forty-three years after the death of Muhammad. His father was an important government official in Damascus at a time when the population was still largely Christian but living under Muslim rule. His grandfather had played an important role in the surrender of Damascus to Muslim troops in 635.

He knew both Arabic and Greek, and worked for about thirty years in the 'Ministry of Finance'. At the age of fifty he left his position, perhaps because top jobs in the civil service were being given only to Muslims, and retired to live in the monastery of St Sabas near Jerusalem. He devoted himself to study and wrote several major theological works.

He is important for our survey, since he was the first Christian theologian to think seriously about Islam and to try to help Christians to know about Islam and see how it differed from Christianity. One part of his large work *The Fount of Wisdom* dealt with heresies, and he included Islam in this section, describing it as the 'heresy of the Ishmaelites'. He thus thought of Islam not as a religion in its own right, but as a kind of Christian heresy.

He has been described as 'one of the most serious originators of Muslim–Christian dialogue'. Generally he avoided polemics, and put forward serious and open-ended theological arguments. He had had close dealings with Muslims from childhood, and had accurate knowledge of the Qur'an and of Muslim beliefs and practices. His writings had a considerable influence on later generations of Christians. Some of his arguments (for example, proving the divinity of Christ from the titles 'Word' and 'spirit' given to Jesus in the Qur'an, and the argument that Muhammad could not have been a prophet because his coming was not foretold in the Bible and because he did not work miracles) became widely accepted in Christian apologetics. Unfortunately, those who followed him seldom had first-hand experience of Islam and Muslims, and often used what John had written simply for political purposes and to stir up the feelings of Christians against Muslims.

23.3 Al-Tabari (died 855)

Al-Tabari was a well-educated Nestorian Christian physician from Baghdad, who converted to Islam at the age of seventy. In the introduction to his book *Refutation of Christianity*, he stated openly that his aim was to destroy the faith of Christians.

The main thrust of his attack was that Christian beliefs about Jesus are absurd and self-contradictory, since Jesus is said by

Christians to be both God and man. He asked Christians questions like these: Do you believe in one God, or is Jesus a second God? Can God experience suffering and death? Is Christ God or man? Is he the Creator or is he simply a creature?

As a Nestorian Christian for most of his life, al-Tabari may well have held a view of Christ which was very close to that of Muslims, namely that he was an ordinary man, a prophet, who was used by God. The weakness of this approach, however, was that it failed to recognize that most Christians have generally understood Jesus to have had two natures, divine and human. It also refused to recognize the possibility of paradox in religious language.

23.4 The correspondence of al-Hashimi and al-Kindi (c. 820)

This work has been described as 'one of the most important writings in the history of Muslim–Christian dialogue' (Jean-Marie Gaudeul). The author of this correspondence must have been a Christian, probably a civil servant living in Baghdad during the time of the Caliph al-Ma'mum (813–833). By writing in the form of a fictional correspondence between a Muslim and a Christian, he was able to state his own views more openly than he could ever have done if he had written in his own name.

The first letter, of thirty-seven pages, is from the Muslim to the Christian, and gives a full and reasonably fair presentation of the beliefs and practices of Islam. It accuses Christians of being in error and unbelief, and invites Christian readers to become Muslims and save themselves from unbelief.

In his reply, of 230 pages, al-Kindi writes about the Christian understanding of the Trinity. He goes on to discuss Muslim claims about the prophet Muhammad, boldly expressing objections and questions which Christians at the time no doubt wanted to put to Muslims, but did not dare to, for fear of death. For example:

■ How could a man who raided caravans and was of doubtful morals be a prophet?

■ Muhammad's claims to be a prophet are not supported by prophecies in the Bible or by miracles.

- Since there is nothing exceptional about the language of the Qur'an, how can Muslims say that the Qur'an is a miracle?

- The Pillars of Islam are useless and cannot purify the heart.

- Although the Qur'an says, 'There is no compulsion in religion', Islam has been spread by the sword.

- Islam is a lax and easy religion compared to the 'narrow way' of Jesus.

In the final section, al-Kindi shows from the gospel of Matthew how the coming of Jesus was predicted by the prophets, and gives an outline of his teaching, his life, death and resurrection, and the coming of the Spirit.

This work had a profound effect on Christian–Muslim relations for centuries. Muslims felt they had to answer the challenges put by al-Kindi, while Christians gained many of their ideas about Islam from these 'letters' and tried to develop al-Kindi's approach to refute Islam.

23.5 Ibn Hazm (994–1064)

This writer is important because he represents 'probably the most violent and systematic attempt to discredit Christianity in the whole history of Christian–Muslim confrontation'. He has been recognized as the 'undisputed Master in the field of anti-Christian polemics' (Jean-Marie Gaudeul).

He came from a Muslim family of Spanish origin and was brought up in the court of the Umayyad caliph in Cordoba. After periods as a prisoner during several *coups*, then as prime minister, and again as a prisoner, he left political life to give himself to religious studies.

Starting from a very strict and literal approach to all Scriptures, which he regarded as the very words dictated by God, he concluded that the text of the Bible had been corrupted. He attacked Christian belief in the Trinity as an invention of Christians and an absurdity: how can three 'things' be one? He also dismissed the doctrine of the incarnation since it implies a 'change of nature': if God *became* man, then he is no longer God. Listing all the discrepancies he could find in the gospels, he concluded that the Christian Scriptures were not revealed by God, but were fabricated by their human authors. Jean-Marie Gaudeul sums up his approach:

> Ibn Hazm does not try to enter into dialogue with Christians or with his other (Muslim) adversaries. He simply tries to crush and destroy his opponents. His method which reduces the meaning of words to simple elementary notions makes it easy for him to win an argument: words are just weapons for him. But this same method prevents him from reaching any real understanding of the thought of others. Consequently, his arguments may be devastating in a public discussion, but they do not touch the real position of his adversaries.
>
> In a way, his approach is totally logical within his own system of thought, but powerless to take into account another set of principles. At the root of all his argument lies the idea he has of what a Revealed Text should look like, and how this Revelation takes place.[1]

23.6 Raymond Lull (1234–1315)

This well-known apologist was born in Majorca, and worked for several years in the service of the king, first as a tutor and later as an adviser. At the age of thirty-one he had a profound conversion experience through a vision of Christ on the cross. Soon after this he began to work out a plan for the evangelism of Muslims, and joined the Franciscan order as a layman. He spent the next twenty-two years preparing himself through the study of theology, Islam and Arabic, and founded a training centre where other Franciscans could prepare themselves for missionary work among Muslims.

At the age of fifty-two he began lecturing at universities in France and Italy, and wrote more than 200 books of Christian apologetics for Muslims. Finally he decided to engage in direct evangelism himself, and at the age of sixty made trips to Tunis, Cyprus and Algeria. In each case he became involved in public controversy, and was arrested and expelled.

His last evangelistic journey (when he was eighty) took him to Sicily and Tunis. He seems to have begun to work in a less confrontational way, and was allowed to engage in debate with Muslim leaders. Before long, however, he changed his style, perhaps out of a desire to die as a martyr. He then moved to Bugia (the modern Bejaia) in Algeria, and began preaching openly in the market. He was stoned by the crowd, who were angry at his criticism of Muhammad, and died either at sea or in his native Majorca.

Lull was in many ways ahead of his time. He recognized, for example, that the Crusades had been a terrible betrayal of the spirit of Christ. He therefore called the whole church, including the Pope, to believe that the Muslim world could not be won for Christ by force. He saw the need for Christians to study Islam carefully and to give missionaries a thorough training. He also worked hard on developing an effective apologetic which would convince Muslims by 'irrefutable logic'. Many Christians today are still challenged by the example of this man who worked so hard to change traditional Christian responses to Islam and who gave his life for Muslims to come to faith in Christ.

At the same time, however, we need to be aware of the limitations of his approach. His apologetic method probably depended too heavily on rational arguments to demonstrate that Christian doctrines are the most reasonable. He may not have been a very good listener, and his reliance on argument combined with his natural impatience tended to make him provocative in his approach to Muslims.

23.7 Henry Martyn (1781–1812)

After his time as a student at Cambridge, Henry went out to India as a chaplain of the East India Company at the age of twenty-four. He was an extremely able linguist, and within seven years had completed a translation of the New Testament into Urdu and a thorough revision of the Persian New Testament, and had also started on a revision of the Arabic New Testament. The only Muslim who became a Christian as a result of his ministry was Sheikh Salih (later known as Abdul Masih, meaning 'servant of Christ'), a gifted evangelist who was the first Christian from a Muslim background to be ordained in India.

Because of his poor health Martyn set out to return to England by land, hoping to meet up with his beloved Lydia, a girl from his home area of Cornwall whom he had known since childhood. During the months he spent in Iran in 1813 on his journey home he spent a considerable time debating with Muslim teachers in Isfahan. After this he set out again on his journey, but died in Turkey.

Part of the significance of Martyn is that while he believed in the need for apologetics, he had real doubts about the value of certain kinds of argument. He was far more at home in personal conversations with small groups of interested Muslims and stressed the need for lasting friendships. It was in this kind of context that he found he could 'share the religious experience of the forgiveness and peace attained through Christ'.

He summed up these convictions in words like these: 'I have now lost all hope of ever convincing Mahomedans by argument . . . I know not what to do but to pray for them.'[2]

23.8 Karl Gottlieb Pfander (1803–65)

Pfander was a German missionary who began his work in Persia at the age of twenty-two. After twelve years he moved to India, where he spoke in public debates and wrote apologetic literature in what came to be known as the Muhammadan Controversy. At the age of fifty-five, he moved to Constantinople to continue his evangelism, until a change of government policy forced missionaries to give up their work.

He wrote his famous *Balance of Truth* in German and Armenian in 1829, when he was only twenty-six. It was later translated into Persian, Urdu, Turkish, Arabic and English, and has been widely used since then as a basic textbook of Christian apologetics with Muslims.

In the introduction, Pfander begins with the question: how can we know whether Christianity or Islam is true, whether the Bible or the Qur'an is the Word of God? He goes on to suggest that any true revelation from God must meet six criteria:

1. It must satisfy the human yearning for eternal happiness.
2. It must accord with the moral law.
3. It must reveal God as just.
4. It must confirm the unity of God.
5. It must make clear the way of salvation.
6. It must reveal God so that people may know him.

Part I is a defence of the text of the Bible, answering the Muslim charge of corruption. Part II outlines the basic teaching of the Bible, showing how biblical doctrine and morals meet the six criteria. Part III, 'A Candid Enquiry into Islam's Claim to be the Final Revelation', answers Muslim arguments about predictions of the coming of Muhammad in the Bible, the miraculous nature of the Qur'an, Muhammad's miracles, and his behaviour. He concludes that Islamic doctrine and beliefs do not meet the criteria for establishing genuine divine revelation. The book ends with a strong appeal to Muslims to recognize the claims of Christ and put their trust in him.

Pfander was once defeated in a public debate in Agra by a Muslim scholar, Rahmatullah al-Hindi, who later (in 1867) wrote a book called *Manifestation of the Truth* as a reply to Pfander's *Balance of Truth*. This book has been reprinted many times and is still used by Muslims today. The book lists what it sees as contradictions and errors in the Old and New Testaments, arguing that they cannot be inspired. It goes on to give evidence not only for false interpretation of the text by Jews and Christians (*tahrif ma'nawi*), but also for falsification or corruption of the text itself (*tahrif lafzi*). The next stage is to argue that many biblical texts are 'immoral' and that certain commands in the Bible have been abrogated or superseded by the Qur'an. There then follows a refutation of the Trinity, and proofs that the Qur'an is the Word of God and that Muhammad is the Prophet of God.

There were several strengths in Pfander's approach in *The Balance of Truth*:

■ He knew a great deal about Islam and could quote from the Qur'an, the *hadith* (tradition) and from many other Muslim sources in different languages.

■ His style was courteous and polite.

■ He could recognize common ground between Christian and Muslim beliefs.

With hindsight, however, we can also recognize certain weaknesses and limitations in his approach:

- His attacks on Muslim beliefs sometimes degenerated into polemics.

- He appealed too much to the reason and the intellect, and not enough to the heart.

- The debate could hardly be an open-ended discussion, because he himself had decided from the beginning the criteria by which genuine revelation is to be determined.

23.9 Temple Gairdner (1873–1928)

Gairdner was an Anglican missionary who worked in Cairo for thirty-one years. He was a gifted linguist and understood Islam well enough to be able to debate publicly in Arabic with sheikhs from the al-Azhar University. In his work with Muslims he believed that 'what was most needed for the redemption of Islam was the living exemplification of Christian brotherhood'. In addition to his work with Muslims, therefore, he spent a great deal of his time in pastoral work in the churches. His approach to Islam and Muslims has been summed up in the words, 'Other teachers taught us how to refute Islam; he taught us how to love Muslims.'

Constance Padwick, in her biography *Temple Gairdner of Cairo*, sums up what was most distinctive about Gairdner's apologetic approach:

> Gairdner ... found that the literature by which the Christian Church had set forth her living truth to Muslims was a curiously arid, machine-made literature. It was as though the compilers, holy men though they were, had been caught into the argumentative machinery of the schoolmen, and had expended all their vital strength in meeting Moslem arguments with juster arguments. The objector himself might be left on the field prostrate but cursing. The books were starved of personality and of appeal to aught save logic and justice. Moreover, he saw, and it was one of his most fruitful perceptions, that the converts made by this literature were often born in its image – with the spirit of disputation rather than of worship and of love, and apt to hammer rather than to woo and win.

Gairdner believed (for was he not nightly battered with anti-Christian arguments?) that there must needs be an apologetic literature, unafraid of controversial points. Silence, he felt, was tantamount to denial of the truth he knew and lived. But the literature must be humanized and written for fellow-men, not only for the defeat of argufiers. Moreover, to Gairdner, stories, history, drama, music, poetry, pictures, all that could bear the impress of the Spirit of Christ, was a reasonable part of the Christian apologetic to the whole man.[3]

23.10 Ahmad Deedat (1918–   )

Deedat is a South African Muslim apologist who has been engaged for over thirty years in public debates with Christians. Video tapes of debates (before large audiences) have been distributed all over the world. Booklets and tracts written by Deedat, with titles such as *What the Bible Says about Muhammad, 50,000 Errors in the Bible?, Resurrection or Resuscitation?*, and *Crucifixion or Cruci-Fiction?* have given Muslims a wide range of arguments to use in discussion with Christians.

Deedat's approach has much in common with that of Ibn Hazm (see 24.5). His style tends to be aggressive and polemical, and he gives the impression of wanting to discredit the Christian faith and make Christian beliefs appear ridiculous.

If this survey points out some of the pitfalls in discussions and debates between Muslims and Christians over the centuries, is it possible to explore more helpful and creative ways of engaging with Muslims in discussion? The next chapter explores other possible models.

24

Exploring dialogue

Is it ever possible to get away from the big theological questions which Christians and Muslims have been arguing about for fourteen centuries? Is it possible to talk freely and frankly with each other about other subjects which are indirectly linked with religious faith, but which avoid starting with the traditional areas of controversy?

In the kind of dialogue that we are exploring in this chapter, we are attempting to break out of our fixed positions to see if there can be a deeper meeting of minds.

The following pages contain a proposed agenda for discussion, outlining possible questions to be discussed – perhaps between a Christian and a Muslim, or a group of Christians and Muslims meeting together over a period of time. If the format seems very formal and artificial, this outline may at least suggest new models for dialogue that can be explored in an appropriate way in different contexts.

24.1 Who are we?

The questions in this section are designed to help us to get to know one another *as people* and to begin to share what our faith means to us. We want to discover each other's humanity before we learn about each other's creed. Thus a meeting of a group could begin with each person giving a kind of 'testimony', saying who they are and speaking about their faith.

1. Who are we?

> We're human beings.
> We belong to a family.
> We belong to a community of faith.
> We live in a particular society.

2. Why is it so important for us to meet one another as people before we get involved in any discussion about religion?

3. What are our basic human needs?

> Health and well-being: what do we do when things go wrong?
>
> Values: how do we know the difference between right and wrong?
>
> Forgiveness: how do we gain forgiveness from God?
>
> Love: we need to be loved by others and to have people to love.
>
> Truth: we want to know as far as we can the truth about ourselves and the world.
>
> A model for humanity: we need an example of the kind of people we ought to be; we need guidance, as we admit in the Fatiha and the Lord's Prayer.
>
> Life beyond death; we want to know what lies beyond the end of our physical life.

4. How are these needs met for us within our own faith?

24.2 What about the past?

Questions under this heading are designed to enable us to think together about how relationships between Muslims and Christians today are affected by what has happened in the past. This is therefore an opportunity for us to try to clear the air and to begin to be open and honest about how we feel about our history and about each other's religion.

In many situations it may be helpful not to discuss these questions in any detail, or not to discuss them at all if we do not have enough background knowledge, or if the discussion simply turns into argument. If the questions do not help us to understand each other's point of view better, they should probably be avoided altogether.

Each of the following events or developments is important because of the way it affects how Christians and Muslims understand their history, and how they see each other.

> The conversion of Constantine, who made Christianity an official religion of the Roman Empire.

The early spread of Islam and the Islamic Empire.
The Crusades and the clash between Christian Europe
    and Islam.
The spread of Islam in the East.
European colonialism.
The Christian missionary movement.
The establishment of the state of Israel.
Secularization in the West.
The Satanic Verses and the Rushdie affair.
The Gulf War (1991).

How do each of these events or developments affect how Christians think about Islam and how Muslims think about Christianity?

Is it true that both Christianity and Islam are missionary religions?

Is it possible to separate religion and politics in Christianity and Islam?

Is there any value in comparing the record of the two religions?

Is it possible to 'let bygones be bygones' and for each generation of Christians and Muslims to start all over again as if nothing had happened in the past? If not, is there anything we can do to help us to understand each other better?

How has it come about that in some countries Christians are a minority living among a Muslim majority, and in others the Muslims are a minority living among a Christian majority? What does it feel like to belong to the minority community? Whichever situation we ourselves are in, can we put ourselves into the shoes of the other community and appreciate how they feel?

24.3 What are we up against?

Instead of constantly thinking in terms of 'us' and 'them' and imagining that we are facing each other across a great divide, can we recognize that because we both believe in one Creator God, we have a great deal in common in a world where most people ignore God and where there is so much suffering? Does it help us to recognize that over many of the following issues we face common dangers? Are there ways in which we can and should work together?

Hunger
War and peace
Stewardship of resources
Human rights
Materialism
Secularization
Racism
Other social problems – poverty, injustice, drugs, *etc.*

How does our faith influence our thinking about these issues?

Are there ways in which we should be joining hands to fight against evils in our society and the world? For instance, how have Muslims and Christians worked together in South Africa to fight apartheid?

24.4 Can we find new ways of bearing witness to our faith?

One way to break out of the deadlock created by centuries of controversy between Muslims and Christians is to start with basic convictions that are common to both faiths, and from there move on to explore differences. Or, to change the metaphor, we try to find how far we can walk along the same road together, and then think about the points at which our paths diverge.

So, for example, we can say that the Muslims and Christians agree with the simple propositions in the overlapping circles below.

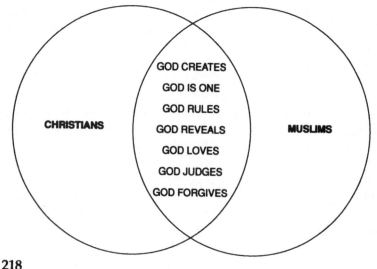

Both Christians and Muslims can assent to these statements without any hesitation. But as Kenneth Cragg has said, 'The question is not *whether*, but *how*'. The issue between us is not *whether* God forgives, but *how* he forgives; not *whether* he reveals, but *what* he reveals and *how*. If we take these propositions one by one, we can see how we can explore them in the context of dialogue.

God creates

Islam has such a clear doctrine of creation that there is no chance of confusing the Creator with his creation. After talking to a Hindu or a Buddhist, it is quite a relief to talk to a Muslim! If we are looking for areas to explore differences, we may want to find out to what extent the Muslim thinks of humans as being created 'in the image of God'. But unless we really know what we are doing, perhaps it is better simply to rejoice in the fact that we have so much in common in our doctrine of creation.

God is one

We can agree with the Muslim that 'there is no god but God'. In the Qur'an Muhammad is commanded to say to the Christians, 'We believe in that which hath been revealed unto us and revealed unto you; our God and your God is One, and unto Him we surrender' (29:46). Because we believe that 'The LORD our God, the LORD is one' (Deuteronomy 6:4), we believe with Muslims in the oneness of God. But the question at issue is: what kind of oneness are we talking about? Are we talking about a strictly mathematical kind of unity? Or can we think of the more complex unity of the atom, or the unity that creates 'one flesh' in marriage?

God rules

God rules as king in complete control of the world he has made. But how does he exercise his kingly rule? And how, in particular, does he react when people reject his lordship over their lives? Christians see God's response coming to a climax in the life of Jesus, whose message is: 'The time has come . . . The kingdom of God is near. Repent and believe the good news!' (Mark 1:15). Jesus enters into his glory as the messianic king only through suffering: 'Did not the Christ have to suffer these things and then enter his glory?' (Luke 24:25). Those who enter the kingdom of God, therefore, are those who live under the authority of Jesus as members of the new community he called into being. Muslims, on the other hand, associate the kingdom of God with the house of Islam, so that entering the kingdom of God means living according to the law revealed through the Prophet.

God reveals

But what does he reveal? We believe that God has revealed *himself*: 'No-one has ever seen God, but God the One and Only, who is at the Father's side, has made him known' (Greek *exēgēsato*, literally, 'has given an exegesis' of God) (John 1:18). In his high-priestly prayer Jesus says: 'I have revealed you [or 'your name'] to those whom you gave me out of the world' (John 17:6).

Muslims, however, cannot generally make such a claim. The ninety-nine 'Names of God' reveal something of the attributes of God. And the Sufis come close to Christian language in speaking about knowing God. The position of orthodox Islam, however, is summed up in these words of Isma'il al-Faruqi:

> He [God] does not reveal Himself to anyone in any way. God reveals only His will . . . But God does not reveal Himself to anyone. Christians talk about the revelation of God Himself – by God of God – but that is the great difference between Christianity and Islam.[1]

(See further chapter 27.)

God loves

John sums up the meaning of the incarnation with the words: 'God so loved the world . . .' (John 3:16). Paul similarly understands it in terms of love: 'God demonstrates his own love for us in this: While we were still sinners, Christ died for us' (Romans 5:8). Christians have sometimes refused to recognize that the Qur'an does speak about the love of God. But while there are many verses which speak about God loving, the crucial question is: whom does he love? We shall see later that the Qur'an states clearly which kinds of people God loves, and which he does not love. (See chapter 34.)

God judges

We both believe in the day of judgment, and look forward either with confidence or with dread to the end of the universe as we know it. But on what basis does God judge? Paul sees that it is the function of the law revealed in Scripture to expose 'the exceeding sinfulness of sin' (Romans 7:13, AV), while those who have not known the law will be judged by the law that is within their hearts (Romans 2:14–15). Either way, all people stand condemned before God (Romans 3:19, 23). While Muslims would see the function of the written law in similar terms, they do not seem to share the Christian conviction that sin is *sinfulness* – that it is more like a fatal disease than simply weakness or a series of mistakes.

God forgives

But whom does he forgive, and how does he forgive? In Islam, when people repent, God forgives, as it were, by a word. But if the sacrificial system of the Old Testament taught the Jews anything, it was that forgiveness involves suffering. Divine forgiveness can never be a simple amnesty or a reassuring *'ma'lesh'* – that wonderful word in colloquial Arabic which means everything from 'Never mind' to 'It doesn't matter'. In the parable of the two lost sons, the father himself suffers as he forgives his son and welcomes him back home.

What, then, have we been doing? We have started from common ground – from seven propositions which Christians and Muslims can affirm together without hesitation. We have also tried to recognize frankly the differences between us in answering questions which arise out of these basic convictions. Instead of trying to dictate the criteria by which we decide whether a particular belief is true or false, we are simply asking: which of these answers makes the most sense of all that we know about the universe and about ourselves? And are we prepared to live with all the consequences of what we believe about God?

If we can have the freedom to explore these issues at this kind of level, there is at least a chance that we may be able to break out of the fixed positions into which we have been forced by confrontation over so many centuries, and experience a new meeting of minds.

If this model for dialogue still sounds too theoretical, the following two examples give some indication of how it can work out in practice. In the first an American student describes how he attended a Qur'an study with some Muslims in London.

There were 6 women and 5 men at the meeting, mainly from South Asia, but a few from Jamaica, all now living in England. The Muslims were studying the Qur'an like I used to study with other college students during my IVCF days. They were asking questions about the text, seeking to interpret it. We studied Surah 55 (The Beneficent), which deals in the latter verses with heaven or paradise. It was interesting to hear how they dealt with the verses about the physical delights of paradise. I felt some of their explanations were quite understandable. I have often heard Christians criticize Islam because of these verses.

After the study they proceeded to ask me questions about the Bible for two hours or so. I tried to be honest with them during the meeting and to explain that I had a real desire to learn something about Islam, not to debate about different religions. I avoided the questions about the deity of Christ and the crucifixion because I felt trying to answer in a few sentences would not be helpful to the Muslims. I told them to read the Injil for themselves and then we would talk about the message it speaks. The meeting opened my eyes to the great value of talking openly and honestly and personally with Muslims. More was accomplished in that meeting than my entire time passing out tracts in London.

At the end of the meeting I again stressed my desire to know more about Islam and to better understand what it was like to be a Muslim in the so-called Christian west. They then apologized to me for not allowing me to think about the questions before I came. They then encouraged me to ask them questions. At the end of the meeting the leader told me I was talking about Islam except for my understanding of Jesus. One of the women then asked me how I deal with sin in my life as a Christian, because she had struggled with sin herself. They invited me back every Wednesday and said if

there were a topic I would like discussed, to let them
know.

I made no apology to them for being a follower of
Messiah Jesus, but through listening and seeking to
understand them, I feel I have gained their respect and
the beginnings of a friendship . . . I am excited about
what God has done.[2]

In the second, Roger Hooker describes how he was able to
enter into this kind of dialogue during his time in India.

In engaging upon this enterprise one discovers that
there are certain areas of human life where Islam is
silent, or by Christian standards, inadequate. One of
these areas is suffering. Two or three years ago I was at
an '*urs* at the *madrasa*, listening to some hauntingly
lovely Urdu poetry. I asked the man next to me what
this particular poem was about. He replied that the poet
was bemoaning the fallen state of Islam and asking God
to put it right. Here is a tension which many a devout
Muslim, like many a devout Christian, must often feel,
the tension between things as they are and things as
they ought to be. A few days later when I was visiting
the mosque I asked one of my friends about this poem
and said: 'If God is really almighty, then why does he
allow Islam to remain in this fallen state, why doesn't
he do something about it?' The only answer I got was a
shrug of the shoulders: 'Only God knows.' Some time
later I asked the same question of another man and this
time the answer went a little further: 'He is testing us to
see if we really believe.' This is the usual theme of the
addresses given in the mosque in *muharram*. Hussein
was subjected to the most fearful sufferings, yet in spite
of all he remained unswervingly loyal to God . . .
Are the stock Muslim answers enough to meet Muslim bewilderment at the course their contemporary
history is taking? Is not this the point at which a Christian who is present as a friend can ask the most searching questions? Yet as he does so he must remember that
his own history poses the same question about the

omnipotence of God. We believe that omnipotence is supremely manifested in the Cross which Islam so tragically misunderstands.[3]

Experiences of this kind show that it really is possible to get beyond the polemics and the arguments to a deeper and more helpful kind of genuine dialogue.

Resources for further study

Christian Mission and Islamic Da'wah: Proceedings of the Chambésy Dialogue Consultation (The Islamic Foundation, 1982)

Anne Cooper, compiler, *In the Family of Abraham* (People International, PO Box 26, Tunbridge Wells, Kent TN2 5AZ, 1989)

Jean-Marie Gaudeul, *Encounters and Clashes: Islam and Christianity in History* (Pontifical Institute for Arab and Islamic Studies, Rome, 1984)

Norman L. Geisler and Abdul Saleeb, *Answering Islam* (Baker, 1993)

John Gilchrist, *Muhammad and the Religion of Islam* (Jesus to Muslims, PO Box 1804, Benoni, South Africa, 1986)

B. D. Kateregga and W. D. Shenk, *Islam and Christianity: A Muslim and a Christian in Dialogue* (Eerdmans, 1980)

Chawkat Georges Moucarry, *Islam and Christianity at the Crossroads* (Lion, 1988)

William J. Saal, *Reaching Muslims for Christ* (Moody Press, 1991)

W. Montgomery Watt, *Muslim–Christian Encounters: Perceptions and Misperceptions* (Routledge, 1991)

Part 4

Facing fundamental issues

The problem in mission to Islam is theological.

Arne Rudvin[1]

There are several ways of establishing contact or communication between man and God. The best would have been incarnation; but Islam has rejected it. It would be too degrading for a transcendent God to become man, to eat, drink, be tortured by His own creatures, and even be put to death. However close a man may approach God in his journeying towards Him, even in his highest ascension, man remains man and very much remote from God.

Muhammad Hamidullah[2]

The call of the minaret must always seem to the Christian a call to retrieval. He yearns to undo the alienation and to make amends for the past by as full a restitution as he can achieve of the Christ to Whom Islam is a stranger. The objective is not, as the Crusaders believed, the repossession of what Christendom has lost, but the restoration to Muslims of the Christ Whom they have missed.

Kenneth Cragg[3]

Islam is a one-way door, you can enter through it but you cannot leave.

Abul A'la Maududi[4]

In Part 4 we consider some of the harder issues that come to the surface in the meeting between the two faiths. In chapter 25 we consider three of the thorny theological questions which the existence of Islam raises for Christians. Chapter 26 explores the perceptions of Jesus in Islam. This leads on in chapter 27 to an attempt to pinpoint the crucial areas of difference in the two faiths.

Chapter 28 discusses biblical models which may help Christians in their thinking about Islam. Chapter 29 deals with some of the implications of conversion to the Christian faith, while chapter 30 explores possible Christian responses to the political challenges presented by Islam in the modern world.

25

Theological questions

Meeting with Muslims and engaging with the religion of Islam is bound to force us to ask fundamental questions about what we believe and what we think about the religion of Islam. This chapter discusses three such questions.

25.1 Is the God of Islam the same as the God of Christianity?

1. The question itself is a kind of trick question, because it forces us to answer with a simple 'Yes' or 'No'. What we need to do is to break the question down into several smaller questions, such as:

■ Is the Christian's *idea of God* the same as the Muslim's idea of God? Most Christians would answer 'No'.

■ Is there *anything in common* between the Christian's idea of God and the Muslim's idea of God? Most would not hesitate to answer 'Yes'.

■ Is there *enough in common* between the Christian's idea of God and the Muslim's idea of God for us to be able to use the same word for 'God'? This is probably the crucial question. Some Christians, like Bishop Rudvin of Karachi, believe that there is not enough in common, while others, like Kenneth Cragg, believe that there is. In the words of Michael Nazir-Ali, 'For Cragg the similarity outweighs the disparity, whereas for Rudvin the disparity clearly outweighs the similarity.'[1]

2. Suppose, for the sake of argument, that there is a country somewhere in the world where the sun is never clearly visible. People are aware of the sun, because they can see the shape of the sun behind the clouds, and know that the sun is the source of heat. But they can never see the sun in a cloudless sky. Contrast this with people who live in the Mediterranean. They see the sun very clearly, and feel its heat. Is it the same sun for both people in both places? It must of course be the same sun, although each group of people has a very different mental image and experience of it.

If the analogy is acceptable (even though somewhat artificial), it would suggest that Muslims and Christians are talking about the same God, even though their ideas of that God and their experience of him may differ considerably. We must not, however, press the analogy too far, since no human being can 'see God' or have complete knowledge of him. As Paul said, 'Now we see but a poor reflection as in a mirror; then we shall see face to face' (1 Corinthians 13:12). There are many shades of experience between the Mediterranean and the country where the sun never shines!

If we cannot accept the analogy, we have to think in terms of two completely different astronomical bodies, such as the sun and the moon, one being the energy centre of a planetary system and the other a planetary satellite, and assume that Christians and Muslims are talking about two totally different beings. That assumption is likely to make communication between Christians and Muslims extremely difficult, if not impossible.

3. When Paul was speaking to a Greek audience at the Areopagus in Acts 17, he did not hesitate to use the word *theos* both for the 'unknown God' and for the God who raised Jesus from the dead (Acts 17:23–24, 30–31). He believed that there is enough in common between the concept of God in the mind of these pagan Greeks and his concept of God for him to use the same word.

4. Very many converts and enquirers from Muslim backgrounds assume that there is some real continuity between their knowledge and experience of God before and after their conversion. They speak as if they had some real knowledge of God as Muslims, and as if Jesus has brought their idea of God into focus in a new way. The experience of Bilquis Sheikh in *I Dared to Call Him Father* points to continuity rather than discontinuity.

When converts take a negative view and want to repudiate everything in Islam, it may well be either because the only way they can feel secure in their new faith is to cut themselves off from everything in their past, or because the Christians who taught them have taken a negative view of Islam.

5. English translations of the Qur'an which keep the Arabic 'Allah' for God seem to want to underline the difference between the God of Islam and the God of Christianity. Muslims are concerned here about the possible confusion between God (with a capital G) and god (with a small g). For these reasons Islamic governments in Malaysia and elsewhere have not allowed Christians to use 'Allah' in recent translations of the Bible. Against this view, however, it can be argued that such practice is not true to the Qur'an and the practice of the Prophet. In one important verse the Prophet is commanded to say to Jews and Christians: 'O People of the Scripture! Come to an agreement between us and you: that we shall worship none but Allah, and that we shall ascribe no partner unto Him . . .' (3:64). Nothing in the Qur'an suggests that Muhammad ever believed that Jews and Christians, the people of the Book, were worshipping a different God.

When Christians today insist on using 'Allah' for the God of Islam, they want to make the theological point that the God of Islam is totally different from the God of Christianity. Fourteen million Arabic-speaking Christians in the Middle East, however, speak of God as Allah, and would never think of using a different word. There can, therefore, be no *linguistic* reason for Christians to choose such a contrived way of speaking about God in Islam and finding a different name for God. And it may be hard to find any *theological* reason for trying to distinguish between the words 'Allah' and 'God' in Christianity.

25.2 Is there any revelation in Islam?

Once again we need to be cautious about the question itself, because it is framed in such a way as to invite a simple 'Yes' or 'No' for an answer. We therefore need to break the question down into a number of smaller questions, which ought at least to alert us to the danger of simplistic answers.

1. Are we speaking about general revelation or special revelation?

Most Christians would reject the view that Muhammad received *special revelation*, in the sense that he received *new* revelations from God which had not been revealed before through the prophets, Jesus or the apostles. No doubt most would also be suspicious of the view that Muhammad's teaching was genuine revelation of God in a form that was specially relevant and appropriate for the Arabs. Many would want to say that if he did receive any special revelation, it did not come to him direct from God, but through what he learned from the Jews and Christians.

If, however, we are simply speaking about *general revelation*, we could say that any revelation Muhammad received was no different from the general revelation that is available to all people. Or we might want to argue that if Muhammad was a sincere seeker after God, any revelation he received was no different in principle from that given (for instance) to Cornelius before his conversion, or to other people who are seeking after God (Acts 17:27).

Or again, using Charles Kraft's memorable phrase, we may want to think of Muhammad as being '*chronologically* AD but *informationally* BC'.[2] In this case, his experiences could have had something in common with people in the Old Testament such as Gideon, or possibly even Elijah, even though he was in no sense part of God's salvation-history which was worked out through the descendants of Abraham.

2. *How did the religion of Islam compare with the religion of Arabia?*

It could be argued that Islam was a distinct improvement on the pre-Islamic polytheism and idolatry of Arabia. If the pre-Islamic religion of Arabia had much in common with Canaanite religion, Islam must have had much in common with the monotheism of the Old Testament. Even so, we may want to argue that it is irrelevant to ask how close Islam was to the religion of the Old Testament or how far it was from it. The final product seems to be 'a denial of Christianity', and this is all that matters.

3. *How are we to understand the development in the experience of Muhammad?*

Many Christians are prepared to acknowledge that earlier in his life Muhammad was a sincere seeker after God. He had come to believe in the one Creator God, but did not have the opportunity to read the Bible or find out the truth about Jesus. Because of choices that he made at certain stages in his ministry, however, he wandered away from the truth that he knew, and was further away from the truth at the end of his life than he was at the beginning. Other Christians answer this question, however, by saying that what matters is 'the finished product', namely his life and teaching as a whole, and that studying the development of his experience is therefore irrelevant.

4. *How are we to understand Muhammad's rejection of Christianity?*

Here again there are at least two possible answers. We can say that what Muhammad rejected was at best a misunderstanding of the gospel, and at worst a travesty of the gospel. We simply do not know how Muhammad would have responded if he had had an opportunity to hear the true gospel. But because the Christianity he rejected was so imperfect, we cannot immediately put Muslims into the same category as Arians or Jehovah's Witnesses. The other answer would be that since Muhammad denied the deity of Christ and the cross, Islam must be seen as a heresy just like any other heresy, ancient or modern. It is irrelevant to ask, 'What would have happened if he had known the true gospel?'

5. *How are we to understand the psychological processes of the so-called 'revelations' which came to Muhammad?*

Some would say that the descriptions of Muhammad's practices and experiences in the Qur'an and the *hadith* suggest that they had strong similarities with those of ascetics, monks, mystics and the like. But since there is not enough clear evidence, we need to look at the content of the revelations rather than speculate over the psychological processes involved. On the other hand, many Christians would not hesitate to say that Muhammad must have had dealings with the occult, and that any 'revelations' he received must have come from evil spirits.

Working through questions like these should force us to recognize all that there is in Islam which is thoroughly consistent with Christian beliefs. We shall probably still want to make a distinction between 'truths' (plural) and 'the truth' (singular), and will remain genuinely puzzled about the mixture of truth and error which Christians find in Islam. But at least we will have been alerted to the danger of simplistic answers which either repel Muslims (because they convey such a negative view of Islam) or alternatively leave them confused (because they blur the distinctives of the two faiths). We may then be in a position to decide between the following four views which are held by different Christians:

1. The Qur'an is inspired by the devil. It doesn't matter how much truth there may be in it, because, *taken as a whole*, it denies the deity of Christ, his crucifixion and resurrection, and therefore takes the heart out of the gospel. It cannot therefore be regarded as being inspired by God in any sense.

2. We should recognize everything in the Qur'an that is consistent with the revelation of God as we know it in the Bible and in Christ. We should be glad of the common ground there is between the Christian faith and Islam, but help Muslims to see where the Muslim understanding of God differs from the Christian understanding.

3. Muhammad should be regarded as a prophet *in some sense*. Since he enabled the Arabs to reject polytheism and idolatry and to accept monotheism, he must have received some genuine revelation from God. He can perhaps therefore be regarded as being comparable to Old Testament characters like Gideon or Elijah, even though he is not part of the biblical 'salvation history' and falls short of the revelation of God given in Christ.

4. Muhammad should be recognized as a genuine prophet for Muslims. In spite of the differences between the revelation of God in the Qur'an and the revelation of God in the Bible and in Christ, the Qur'an should be recognized as a revelation of God that was appropriate for the Arabs in its original context and is still appropriate for Muslims all over the world today.

25.3 Is Islam inspired by the devil?

Some Christians would never think in these terms, and would be embarrassed to think that Muslims might overhear Christians posing the question in such a blunt way. Others, however, feel compelled to ask the question at one time or another, because they need to explain the source of the error they perceive in Islam.

One possible starting-point would be to take texts such as these from the letters of Paul: 'The god of this age has blinded the minds of unbelievers' (2 Corinthians 4:4); 'Our struggle is . . . against the powers of this dark world and against the spiritual forces of evil in the heavenly realms' (Ephesians 6:12); and 'Satan himself masquerades as an angel of light' (2 Corinthians 11:14).

All these verses are no doubt thoroughly relevant to our thinking about *all* faiths and ideologies.

There are several reasons, however, for suggesting that there can be real dangers in Christians coming too easily and too quickly to the conclusion that Islam is a religion 'inspired by the devil'.

1. Why single out Islam for special mention? What about the godless humanism and materialism of the West today? What about some of the demonic forces at work in parts of the *Christian* world? When some Christians speak as if Islam is 'enemy number one' in the world today, there is a real danger of getting things out of proportion.

2. An overemphasis on the role of Satan in Islam can easily prevent Christians from facing up to the terrible record of the Christian church in its relations with Muhammad and his followers. Attributing everything we dislike or disagree with in Islam to demonic forces allows us, so to speak, to 'pass the buck', and fail to recognize the responsibility of the Christian church in much of what has happened. The very existence of Islam can be seen as a judgment on the Christian church, and the record of the church over fourteen centuries in its relations with Islam should leave us with a sense of shame.

In talking with Muslims we will of course want to disassociate ourselves from the Crusades, just as some Muslims have disassociated themselves from the Amins, the Khomeinis or the Qadhdhafis of the Muslim world. But resorting too quickly to the explanation that Islam is inspired by the devil may mean that we are letting ourselves off the hook too lightly, and that we never recognize the responsibility of the Christian church for much that has happened in the past.

3. If we teach that non-Christian religions are inspired by the devil, some Christians jump to the conclusion that people of these faiths must therefore by definition be possessed by evil powers. It is obvious that there are occult practices in some forms of 'folk Islam', and many Christians have no difficulty whatever in believing in demon possession. But it is neither true nor helpful to suggest that every Muslim must be treated as a case of demonic possession.

234

4. We are probably influenced more than we realize by stereotypes of Islam which we have inherited from the past. It was not for purely biblical and theological reasons that our forefathers in the eastern churches and in Europe thought of Islam in these terms. There were many other cultural, political and psychological factors which were at work not so far below the surface. This is how Jean-Marie Gaudeul makes the point, writing about the Middle Ages:

> Europe elaborated instinctively an image of everything it repudiated and projected this image on Islam, the symbol of all that was 'un-Christian' . . . This was not deliberate, but instinctive: Europe had felt inferior to the Islamic civilization, it had received much from it: philosophy, the sciences, technology; unable as yet to express its own culture in positive terms, Europe rejected in Islam whatever seemed to threaten its Christian identity.[3]

Norman Daniels, in his book *Islam and the West: the Making of an Image*, shows that many of the popular images and stereotypes of Muslims and Islam in the minds of Europeans and westerners today can be traced back to the writings of Christians in the Middle East and Europe in the Middle Ages.

5. When Christians interpret the contemporary resurgence of Islam, especially in the Middle East, simply in terms of the work of Satan, they are probably guilty of resorting to a terrible over-simplification of complex issues. This revival is to some extent a response to centuries of European colonialism, and we cannot understand what has been happening in countries such as Iran and Iraq if we do not appreciate the many cultural, political and economic factors that have been involved. Simple explanations expressed in purely spiritual terms can easily prevent us from getting to grips with the complexities of history and politics.

6. Explaining Islam in terms of the demonic can sometimes simply be a way of coming to terms with all that is culturally strange and foreign in Islam. Simple explanations of this kind seem to save us from the hard work of coming to terms with all those pastoral, psychological, political and cultural factors which come into the equation.

If some Christians, then, refuse to answer the question 'Is Islam inspired by the devil?', others will answer with a simple 'Yes', because they can find no other way of explaining the fact that Islam seems to deny some of the most fundamental and essential Christian beliefs. But there will be others who will want to answer, 'Maybe, but . . .' These 'buts' will probably not turn the 'Maybe' into a 'No'. But they should at least make us recognize that simple categories of 'all good' and 'all bad' cannot really help us in coming to terms with all that we find both in the religion of Islam and in the actual Muslims whom we meet.

26

The Islamic view of Jesus

'We believe in Jesus and all the prophets,' says the Muslim to the Christian.

'But what kind of Jesus do you believe in?' replies the Christian. 'What precisely is your picture of him?'

This is an area where Christians and Muslims appear to have much in common because of the important place they give to Jesus. But how significant are the differences in the way the two faiths think of Jesus? Does the amount of common ground make the differences seem minimal? Or are the differences so important that they point to fundamental differences between the two faiths?

The Islamic view of Jesus is based primarily on the Qur'an, but has also been coloured by centuries of tradition.

26.1 Jesus in the Qur'an

The following are the main features of the picture of Jesus which emerges from the ninety-three verses in the Qur'an which speak about him. The quotations in this chapter are taken from Kenneth Cragg's translation, *Readings in the Qur'an*.[1]

1. Jesus is seen as one in the line of prophets sent by God.

> We have granted revelation to you [singular, *i.e.* Muhammad] as We gave revelation to Noah and the prophets who came after him. To Abraham also We gave revelation, and to Ishmael, Isaac, Jacob and the tribes, to Jesus and to Job, to Jonah, Aaron and Solomon. To David We brought the Psalms (4:163).

> Say: 'We believe in God and in what He has revealed to us and His revelations to Abraham and Ishmael, to

Isaac and Jacob and the tribes, and in what was brought to Moses, Jesus and the prophets, from their Lord. We do not discriminate between any of them and to God do we surrender' (3:84–85).

2. Jesus was born of a virgin; his birth was announced to Mary by an angel.

To Mary the angel said: 'Mary, God gives you glad news of a word from Him. His name is the Messiah Jesus, son of Mary. Eminent will he be in this world and in the age to come, and he will have his place among those who are brought near to God's Throne. He will speak to men in the cradle and in his mature years, and he will be among the righteous.'

Mary said: 'Lord, how shall I bear a son when no man has known me?' He replied: 'The will of God is so, for He creates as He wills. When His purpose is decreed He only says: "Be!" and it is. God will teach him the Scripture, the wisdom, the Torah and the Gospel, making him a messenger to the people of Israel' (3:45–49).

3. He performed many miracles.

And to Jesus He will say: 'Jesus, son of Mary, remember My grace towards your mother when I aided you with the holy spirit, so that in your cradle and in your mature years you spoke to men. Remember how I gave you knowledge of the Book, and the wisdom, the Torah and the Gospel, and how by My leave you fashioned clay into the shape of the bird and when you breathed into it it became a bird by My leave, and how, by My leave too, you healed those born blind and the lepers and how, by My leave again, you brought the dead to life once more' (5:110).

4. It is blasphemy to elevate Jesus to the level of God.

Truly they have lied against the truth who say: 'God, He is the Messiah, son of Mary.' Say: 'Who can arrogate sovereignty from God in anything? If God but wills it

His power could annihilate the Messiah and his mother and every one else in the world. To God belongs the sovereignty of the heavens and of the earth and all that is within them and He is omnipotent over all' (5:17).

They have ascribed invisible beings as partners to God, though He created them, and in their total ignorance they have attributed to Him sons and daughters. Glory to Him and exalted be He above what they allege. The very Creator of the heavens and of the earth, how could there be a 'son' to Him there never having been a 'spouse' to Him – He who created everything and who is omniscient over all things? (6:101–102).

5. While Jesus is not divine in any sense, he is unique among the prophets of God and is given titles such as 'word' and 'spirit' which are not given to any other human beings:

People of the Book, do not go to unwarranted lengths in your religion and get involved in false utterances relating to God. Truly, Jesus, Mary's son, was the messenger of God and His word – the word which He imparted to Mary – and a spirit from Him. Believe, then, in God and His Messengers and do not talk of three gods. You are well advised to abandon such ideas. Truly God is one God. Glory be to Him and no 'son' to Him whose are all things in the heavens and the earth, their one and only guardian.

That He should be servant to God will never be disdained by the Messiah as beneath his dignity, nor indeed by the angels who dwell in the divine presence. Servants of His who take on arrogant airs and think themselves above serving – well, God will have them all summoned to answer for it (4:171–172).

6. Jesus is to be thought of as similar to Adam in that they were both created by the word of God:

God would have you think of Jesus as you think of Adam, created by God from the dust, saying to him 'Be' and into being he came. This is the truth from your

Lord, so do not be among those who are dubious (3:59–60).

7. Jesus was not crucified. In a passage about the Jews we are told:

> As for their claim that they killed the Messiah Jesus, son of Mary, the messenger of God, the truth is they did not kill him nor did they crucify him. They were under the illusion that they had. There is a lot of doubt about this matter among those who are at odds over it. They have no real knowledge but follow only surmise. Assuredly, they did not kill him. On the contrary, God raised him to Himself – God whose are all wisdom and power. And before they come to die, the people of the Book, to a man, will surely believe on him. On the Day of Resurrection he will be a witness against them (4:157–159).

The picture of Jesus that emerges from the Qur'an is summed up by M. Ali Merad, a Muslim scholar of Algerian origin, as follows:

> Prophet, Apostle of God, servant of God, these are titles which are applied in the Qur'an to many other prophetic figures. But Christ is more than that. Everything in the Qur'an inclines us to represent him as being above the common condition of men . . . An exceptional divine work, an exceptional messenger, favoured in all things by God, Christ witnesses to an exceptional divine concern. Through all that the Qur'an has to say about Jesus, we cannot fail to recognize an unquestionable convergence: everything it gives leads to the declaration of Christ's surpassing greatness.[2]

The traditional Islamic interpretation of the death of Jesus is summed up by the same writer in this way:

> The Muslim's conviction is . . . strengthened by everything he reads in the Qur'an, namely that God does not abandon His own: how then could He have abandoned

Jesus, a being whom he produced miraculously, by His *Kalima*, a being whom He assisted by His Spirit, whom He had singularly favoured, conferring on him the remarkable power of giving life and of raising from the dead? God cannot hand over to the fury of some executioners a being with a nature like Jesus.

Islam refuses to accept this tragic image of the Passion. Not simply because it has no place for the dogma of the Redemption, but because the Passion would imply in its eyes that God had failed.

Islam rejects the idea of the death of Christ. This attitude safeguards at one and the same time the idea found in the Qur'an of God's honour and of man's dignity. For in Jesus mankind attains its supreme dignity, its consummation.[3]

26.2 Jesus in later Islamic tradition

Since Jesus in the Qur'an is such an enigmatic figure, Muslims after the time of Muhammad felt the need to explain the references to Jesus in the Qur'an in order to add to and fill out its picture of Jesus. In the traditions which developed, the main focus of interest was on three areas:

1. His miraculous powers. One story tells how he dyed ten garments in different colours in one single vat. Another story tells how he turned a group of children into pigs.

2. His asceticism. Jesus is described as wearing a robe of wool, which indicates that he lived very simply. He is quoted as saying, 'I have become worn out by my labours, and there is no poor person poorer than I am.' He has no human ties, except to his mother, and is known as 'the prince of wanderers'.

3. His role at the end of history. Various traditions say that he will come down to earth at the eastern gate of the Great Mosque at Damascus. He will then go to Jerusalem to worship God in a mosque along with other Muslims. He will kill all the pigs, break the crosses, destroy Jewish synagogues and Christian churches, and kill all the Christians who do not believe in him, and kill the

Antichrist. All the People of the Book will thus believe in him. Justice and peace will reign all over the world, and after forty years Jesus will die a natural death and be buried in Medina alongside Muhammad. The purpose of the second coming of Jesus, then, is to vindicate Islam and demonstrate its triumph to the whole world.

Another significant development that took place over centuries was that the Muslims' picture of Muhammad became deeply influenced by the Christians' picture of Christ. Samuel Zwemer speaks of Muhammad as being 'transformed at least in measure into the character if not into the image of Christ':

> The sin and guilt of the Muslim world is that they give Christ's glory to another, *and that for all practical purposes Muhammad himself is the Muslim Christ*. The life and character of Muhammad as portrayed for us by his earliest biographers, who were all his faithful followers and admirers, leaves no doubt that he was thoroughly human and liable to error. Later tradition has changed all this, and made him sinless and almost divine. Two hundred and one titles of honour given to Muhammad proclaim his apotheosis [deification].[4]

The Ahmadiyya movement, which began in Pakistan in 1879, has taught that Jesus was taken down from the cross before he actually died, and later revived in the tomb. He then escaped from Jerusalem, and travelled to Kashmir, where he died. Although the Ahmadis are a strong missionary group, they have been officially declared non-Muslims by the government of Pakistan.

Early in this century Muslim apologists began to use the so-called *Gospel of Barnabas*, claiming that this is the only authentic account of the life of Jesus. It can easily be demonstrated, however, from its historical and geographical errors, and from teaching which contradicts the Qur'an, that the book is a medieval forgery. The author was probably an Italian Franciscan monk who converted to Islam in the sixteenth century. (See further chapter 22.)

If Muslims today know only the Jesus of the Qur'an and of

later Muslim tradition, they insist that he was no more than a prophet and that he did not die on the cross. Many of them have little or no desire to read the gospels or to explore Christian beliefs about him, because they think that all they need to know about him is revealed in the Qur'an. If they do read the gospels and admire his teaching, they tend to regard it as hopelessly unrealistic. Although they are often impressed by his miraculous powers and may even be moved by the story of the crucifixion, they find it impossible to believe that God could have allowed it to happen, or to see Jesus as anything more than an ordinary man and a great prophet.

26.3 Christian responses

1. While some aspects of the Qur'anic Jesus fit with the picture given in the New Testament (for instance, the Virgin Birth and some of the miracles), several other aspects appear to have come from unorthodox, if not heretical, Christian sources (such as the miracles performed during the childhood of Jesus, and the idea of a substitute who was crucified in place of Jesus). Christians have to recognize, however, that such an interpretation is totally unacceptable to Muslims who believe that the Qur'an was revealed directly by God to the mind of the Prophet, and that the contents of the Qur'an cannot therefore be traced back to human sources.

2. The basic reason Jesus cannot be seen by the Qur'an as 'more than a prophet' is that he does not fit into the Islamic understanding of how God has revealed himself to the world. The contrast between the two faiths at this point is summed up vividly by Jens Christensen when he writes: 'Islam says: Book from God = revelation from God. Christianity says: Christ from God = revelation of God.' Islam rules out the possibility of God revealing himself through an incarnation. For Muslims, therefore, however exalted Jesus may be, he cannot possibly be anything more than a person of 'surpassing greatness'.

3. Christians feel compelled to point out to Muslims that the Jesus of the Qur'an is a very pale reflection of the Jesus of the New Testament. This feeling is expressed by Kenneth Cragg:

> This is the inward tragedy, from the Christian angle, of the rise of Islam, the genesis and dissemination of a new

belief which claimed to displace what it had never effectively known. The state of being a stranger to the Christian's Christ has been intensified by further failures of love and loyalty on the part of institutional Christianity in the long and often bitter external relations of the two faiths through the centuries.

It is for these reasons that the call of the minaret must always seem to the Christian a call to retrieval. He yearns to undo the alienation and to make amends for the past by as full a restitution as he can achieve of the Christ to Whom Islam is a stranger. The objective is not, as the Crusaders believed, the repossesion of what Christendom has lost, but the restoration to Muslims of the Christ Whom they have missed.[5]

4. Instead of putting an end to the discussion, the Qur'anic picture of Jesus can be used effectively as a starting-point by Christians who know what they are doing. Henri Michaud makes this point in a study of Jesus in the Qur'an :

After having tried to understand what the Qur'an says about Jesus, we shall ask our brothers of Islam with very great anxiety: 'Is this indeed what you believe about Jesus?' If there is a reply without ambiguity, then an eirenical dialogue can begin.[6]

27

Crucial differences: the parting of the ways

If some Christians concentrate on the differences between Christianity and Islam, others tend to emphasize the common ground without ever getting to grips with the areas of disagreement. Is it ever possible to strike the right balance between these two approaches? While attempting to be scrupulously fair and honest, is it possible to recognize and rejoice in what is common between the two faiths, and at the same time to articulate the fundamentally different assumptions which lie behind the disagreements in other areas of belief?

What we find in practice is that in their discussions with one another, Christians and Muslims can often feel that, for part of their journey at least, they are walking together in the same direction along the same road. But then they come to a fork in the road, and find themselves going in different directions. Where then are these forks in the road, and what are the issues over which Christians and Muslims discover that their paths diverge?

In this chapter we take six different subjects, and attempt to summarize what most Muslims believe (the column on the left) alongside what most Christians believe (the column on the right). The summary of beliefs on both sides is followed by further reflection on the similarities and differences.

27.1 Revelation: can God be known?

While the Qur'an uses expressions such as 'seeking the face of God' (e.g. 2:272), orthodox Islamic theology teaches that God himself cannot be known; only his will can be known.

Christian theology teaches that God can be known because he has revealed himself – through the universe, through human conscience, through the Bible, and supremely through Jesus.

The 'names of God' reveal something of the character and attributes of God; but God is so 'wholly other', so different from humans, that the meaning of these names when applied to God is not the same as when applied to people.	We need not be so sceptical about the meaning of words used about God. When God says, 'Be holy, for I am holy', he defines the meaning he gives to the word 'holy', and does not leave it to humans to decide what it may mean.
God has revealed his will for the human race through the Qur'an.	Jesus spoke about the possibility of knowing God, and related this possibility to his own coming into the world (John 17:3).

The Christian perception of orthodox Islamic teaching about revelation is summed up by Michael Nazir-Ali:

> Islam not only believes in the hiddenness of God, but, more seriously, in the impossibility of ever knowing Him. The most that can be said is that believers know His will which he has revealed to them.[1]

In case it is suggested that this misrepresents orthodox Muslim teaching at this point, it is worth quoting from a recent Muslim theologian. In response to a Christian speaker at the Chambésy Consultation on 'Christian Mission and Islamic *Da'wah*', held in 1976, Isma'il al-Faruqi summed up orthodox teaching about the possibility of knowing God as follows:

> You spoke of God 'willing and wanting to reveal Himself to man'. God does *not* reveal Himself. He does not reveal Himself to anyone in any way. God reveals only His will. Remember one of the prophets asked God to reveal Himself and God told him, 'No, it is not possible for Me to reveal Myself to anyone . . .'
> This is God's will and that is all we have – and we have it in perfection in the Qur'an. But Islam does not equate the Qur'an with the nature or essence of God. It is the Word of God, the Commandment of God, the Will of God. But God does not reveal Himself to anyone. Christians talk about the revelation of God Himself

– by God of God – but that is the great difference between Christianity and Islam. God is transcendent, and once you talk about self-revelation you have hierophancy and immanence, and then the transcendence of God is compromised. You may not have complete transcendence and self-revelation at the same time.[2]

27.2 Inspiration: in what sense is Scripture the Word of God?

The very words of the Qur'an were revealed to Muhammad (12:2–3). Muhammad did not write the Qur'an; he simply received it and recited it, so that his own thoughts and ideas did not contribute to the revelations (7:157; 29:48).

The writers of the Bible were inspired by the Holy Spirit. 'Men spoke from God' (2 Peter 1:21). The Bible is therefore both the Word of God and the word of people. The writers were not passive instruments used by God like wordprocessors; they thought about what they were doing and wrote in their own individual style.

It is unnecessary and wrong to try to find the 'sources' of the Qur'an, since it came directly from God to the Prophet Muhammad.

Although the biblical writings were inspired, there is no reason why we should not ask questions about sources.

Because the Qur'an was revealed in Arabic, it is vital to read and recite it in Arabic. Translations of the Qur'an may or may not be permitted; but even when permitted, they do not convey the full meaning of the original.

Almost all the OT was written in Hebrew, and the NT writers wrote in Greek and used Greek translations of the OT. We encourage translations of the Bible because we believe God wants all people to understand as best as they can. A translation of the Bible is just as much 'the Bible' as the original Hebrew and Greek. The meaning of the original can be conveyed adequately in any language.

Underlying all the Muslim's questions and objections about the Old and New Testaments is the Islamic understanding of what Scripture is. Anything that claims to be Scripture but does not read like the Qur'an or have the same message as the Qur'an cannot be Scripture inspired by God. Everything in the Qur'an –

including stories about the prophets, warnings of judgment, and the detailed provisions of the law – comes directly from God. So if the Jewish and Christian Scriptures record immoral actions done by the prophets, include love poetry (as in the Song of Songs) and letters written by the apostles, and give four different versions of the life of Jesus, how, ask Muslims, can such a variety of literature be regarded as revealed Scripture? In short, Muslims are critical of the Jewish and Christian Scriptures because they judge them by the standard of the Qur'an.

In this situation Christians want to point out, first, that Christians have a different understanding of the process of inspiration. Then, secondly, they will want to say that the supreme revelation of God to the human race came not in the form of Scripture, but in the form of a person, that is, Jesus of Nazareth. Christians can say with the apostle John, 'The Word became flesh and made his dwelling among us' (John 1:14), whereas Muslims would no doubt have to say, 'The Word became *book*.'

27.3 The unity of God: what do we understand by it?

God is One; he cannot possibly have a 'son' (112:1–4)

Christians are as convinced monotheists as Muslims and Jews; they accept the basic monotheism of the Old Testament: 'The LORD our God, the LORD is one' (Deuteronomy 6:4).

Idolatry (*shirk*) means putting anything (a human being, an angel or any other 'god') on the same level as the one true God, or associating them with God in any way (7:191–194).

Christians think of God the Father, God the Son and God the Holy Spirit as three 'persons' within the one God, bound together in a relationship of love, not as three distinct 'gods'.

'God is greater' – greater, for example, than all our ideas of him. He is 'the Lord of all worlds', the Creator and Sustainer of the universe (3:189). Although there is a radical difference between God and humans, God is nearer to man 'than the jugular vein' (50:16).

Christians have a similar belief about the sovereignty of God, but tend to put more emphasis on the nearness of God to humans, and use more personal terms for God such as 'Father'.

God is almighty and predestines everything in the universe, including both good and evil. At the same time humans are still held responsible for their actions (4:79).	Christians also try to maintain a balance between God's predestination and human freedom and responsibility; but they tend to put less emphasis than Muslims on God's predestination of everything, and never speak of God decreeing or creating evil.

If we have listened to Muslims long enough to understand the passionate protest against idolatry that is implied in the words 'There is no god but God' and 'God is greater', we may remember that our own Scriptures sound the same call in many different ways. There is the uncompromising demand of the law: 'I am the LORD your God . . . You shall have no other gods before me. You shall not make for yourself an idol in the form of anything in heaven above or on the earth beneath or in the waters below. You shall not bow down to them or worship them; for I, the LORD your God, am a jealous God' (Exodus 20:2–5). The prophets speak with the same voice: 'I am the LORD; that is my name! I will not give my glory to another or my praise to idols' (Isaiah 42:8). We find that Jesus himself reaffirmed the Old Testament command to worship God alone: 'It is written: "Worship the Lord your God, and serve him only"' (Matthew 4:10). And the apostle John ends his first letter with the urgent plea, 'Little children, keep yourselves from idols' (1 John 5:21, RSV).

If Muslims and Christians agree in denouncing idolatry, how much further can we go before finding ourselves entangled in misunderstanding and disagreement? It should not take us long to realize that we are not the first to have passed this way. If the disciples were orthodox Jews who recited daily, 'Hear, O Israel, the LORD our God is one Lord' (Deuteronomy 6:4, RSV), did they not start with the very same assumption as Muslims about the oneness of God? Yet they were constantly being forced to say about Jesus, 'What manner of man is this?' (Mark 4:41, AV). It took Peter some time before he could say, 'You are the Christ' (Mark 8:29); and it was only at the end of three years and after the resurrection that Thomas could say, 'My Lord and my God!' (John 20:28). Because we have the advantage (or disadvantage?) of many centuries of Christian theology and devotion behind us, it is hard for us to realize how much of a revolution had to take place in the minds of the disciples before they could see Jesus as anything more than 'a man sent from God'. It was a gradual process, with each of them making the necessary adjustments at his own speed to enable him to reconcile all that Jesus was saying and doing with the basic conviction that God is one.

If, therefore, we find in the gospels that Jesus himself affirmed the Old Testament command to worship the one true God, and at the same time said and did things which challenge our interpretation of what God is like, our search for truth should make us look for the simplest theory which can hold together all the different data. Instead of abandoning our belief that God is one, we will have to go through the painful (and probably slow) process of redefining what that oneness means. If in the end we can still declare that 'the LORD our God is one LORD', and at the same time say to Jesus, 'My Lord and my God!' we will not be guilty of misusing words any more than we do when we say that a man and a woman become 'one flesh' in marriage. We have not rejected our basic assumption about the oneness of God; we have only redefined it or reinterpreted it in the light of all that we have seen and heard.

27.4 Human nature: what is the true diagnosis of the human condition?

The proper relationship of humankind to God is that of a servant to his Master. 'To be the slave of Allah is the proudest boast of the Muslim, bondage to Allah liberating from all other servitudes' (Pickthall).

People are creatures created in the image and likeness of God (Genesis 1:26). This image has been spoiled and marred, but not completely destroyed. God wants people to be his 'sons and daughters' who know him as 'Father'.

People have been created as stewards to look after the world God has made (2:30).

Christians believe similarly that people were created to 'subdue the earth' (Genesis 1:28).

When Adam sinned, this did not amount to a 'fall' for the whole human race.

Original sin means that we inherit the fallen human nature of our parents, and are born in a state of alienation from God. We are not guilty before God because of our parents' sin, but we inherit the tendency to sin.

God's requirements for people are contained in the law (*shari'a*); and the most important are summed up in the Five Pillars.	God's requirements are revealed supremely in the Ten Commandments which cover our relationship with God and with our neighbours. This basic law is explained and amplified in the rest of the OT and the teaching of Jesus.
Repentance means confessing our sins and turning from the wrong that we have done.	Repentance needs to go deeper than the confession of sins and include the confession that there is something wrong not only with our actions, but also with our nature.
Apart from what is prescribed in the law, the life and teaching of Muhammad as revealed in the Qur'an and the traditions give us a standard of the way we should live as individuals and as a community. (Some Muslims believe that Muhammad was sinless and even pre-existent, though this is not supported by the Qur'an.)	Christians think of Jesus as the supreme example of the kind of person God wants us to be. They believe that the Holy Spirit of God lives in the hearts of those who want to be followers of Jesus, helping them to become more and more like him in their attitudes and behaviour.

If Christians trace the problem of human nature back to the fall of Adam and the inherent sinfulness of human nature, Muslims believe that we take an unnecessarily serious view of the human condition. They do not see Adam's sin as a 'fall' affecting the whole human race, but rather believe that every person starts life with a clean sheet, completely innocent before God. People need the law of God, as revealed in the Qur'an; and when they break it, they need to turn to God in repentance and faith to seek forgiveness. Muslims thus see divine law and divine forgiveness as being sufficient remedy for human disobedience.

Christians who understand anything of the moral conflict described by Paul in Romans 7 feel bound to say that the Muslim diagnosis is too optimistic, and does not make sense of the facts of our moral experience. Instead of solving the problem of human disobedience, the law seems only to intensify it, by showing that our problem is not simply individual 'sins', but rather our 'sin' – our sinful human nature which is constantly dragging us down.

This does not mean that there is anything wrong with the law; it merely means that it was never intended to provide the final solution. Its purpose was rather to expose the problem in its true light; 'The law itself is holy, and the commandment is holy, right, and good. But does this mean that what is good caused my death? By no means! It was sin that did it; by using what is good, sin brought death to me, in order that its true nature as sin might be revealed. And so, by means of the commandment sin is shown to be even more terribly sinful' (Romans 7:12–13, GNB). The more intense the conflict between our desire to obey God's law and the downward pull of our human nature, the more we will find ourselves agreeing with Paul's final analysis of the problem: 'This, then, is my condition: on my own I can serve God's law only with my mind, while my human nature serves the law of sin' (Romans 7:25, GNB).

The difference between the two faiths on this issue has far-reaching consequences in many areas. When we put ourselves under the law of God, what do we find? Do we find ourselves nearer to the confidence and optimism of the man who said to Jesus, 'Ever since I was young, I have obeyed all these commandments' (Mark 10:20, GNB)? Or do we find ourselves echoing Paul's cry of desperation, 'What an unhappy man I am! Who will rescue me from this body that is taking me to death?' (Romans 7:24, GNB).

27.5 Forgiveness and salvation: how does God forgive? What is the meaning of salvation?

God is merciful and willing to forgive all people who sincerely repent, believe and devote themselves to good works. God forgives simply by pronouncing forgiveness. There is no need for any sacrifice or atonement. Forgiveness depends simply on the mercy of God and his declaration of forgiveness. God forgives as he wills.

Since God is both loving and holy, forgiveness cannot depend on a mere verbal declaration. If the laws of the holy God have been broken, simple forgiveness would undermine those laws. So how can God remain just and holy, and at the same time pardon sinful people who have turned their backs on him?

252

Our good deeds and our bad deeds will be weighed in the balance by God on the day of judgment. But we can trust that if we live a good life, our good deeds will outweigh our bad; but we cannot know until the day itself (2:82), since God forgives as he pleases. (Many Muslims believe they can trust the intercession of the Prophet to help them.) All who are accepted by God will be admitted to Paradise; those not accepted go to hell (7:40–46). (Some Muslims are more universalist and believe that God's mercy will reach to all.)

It is in the death of Jesus on the cross that we get a clue to the way this tension is resolved; Jesus in his death bore the judgment on all human sin, and at the same time demonstrated his self-giving, sacrificial love for all people. Anyone who believes that Jesus has already taken upon himself the judgment that each of us deserves has no reason to be afraid of the day of judgment. This assurance of forgiveness and this confidence about the day of judgment produce a profound gratitude and peace, and need never turn into complacency or presumption.

Christians take it for granted that some kind of atonement was needed, and spend a great deal of time trying to explain the rationale for that atonement. Muslims, however, are not interested in challenging any particular theory of the atonement; they cannot see the need for *any* atonement.

If the law of God can be obeyed by all who genuinely desire to live by it, and if any disobedience to the law is simply seen as individual 'sins', it is natural to believe that these sins can be forgiven simply by a 'word' from God. Provided we are sincere in our repentance and trust in God's mercy and compassion, he can forgive us, so to speak, by divine decree. There is no need for any sacrifice to atone for our sins.

This understanding of forgiveness, however, leaves us open to a frightening uncertainty, since we can never have any assurance about God's verdict for each individual on the day of judgment. This is how Jens Christensen comments on this uncertainty:

One of the things that often surprised me in my first studies of Islam was the note of despondency and insecurity that is found in the deathbed utterances of so many of Islam's great men. For example: Abu Bakr was a prince among men of sterling character and a true Muslim. It is said of him that he was so fearful of the

253

future and laboured so much under distress that his breath was often as of a roasted liver. According to two traditions he is supposed to have said to Aisha on the day of his death: 'O my daughter, this is the day of my release and of obtaining my desert; – if gladness it will be lasting; if sorrow it will never cease' . . .

Likewise when Umar was lying on his deathbed he is reported to have said: '. . . I am none other than as a drowning man who sees possibility of escape with life, and hopeth for it, but feareth he may die and lose it, and so plungeth about with hands and feet. More desperate than the drowning man is he who at the sight of heaven and hell is buried in the vision . . . Had I the whole East and West, gladly would I give up all to be delivered from this awful terror that is hanging over me.' And finally touching his face against the ground he cried aloud: 'Alas for Umar, and alas for the mother of Umar, if it should not please the Lord to pardon me.'[3]

The Christian answer to the question about forgiveness and salvation speaks of the possibility of real assurance about the day of judgment. If the gospel can hold out a clear hope, however, it can do so only (1) because it starts out with a more radical diagnosis of the human condition (see 28.4), and (2) because the basis for divine forgiveness is not a divine decree on the day of judgment, but the death of the supreme mediator at a particular place and time in history; the ground of God's forgiveness and the supreme demonstration of his willingness to forgive are to be seen in the death of Jesus on the cross.

This Christian understanding of forgiveness is not totally unrelated to our experience of forgiveness in human relationships, where we find that forgiveness usually *costs* something. The greater the wrong that is done to me, and the deeper the wound, the more it costs me to forgive and to bear the wrong and the injury without hitting back. If God is the lawgiver, there must surely be some problem with how he can both uphold his own laws and at the same time forgive those who break them. If God is also the personal Creator who has made people in his own image, would we not expect his way of forgiving to have something in common with forgiveness between people as we know it, and not to be like the pardon extended by an all-powerful ruler to his subjects at little or no cost to himself?

Even after the disciples had met the risen Jesus, they were still slow to understand the meaning of his death. Jesus therefore had to explain *why* he had to die: '"O foolish men, and slow of heart to believe all that the prophets had spoken! *Was it not necessary* that the Christ should suffer these things and enter into his glory?" And beginning with Moses and all the prophets he interpreted to them in all the Scriptures the things concerning himself' (Luke 24:26–27, RSV). The Scriptures said that this is how it must be. But why did it have to be this way? This is a legitimate question which demands some kind of answer. The Old Testament proof-texts will not by themselves help us to meet the Muslim challenge unless they enable us to grasp something of the divine logic which demands that forgiveness can be proclaimed to people only in the name of one who suffered and died.

The New Testament understanding of the atonement, however, is even more comprehensive than this, since it also introduces us to the Holy Spirit, who is given to enable us to live up to the righteous demands of the law: 'What the Law could not do, because human nature was weak, God did. He condemned sin in human nature by sending his own Son, who came with a nature like man's sinful nature, to do away with sin. God did this so that the righteous demands of the Law might be fully satisfied in us who live according to the Spirit, and not according to human nature' (Romans 8:3–4, GNB).

If, therefore, the Christian understanding of the divine remedy covers every dimension of the human problem and involves the work of the whole Trinity, our ability to enjoy this remedy depends on our willingness to accept the Christian diagnosis of our need, and our willingness to try to grasp the divine logic which demanded that our need could be met only in this way.

27.6 Politics and the state: what is the place of the state in the kingdom of God?

Muhammad was both 'prophet' and 'statesman'. Not only did he receive the revelation from God in the Qur'an; he believed he was called to establish an Islamic society in Medina.

While Jesus was certainly a prophet, he was not a statesman in the sense that Muhammad was. He taught that the kingdom of God was being established on earth through him (Mark 1:15); and in the Sermon on the Mount he explained what it means for individuals and communities to live under his authority.

Muslims therefore find it difficult, if not impossible, to separate 'mosque' and 'state', 'what is Caesar's' and 'what is God's', what is religious and what is secular. Muslims generally believe that the rule of God in the world needs to be embodied in an Islamic state, and have the conviction that 'Islam must rule'.

Jesus' words, 'Give to Caesar what is Caesar's and to God what is God's' (Mark 12:17) suggest that there can often be a tension, if not a conflict, between obedience to the state and obedience to God. During his trial before Pilate, Jesus said, 'My kingdom is not of this world. If it were, my servants would fight to prevent my arrest by the Jews. But now my kingdom is from another place' (John 18:36).

In the early years of Muhammad's ministry in Mecca, he had a limited number of followers, and was despised and rejected by the majority of his own people. He must have realized that the whole Islamic movement could easily be suppressed by persecution. What was he to do? Was he to be patient and trust that God would vindicate him in his own time and in his own way? Or would he be cowardly and irresponsible if he were to take such an enormous risk with the final revelation from God? The answer to this dilemma seemed to come through the overtures of the delegation from Medina who invited him to take over the leadership of their city, and so bring to an end the feuds between its different groups. Muhammad must have seen that this invitation offered him the possibility of establishing as a political leader the kind of society which he had until now been calling for simply as a prophet. In this way the Prophet became both prophet and statesman.

The Jewish–Christian scriptural tradition, however, has generally been suspicious of such a union of different kinds of power. As prophet and lawgiver, Moses had complete authority over every aspect of the people's life. But in the period of the monarchy there were certain safeguards to prevent the king from assuming absolute power. The book of Deuteronomy, for example, speaks of any future kings not as lawgivers, but as those who submit to the law that has already been revealed to Moses: 'When he becomes king, he is to have a copy of the book of God's laws and teachings made from the original copy kept by the levitical priests. He is to keep this book near him and read from it all his life, so that he will learn to honour the LORD and obey faithfully everything that is commanded in it' (Deuteronomy 17:18–19, GNB).

Moreover, God frequently raised up prophets who spoke with an independent voice, condemning disobedience to the revealed law, and at times calling for particular policies and actions. Nathan, for example, had to challenge the great king David and condemn him for adultery and murder (2 Samuel 11:1 – 12:15), while Jeremiah had the unwelcome task of telling king Zedekiah to surrender to the Babylonian invaders (Jeremiah 27:12ff.).

In Islam, however, the one who begins simply as a prophet soon assumes in addition the role of the 'king'; for after the Hijra, there can no longer be any distinction between 'what is Caesar's' and 'what is God's'. If God's kingdom is to be established on earth, what is God's must coincide with what is Caesar's. The law of God must be embodied in a particular kind of society; it must be commended and enforced by some executive power and not left to the conscience of the individual or entrusted to a minority group.

The difference between these two ways of thinking is also evident in the confrontation between Jesus and Pilate. When Jesus was asked what he had done, he replied, 'My kingdom does not belong to this world; if my kingdom belonged to this world, my followers would fight to keep me from being handed over to the Jewish authorities. No, my kingdom does not belong here!' (John 18:36, GNB). Muhammad would not have accepted this distinction between the different kinds of kingdom. Once he had concluded that the kingdom he was concerned about *did* belong to this world, it was an inevitable corollary that his followers would fight to protect him and to extend his authority.

This factor – the attitude to political power – makes Islam significantly different from Judaism and Christianity, and goes a long way towards explaining the importance of the political face of Islam in the modern world. In the New Testament period, although the first Jewish Christians were tolerated by the Roman authorities as a sect within Judaism (the followers of 'the Way') they frequently found themselves up against the power of the synagogue and the Sanhedrin. From the early 60s, however, the Roman authorities became more and more intolerant towards them, and, as the emperors increased their powers and made bolder claims for themselves, Christians found themselves in a persecuted minority.

Thus, whereas Paul in the 50s and 60s had been able to enjoy some of the privileges of being a Roman citizen and could appeal to Caesar for protection against the plots of the Jews, by the time we come to the Revelation to John in the 90s, Rome has become more like a totalitarian state. It is symbolized as 'the beast', whose ways are totally opposed to those of 'the Lamb'; and only those who bear the mark of the beast and consent to all that it stands for can live as full members of society.

In many parts of the Muslim world today Christians enjoy very considerable freedoms. There are other situations, however, in which Christians have good reason to feel they are up against the combined powers of mosque and state. Whenever there is such an alliance, Muslims are simply working out the logic of Muhammad's thinking about what is Caesar's and what is God's.

In this situation Christians need to sit with the apostle John and hear the voice in heaven which gives a different understanding of the way by which God establishes his kingdom on earth: 'Now God's salvation has come! Now God has shown his power as King! Now his Messiah has shown his authority! For the one who stood before our God and accused our brothers day and night has been thrown out of heaven. Our brothers won the victory over him by the blood of the Lamb and by the truth which they proclaimed; and they were willing to give up their lives and die. And be glad, you heavens, and all you that live there!' (Revelation 12:10–12).

In discussing this issue, however, Christians cannot simply stop at the New Testament period. They need to look at later history and recognize the many situations in which Christians have been in positions of political power, and have developed a relationship between church and state that is close to the Islamic understanding of the relationship between mosque and state. Examples here would include Constantine's Holy Roman Empire, Luther and the state churches of Germany, and Calvin's Geneva.

But if Muslims and Christians go back to their Scriptures, they can hardly fail to recognize the clear contrast between the attitude of Jesus and the attitude of Muhammad to political power. It is in pointing out these differences that Kenneth Cragg, in spite of his eirenic approach, feels compelled to say:

> In their origins, an abiding, and irreducible, disparity persists. It must be allowed to stand without compromise and without concealment.[4]

Is there any common denominator in our discussion of these six issues? Where there has been a parting of the ways between Christians and Muslims, perhaps it is because we are faced ultimately with a choice between two ways of thinking which cannot be reconciled. From the Christian perspective, Islam is utterly rational and reasonable in each of these areas – but only by the standards of human reason.

Jesus had to rebuke Peter for his very 'Islamic' thinking over the question of his suffering and death with the words, 'You think as men think, not as God thinks' (Mark 8:33, NEB). Could we apply this to the thinking of Islam at these points as well? *From the standpoint of the revelation of God in Christ*, Islam seems to be thinking 'as men think' in each of the six areas considered in this chapter.

■ By ruling out the possibility of incarnation and by reducing Jesus to the level of a prophet, it claims to be able to tell God what he can and cannot do in revealing himself to the human race. 'There are several ways of establishing contact or communication between man and God. The best would have been incarnation; but Islam has rejected it' (Muhammad Hamidullah).

- In its concept of inspiration it is ruled by an almost mechanical view of divine communication through a book as the final and supreme disclosure of God and the only guarantee of a reliable revelation.

- It refuses to contemplate the possibility that the oneness could be more complex than that of a single mathematical unit.

- Its diagnosis of human nature is too superficial and optimistic, and hardly touches the root of the problem, since it has little or nothing to say about its deep-seated corruption.

- Its message about forgiveness generally seems to leave people at best in uncertainty or complacency, and at worst in abject fear of what to expect on the day of judgment, and refuses to see in the life, death and resurrection of Jesus a demonstration of God's love.

- By linking truth to power, it seems blind to the corruption that so often goes with political power; and in offering the world its vision of a society under Islamic law, it associates the kingdom of God too closely with 'what is Caesar's'.

What we know of Peter after that decisive encounter at Caesarea Philippi suggests that he must have accepted this stinging rebuke from Jesus. 'You think as men think, not as God thinks'. *He must have changed his thinking about God because of what he saw in Jesus.*

28

Thinking biblically about Islam

Are there any ways in which we can use our own Scriptures to help us to evaluate Islam? Our own thinking about Islam is coloured by historical, political and sociological factors (whether we live in the East or the West). Should we not be able to find in the Bible a more objective reference point which will challenge our prejudices and help us to think in a more deeply Christian way about Islam?

The attempt to 'think biblically' may turn out to be a new discipline which cannot be taught by textbooks and cannot be included under any one of the basic disciplines of traditional theological study. There will be little place for simply collecting proof-texts. We shall rather need to draw on all the resources of biblical scholarship at our disposal to help us to understand the text in its proper historical context and then draw legitimate parallels with Islam.

We focus here on four specific points at which Christians have tried to relate the biblical text to the life and teaching of Muhammad.

28.1 'False prophets' and 'the Antichrist'

Many Christians turn instinctively to Matthew 24:23–27, believing that it provides the only truly biblical category for understanding Muhammad: 'False Messiahs and false prophets will appear.' They might also turn to 1 John 2:22–23: 'Who, then, is the liar? It is anyone who says that Jesus is not the Messiah. Such a person is the Enemy of Christ – he rejects both the Father and the Son. For whoever rejects the Son also rejects the Father; whoever accepts the Son has the Father also.'

There is a certain danger, however, in thinking that this is the beginning and end of thinking biblically about Islam. If we bind ourselves exclusively to these categories, we may find it impossible to enter sympathetically into the mind of Muslims. We will find it hard to appreciate the development of Muhammad's teaching; and we may fail to understand the true context and the real intention of Muhammad's denial of the divinity of Jesus.

Muhammad's public ministry did not begin with a rejection of Christian beliefs. It began with a passionate rejection of the idolatry of Mecca and a recall to the worship of the one Creator God. Muhammad must have been in contact with individual Christians and groups of Christians at many stages of his life. But it was only later in his public ministry, when he came in closer contact with Christians at Medina and elsewhere, that he felt compelled to extend his denunciation of idolatry to include Christian beliefs about Jesus as the Son of God.

There are good reasons for believing, however, that Muhammad did not really understand the Christian claim that Jesus was the Son of God. He may have rejected what he thought was a Christian belief because it seemed to be as crude as the polytheistic beliefs of the Meccans. We do not know how Muhammad would have responded if he had had first-hand knowledge of the gospel, and had understood how the Christian faith can be both monotheistic and trinitarian at the same time. But if what he rejected as blasphemous was at best a distortion, and at worst a travesty of Christian beliefs, are we really justified in thinking of Muhammad simply as a post-Christian heretic? Could it be that we are influenced too much by our historical sense which tells us that since Muhammad lived centuries after Jesus, he must be considered simply as a false prophet who rejected the New Testament gospel about Jesus?

28.2 Allah – the God of Islam?

Christians often feel uneasy with the word 'Allah', because it sounds so foreign, and 'Allah' is thought of simply as 'the God of Islam'. Since we have discussed some of the theological issues (chapter 25), our discussion here can focus on some of the words for 'God' used in the Bible, particularly in the Old Testament.

Allah in Arabic probably originally meant something like 'the God', that is 'the High God', the highest deity at the head of the whole pantheon of gods and goddesses in Arabia at the time of Muhammad, 'the supreme but ignored deity of the Arabs' (Michael Nazir-Ali).

Arabic and Hebrew are both Semitic languages and have a great deal in common, just as two Romance languages, such as French and Spanish, have much in common. The Hebrew word *'ēl* is translated either 'god' or 'God', depending on the context. The Arabic word for a 'god' is *ilah*. *Allah* is probably this same word combined with the definite article, meaning 'the God', that is 'the one and only God'. The Shahada (the Confession) uses both words: *la illaha* (there is no 'god') *ill-allah* (except 'God', Allah).

The Hebrew *'ēl* is sometimes found with the article, and becomes *ha'ēl*, as in Genesis 46:3: 'I am God [literally the God], the God of your fathers' (*cf.* Genesis 31:13; 35:1; 2 Samuel 22:31, 33, 48; Psalms 68:20–21; 77:15, *etc.*). The more common word for God in the Old Testament, however, is the plural form *'ᵉlōhîm*.

It seems that *'ēl* was thought of as the High God of *all* the Semitic peoples of the ancient Middle East. This is reflected in the account of Abraham's meeting with Melchizedek in Genesis 14. We are told that Melchizedek, the king of Salem, was 'priest of God Most High' (*'ēl 'elyôn*), and that he blessed Abraham with the words 'Blessed be Abram by God Most High, Creator of heaven and earth. And blessed be God Most High, who delivered your enemies into your hands' (14:19–20). Abraham did not assume that Melchizedek was worshipping a god who was totally different from the God he himself worshipped. He seemed to assume that they were worshipping one and the same God when he went on to say, 'I have raised my hand to the LORD [*i.e.* Yahweh], God Most High, Creator of heaven and earth' (Genesis 14:22).

If *'ēl* and *'ᵉlōhîm* are the Hebrew words for 'God', 'Yahweh' is his *personal name*, the name that distinguishes him from the gods of other peoples, such as Baal and Astarte (Canaanites), Dagon (Philistines), Chemosh (Moabites and Ammonites) and Molech (Ammonites). According to Exodus 3 and 6, the name 'Yahweh' was first revealed to Moses when God met him in the desert and commissioned him to lead the people of Israel out of Egypt: 'I am the LORD [*i.e.* Yahweh]. I appeared to Abraham, to Isaac and to Jacob as God Almighty, but by my name the LORD [Yahweh] I did not make myself known to them' (6:2–3).

If, however, the name 'Yahweh' was first revealed to Moses, how are we to explain the references to Yahweh before the time of Moses? How, for example, do we explain the sentence in Genesis 4:26, 'At that time men began to call on the name of the LORD' (*i.e.* Yahweh)? The apparent inconsistency is removed if we understand that the writer of Genesis assumed that the God who had revealed himself more fully to Moses as Yahweh was the one God who had been worshipped since the beginning. The revelation of the name 'Yahweh' did not introduce a new god to Moses and the people of Israel; rather, the one true God who had been worshipped from the beginning was now, through the experience of Moses, revealing more of himself and his nature as a holy and loving God who cares for his people.

This would also explain why Job is portrayed as someone who has personal dealings with Yahweh, in spite of the fact that he is a foreigner from the land of Uz (perhaps Edom or Aram?), with no connections with Israel, and living around the time of the patriarchs. At the beginning of the book we are told that Job 'fears God (*'elōhîm*) and shuns evil' (Job 1:8). But at the end of the book it is Yahweh, the covenant God of Israel, who speaks to Job out of the storm (38:1; 40:1; 42:1).

The message of the Old Testament, therefore, is that there is only one true God, and that this God has revealed himself in a unique way through the history of the people of Israel. The prophets constantly denounce the lower gods and goddesses, such as Baal and Astarte, who are worshipped by the surrounding peoples. They recall people to the worship of the one and only God who has revealed himself in a special way to the people of Israel in order to reveal himself more fully to the nations. Since there is no God apart from him, the prophets feel secure in pouring scorn on the gods of the nations who are nothing but 'idols' (Psalm 96:5; Deuteronomy 32:16–17; Isaiah 44:9–20).

At this point we can recognize similarities between the work of some of the Old Testament prophets and Muhammad. Just as the prophets campaigned vigorously against idolatry in all its forms, and called the people back to acknowledge the one God, so Muhammad called his people to worship Allah, the High God of the Arabs, who had become obscured by the three hundred or more gods and goddesses who were worshipped by the people of Mecca.

There is also a parallel with what happened when the Christian gospel first came to western and northern Europe. Christian missionaries used the words for the High God in the pantheon of different tribes, and it is from these that we get the words that we use today for 'God' – *Gott, Dieu* and the like. As the Christian faith became more widely accepted, the other gods and goddesses lost much of the power that they had had in people's minds, and eventually came to be remembered only, for example, in Norse mythology and in the English names of the days of the week (Tiw, Tuesday; Odin, Wednesday; Thor, Thursday; Frigga, Friday; Saturn, Saturday).

Much of the foreignness in the name 'Allah' begins to disappear when we see how close it is linguistically to the Hebrew words for 'God'. We should not, however, fall into the trap of saying that the God of the Bible is therefore the same as Allah, the God of Islam (see chapter 25). But this study of the words for God in the Old Testament should at least clear the air and help us to tackle the bigger theological questions involved in discussions of this kind.

28.3 Gideon

The picture of Muhammad which emerges from the earliest Meccan *suras* of the Qur'an and from the earliest traditions is of a man who combined a strong protest against idolatry with an attempt to bring unity among the tribes around Mecca and further afield in the Arabian peninsula. When we remember the thoroughly degenerate state of Arabian religion at the time of Muhammad, as well as the continuous conflicts between the tribes, we cannot but feel genuine amazement and admiration for all that he achieved in his lifetime in both these areas.

This picture bears a striking resemblance to the picture of Gideon in Judges. Here too is a man who combined a protest against idolatry ('Tear down your father's altar to Baal', 6:25ff.) with political and military action for his people ('Save Israel out of Midian's hand', 6:14).

If Muhammad's ministry began with the same fervour as Gideon's ministry, something certainly went wrong (from a Christian perspective) at a later stage. It is only right to remember that something also went wrong later in Gideon's life; 'Gideon made an idol from the gold and put it in his home town, Ophrah. All the Israelites abandoned God and went there to worship the idol. It was a trap for Gideon and his family' (8:22–28).

Is it too dangerous to draw such a parallel between Muhammad and Gideon? It must be emphasized that we are saying only that the cases are similar, not identical. Moreover, while we can see how Gideon fits into the plan of biblical history from Abraham to Jesus, we cannot of course fit Muhammad into the same scheme. But if there is any parallel at all, it should help us at the very least to feel more sympathy for the vision with which Muhammad began his ministry – the vision of the Arabian tribes united as one people, and united in the worship of the one true God.

28.4 Judaism and Islam

From his early contact with Jews, particularly with the Jewish community in Medina after the Hijra in 622, Muhammad must have absorbed something of the spirit and ritual of Jewish worship, as well as many stories from the Old Testament and later rabbinic legends. This background should help us to understand not only the most obvious similarities between the doctrines of Judaism and Islam (such as their understanding of the oneness of God), but also some of the deeper similarities between the spirit of the two religions (such as their understanding of the role of the law). It should therefore make it easier for us to put ourselves in the place of Muslims and to see Jesus as they see him.

It requires effort and discipline, however, to read the gospels in this way. We naturally tend to think of the disciples as Christian believers right from the start instead of seeing them as devout, orthodox Jews. But what if we take off our 'Christian spectacles' for a moment and try to see Jesus against the background of Old Testament assumptions and several centuries of Jewish traditions? We then begin to realize that Muslims react to Christian claims about Jesus (if they have not misunderstood them) in the same way as the High Priest reacted to Jesus' claims about himself: 'You have heard his blasphemy' (Mark 14:63–64). It is the same instinct, the same jealous concern for the oneness of God, that makes it unthinkable that a mere human being could be associated with God in anything other than a creature–Creator relationship. We begin to see also that there is an understandable logic behind Peter's objection to the idea that the Messiah must suffer and die: how *could* God let his representative on earth be so humiliated? Surely God must vindicate his servants the prophets in the eyes of the world!

This parallel between Judaism and Islam needs to be qualified at three points. In the first place, Muhammad was too much of a creative genius to be described as one who simply 'borrowed' from Jewish sources. Everything that he absorbed was stamped with the imprint of his own creative mind, as we see in the distinctive thrust that is given to the story of Joseph (*sura* 12).

Secondly, some of Muhammad's teaching was influenced, if not actually determined, by the negative response he received from the Jews in Medina. His early openness soon turned to bitter hostility when he finally saw that he had no chance of winning them over as a community. Thus, for example, having earlier prayed with his face to Jerusalem as the Jews did, he now began to pray facing Mecca. There had been nothing in the Old Testament or in rabbinic tradition which linked Abraham with Mecca. But Muhammad now claimed that Abraham and Ishmael had been associated with the building of the Ka'ba in Mecca. He claimed that Abraham was a Muslim, and in the words of Alfred Guillaume, 'thus at a stroke the primitive and apostolic character of Islam was established'. Any attempt to draw a parallel between Judaism and Islam, then, must take into account this tortuous love–hate relationship between Muhammad and the Jews which has coloured relations between Muslims (particularly Arabs) and Jews ever since, not least in the twentieth century.

Thirdly, in spite of the similarities between the two religions, the Jewish people had special privileges because of their place in God's plan of salvation: 'They are God's people . . . he made his covenants with them and gave them the Law; they have the true worship; they have received God's promises; they are descended from the famous Hebrew ancestors: and Christ, as a human being, belongs to their race' (Romans 9:4–5, GNB). This was Paul's understanding of the privileges of the Jewish people simply by virtue of being descended from Abraham through the line of Isaac, and can be applied to the Muslim only in the sense that the covenant promises of God are now open to all who turn to Jesus, as Peter says on the day of Pentecost: 'God's promise was made to you and your children, and to all who are far away – all whom the Lord our God calls to himself' (Acts 2:39, GNB).

If, however, these qualifications are not serious enough to make us abandon the attempt to see Islam in the light of New Testament Judaism, this approach may also help us to come to terms with the bewildering variety of Christian responses to Islam. Is it a religion inspired by the devil, or a 'valid' religion which offers valuable insights for all? Is it a Christian heresy like Jehovah's Witnesses, or can it sometimes be a genuine preparation for the gospel?

We find similar problems in the responses to Judaism in the pages of the New Testament. Paul's verdict about the Jews in his letter to the Thessalonians (written in about 50 or 51 AD) sounds very harsh: 'The Jews . . . killed the Lord Jesus and the prophets, and persecuted us. How displeasing they are to God! How hostile they are to everyone! They even tried to stop us from preaching to the Gentiles the message that would bring them salvation. In this way they have brought to completion all the sins they have always committed. And now God's anger has at last come down on them!' (1 Thessalonians 2:14–16, GNB). In his letter to the Romans (written in 57 AD), however, he reveals how he actually prays for his fellow Jews: 'I am speaking the truth; I belong to Christ and I do not lie. My conscience, ruled by the Holy Spirit, also assures me that I am not lying when I say how great is my sorrow, how endless the pain in my heart for my people, my own flesh and blood! For their sake I could wish that I myself were under God's curse and separated from Christ' (Romans 9:1–3, GNB).

In his travels in Asia Minor Paul made it a matter of policy to go first to the synagogue in every city, believing that those who knew the Old Testament Scriptures would be the first to respond to the good news about Jesus. When we come to the book of Revelation (written some thirty years after Paul's death), however, the risen Lord's description of one particular synagogue in Asia Minor paints it in a very different light: 'I will make those of Satan's synagogue, who claim to be Jews but are lying frauds, come and fall down at your feet; and they shall know that you are my beloved people' (Revelation 3:9, NEB).

If we are confused by this ambivalence, we need to go back to the words of Jesus himself and ask how it was that he could say to one Jew, 'You are not far from the kingdom of God' (Mark 12:34), but on another occasion to a group of Jews, 'You are of your father the devil' (John 8:44, RSV). Part of the answer needs to be that there is a difference between 'Judaism' and 'Jews' – between the body of beliefs and traditions, and the people who hold them with varying degrees of conviction. We also need to be suspicious of sweeping generalizations and simple categories, whether they spring from an attitude that is excessively generous or excessively negative.

If we base our understanding of Judaism only on the scribes and the Pharisees described in the New Testament, we may be incapable of recognizing a Nicodemus who has grown up in the same tradition but is reaching out for something more (John 3:1–13). If we think that all our Muslim friends are as dogmatic as Caiaphas (Mark 14:63–64), we will fail to notice those who are as open, but as cautious, as Gamaliel (Acts 5:33–39). If we think that all Muslims are in the same category as the members of the synagogue of Philadelphia (Revelation 3:9), we can hardly fail to rebuff any leader (such as Jairus) who comes with his deep personal need and a faith that reaches out to Jesus (Mark 5:22ff.). If the practice of Islam can make some Muslims as self-confident as the Pharisee (Luke 18:11ff.), can it not sometimes lead others to the point where God can say to them, as he did to the God-fearing proselyte Cornelius, 'God is pleased with your prayers and works of charity, and is ready to answer you. And now send some men to Joppa for a certain man whose full name is Simon Peter . . .' (Acts 10:4ff.).

29

Counting the cost of conversion

We have already noted the statement of Abul A'la Mawdudi: 'Islam is a one-way door, you can enter through it but you cannot leave.'[1] A Christian response to this assumption is summed up just as sharply by Kenneth Cragg: 'A faith which you are not free to leave becomes a prison, and no self-respecting faith should be a prison for those within it.'[2]

It is a sad fact that in spite of its tolerant attitudes in many areas, Islam does not find it easy to accept the idea of Muslims becoming Christians. Conversion to Christianity (or to any other religion) is generally regarded as a betrayal of family and community, and as apostasy which deserves the severest punishment.

Muslims who express an interest in the Christian faith are often subject to strong pressures, and those who take the step of being baptized frequently experience opposition and hostility in the home, at work and in the wider community. Many converts in the past have had to leave their homes for safety, and some have been killed. In some communities attitudes are becoming more liberal and tolerant.

Christians also find it hard to accept the idea of fellow Christians renouncing their faith to accept a different one. Even so, we can hardly escape the conclusion that Islam seems to have its own special reasons for reacting strongly to the idea of conversion.

At some stage in our study, therefore, we need to stop and consider the possible implications of what we are doing. Does our concern for Muslims go beyond good-neighbourliness and the desire for mutual understanding and tolerance? Are we working for anything more than racial harmony and social justice? What if Muslims are attracted by the person of Christ and want to express their faith openly in some way? Do we have any idea of the possible cost for Muslims who want to become disciples of Jesus? And if we personally are involved in any way in the process, do we appreciate the possible cost to ourselves?

In facing these questions, we need, first, to understand how Muslims view the thought of fellow Muslims leaving their faith and their community, and secondly, how to think through several specific issues that may need to be faced.

'Conversion' as seen by Islam

1. The following are the main passages in the Qur'an which teach how Muslims should deal with those who renounce the faith of Islam:

> They long that ye should disbelieve even as they disbelieve, that ye may be upon a level (with them). So choose not friends from them till they forsake their homes in the way of Allah; if they turn back (to enmity) then take them and kill them wherever ye find them, and choose no friend nor helper from among them (4:89).

> Lo! those who disbelieve after their (profession of) belief, and afterward grow violent in disbelief: their repentance will not be accepted. And such are those who are astray.
> Lo! those who disbelieve, and die in disbelief, the (whole) earth full of gold would not be accepted from such an one if it were offered as a ransom (for his soul). Theirs will be a painful doom and they will have no helpers (3:90–91).

> Whoso becometh a renegade and dieth in his disbelief: such are they whose works have fallen both in the world and the Hereafter. Such are rightful owners of the Fire: they will abide therein (2:217).

If we want to find out how Muslims in the past and present have interpreted these verses and applied them to the issue of conversion, we need to consult Qur'anic commentaries, the *hadith* literature (tradition), and *shari'a* law, and note the variety of modern statements on the subject.

2. A study of Muslim commentaries shows that, in their original context, none of these verses is concerned with Muslims becoming Christians. Most of them deal with those who were known as 'hypocrites' – idolaters who made a profession of Islam, but who were not sincere and later went back to their former way of life.

There is considerable diversity among Muslim commentators in their interpretation of the key verses. Al-Baidhawi, the famous commentator of the thirteenth century, gives a very strict interpretation in his comment on the verse 4:89:

> Whoever turns back from his belief (*irtadda*), openly or secretly, take him and kill him wheresoever ye find him, like any other infidel. Separate yourself from him altogether. Do not accept intercession in his regard.[3]

Yusuf Ali, a modern commentator, relates the same verse (4:89) to the special circumstances after the Battle of Uhud:

> When the desertion of the Hypocrites at Uhud nearly caused a disaster to the Muslim cause, there was great feeling among the Muslims of Medina against them. One party wanted to put them to the sword; another to leave them alone. The actual policy pursued avoided both extremes, and was determined by these verses. It was clear that they were a danger to the Muslim community if they were admitted into its counsels, and in any case they were a source of demoralisation. But while every caution was used, no extreme measures were taken against them. On the contrary, they were given a chance of making good. If they made sacrifice for the cause ('flee from what is forbidden'), their conduct purged their previous cowardice, and their sincerity entitled them to be taken back. But if they deserted the Muslim community again, they were treated as enemies, with the additional penalty of desertion which is enforced by all nations actually at war.[4]

Maulvi Muhammad Ali's comment on 2:217 probably represents the attitude of many moral liberal (but orthodox) Muslims:

The persons spoken of in this passage are the apostates, or those who 'turn from their religion'. A wrong impression exists among non-Muslims, and among some Muslims as well, that the Holy Qur'an requires those who apostatize from Islam to be put to death, but this is not true ... As the plain words of the Qur'an show, what is stated here is that the opponents of Islam exerted themselves to the utmost to turn back the Muslims from their faith, by their cruel persecutions, and therefore if a Muslim actually went back to unbelief he would be a loser in this life as well as in the next, because the desertion of Islam would not only deprive him of the spiritual advantages which he could obtain by remaining a Muslim, but also of the physical advantages which must accrue to the Muslims through the triumph of Islam. And neither here nor anywhere else in the Qur'an is there even a hint of the infliction of capital or any other punishment on the apostate.[5]

3. The *hadith* literature (tradition) contains a variety of sayings of the Prophet about apostasy, and it is here that we find reference to the death penalty, which is not mentioned in the Qur'an. One saying reported by al-Bukhari (ninth century) has been widely quoted both by Muslims and by critics of Islam:

It is related from Ikrimah that he said, 'Hypocrites were brought to Ali and he burnt them.' The news of that reached Ibn Abbas, and he said, 'If it had been I, I would not have burnt them, because of the prohibition of the Apostle of God: Do not punish with the punishment of God; but I would certainly have killed them according to the word of the Apostle: Whoever changes his religion, kill him.'[6]

The *Shorter Encyclopedia of Islam* quotes this saying of the Prophet reported by Ibn Abbas: 'Slay (or behead) him who changes his religion.'[7] According to another tradition reported by Ibn Abbas and 'A'isha, the Prophet said that the blood of a fellow Muslim should never be shed except in the case of the adulterer, the murderer and the person 'who abandons his religion and separates himself from the community.'[8] The traditions differ, however, on whether or not apostates should be given an opportunity to repent. Some traditions say that God does not accept the repentance of an apostate, while others say that in some cases even the Prophet forgave apostates.

4. The traditional response to apostasy in *shari'a* law is summed up by a Sudanese Islamic scholar, Abdullahi Ahmed An-Na'im, in these terms:

> On the basis of these *Sunna*, and standard commentaries on the Qur'an, traditional Islamic schools of jurisprudence are unanimous in holding that apostasy is punishable by death, although they differ on such questions as to whether to execute the sentence immediately or grant the apostate a reprieve of a few days in order to allow him time to reflect and reconsider his position in the hope that he may recant and re-embrace Islam, thereby saving his life as well as his soul. There is also disagreement on whether a female apostate is to be killed or merely imprisoned until she returns to the faith. Her offense is not regarded by any school or jurist to be of less magnitude, the disagreement merely relates to whether the appropriate punishment is death or life imprisonment.[9]

The *Shorter Encyclopedia of Islam* describes the situation that has prevailed since the last century:

> In former Turkish territory and Egypt as well as in Muslim lands under European rule since the middle of the nineteenth century, under European influence the execution of an apostate on a kadi's [judge's] sentence has been abolished, but we still have imprisonment and deportation; nevertheless renegades are not sure of their lives as their Muslim relatives endeavour secretly to dispose of them by poison or otherwise. Occasionally modern Islamic writers (Ahmadiya movement) endeavour to prove that Islam knows of no death penalty for apostasy; the Indian apologist Muhammad Ali

lays great stress on the fact that there is not once an indication of the death penalty in the Qur'an.[10]

5. Muslim views today cover the same spectrum of positions that we have noted in the past. Rafiq Zakaria, for example, an Indian Muslim, writing after the Salman Rushdie affair, is at pains to give a very liberal interpretation of Islamic teaching on apostasy:

> For an apostate, or *murtadd*, 'one who turns back' from Islam, there is no punishment in the Qur'an. According to one verse: 'O true believers, whoever of you apostatizes from his religion, God will certainly bring other people to take his place, whom He will love and who will love Him, who shall be humble towards the believers, but severe to the unbelievers. They shall fight for the religion of God and shall not fear the obloquy of the detractor' (5:54). There are no recorded cases of the Prophet punishing those Muslims who renege upon their faith. There is, however, misconception about the punishment for apostasy, which has distorted the image of Islam. It has arisen because of classical jurists who have opined that the punishment for apostasy in Islam is death. But Muslims subscribe to the concept of 'freedom of worship', and demand the right to convert non-Muslims. The Qur'an makes it clear that 'there is no compulsion in religion'; how then can it pronounce the death penalty on those who 'turn away' from Islam, or 'turn back' on it? On the contrary, the Qur'an mentions that in place of those who have given up the right path, God will bring better and more faithful ones . . .
>
> It is true that if, during a war, some Muslims committed treason and went over to the other side, then they were put to death on being captured. But that was for being traitors, not apostates. This is clear from many traditions reported in *Sahih al-Bukhari*, the most reliable book of traditions. Unfortunately, there is one tradition – 'Whoever changes his religion shall be put to death' – which contradicts the entire tenor of a mass of other traditions and, therefore, cannot be relied upon. It also

contradicts the verses in the Qur'an that speak of freedom of worship. Besides, it makes a general proposition
and does not specifically refer to a change of religion by
Muslims alone. The *Encyclopedia of Islam* has correctly
pointed out: 'In the Qur'an, the apostate is threatened
with punishment in the next world.' He can be killed if
he joins the enemies of God and forsakes his religion,
but that would not be merely for changing religion.[11]

The late Isma'il al-Faruqi, a professor of Islamic studies in the
USA, sums up the attitude of most orthodox Muslims:

Islamic law *does* allow a person to exit from the Islamic
state.

However, the Islamic state has, of course, to protect
itself – and . . . conversion so often seems to be tantamount to subversion of Islamic values and existence.

This was the situation certainly which existed in the
original Islamic state in Madinah [Medina] during the
prophet's life, where for a person to convert out of
Islam meant joining the polytheistic camp of Makkah
[Mecca] which was in a constant state of war against the
Muslims. Now obviously that was the situation in
which, for political reasons, legislation was formulated
that conversion out of Islam is not to be tolerated.
When, later, Islam became dominant in Madinah and
Makkah, and subsequently built an empire for itself,
this legislation continued to be observed although you
might argue that there was empirically no use for it;
conversion represented no threat at all to the security of
the Muslim community.

But would you really consider revoking that legislation altogether and grant unrestricted freedom to anyone to change his religion according to the Islamic
principle that everyone has the right to 'convince and be
convinced', when we have heard of what is happening
in Indonesia? What we have heard about the situation
confronting Islam in Indonesia is like a re-enactment of
Madinah and Makkah. When politics get so inter-
mingled with Christian mission, what sort of situation

would you expect if total religious freedom were allowed? Give us the assurance that political involvement in mission will cease, and that power politics will no longer intrude, then the principles of religious freedom would be approved by every sensible Muslim on earth. We Muslims are at the receiving end of the line of injustice. We haven't emerged yet from two centuries of colonialization.[12]

Dr Syed M. Darsh, an Egyptian Muslim living in London, sums up the orthodox attitude to apostasy by quoting Aisha Abdul-Rahman, professor of Tafsir and Higher Studies at the al-Azhar University in Cairo, in an article about Salman Rushdie written in February 1994:

> She chides 'those who have fallen into the trap of apostasy'. They 'confuse what is established as a fundamental Islamic law that there is no compulsion in religion, that we Muslims are not allowed to force any one to abandon his religion', with the Islamic law about *riddah*, apostasy. She says, 'The apostate is a person of treason: treason to his family, his people and his nation. He is an avowed enemy of them all.'[13]

6. The most significant test of Muslim attitudes to conversion, however, is not the statements of jurists and theologians of the past and present, but what actually happens in practice. However liberal and tolerant Muslim leaders can be, what really seems to count at the end of the day is the attitude of a particular family to one or more of their number who seem to be turning their backs on their religion, and bringing shame and dishonour on the whole family.

Al-Faruqi explains that when this happens, 'we are not talking about an Islamic state acting under Islamic law, but a village group or a city group aroused by the idea that they have lost one of their fellow members so they go and kill him or put difficulties in his path. This is not an application of the Islamic law.'[14] In many cases, however, it is hard to draw a clear dividing line between what happens in a local community and what is done by the group in the name of Islam. However charitable we want to be, we have to reckon with the fact that in the majority of cases Muslims who want to become disciples of Christ are thought of and treated as apostates and outcasts from their family and community.

7. It needs to be pointed out that there is a real tension, if not an inconsistency, at this point between the traditional Islamic responses to conversion and the UN Universal Declaration of Human Rights. This charter has been officially accepted by most countries, including Islamic states, and states in which Muslims are a majority. It allows the freedom not only to hold and practise one's own religion, but also to change one's religion. Article 18 states:

> Everyone has the right to freedom of thought, conscience and religion; this right includes freedom to change his religion or belief, and freedom, either alone or in community with others and in public or private, to manifest his religion or belief in teaching, practice, worship and observance.

The inconsistency between this Declaration of Human Rights and the practice of many Muslim states has been pointed out by Abdullahi Ahmed An-Na'im:

> The inescapable conclusion . . . is that it is inconsistent with modern notions of religious freedom, an internationally acknowledged basic human right and generally accepted fundamental civil liberty guaranteed by most constitutions throughout the world.[15]

30

Facing the political challenge of Islam

'In our day,' says Jens Christensen, 'the subject of politics is one of the most fundamental and difficult problems we have to contend with in coming to grips with Islam.'[1] This is particularly the case in situations where Christians are a small minority living among Muslim majorities or in Islamic states. But even in western countries where Muslims are minorities, as we have already noted, they are making their presence felt through requests and demands in various areas of public life. In education and family law, for example, they are asking for certain rights to be granted to them.

We are therefore forced to ask general questions such as these:

■ Why does Islam seem to be such a political religion – so much more political than Christianity as we know it today?

■ What is the Muslim vision for the world? Do all Muslims want or expect Islam to triumph? If so, is it to triumph through persuasion or through force, or through both?

We also need to ask detailed questions such as these:

■ How are Christian minorities treated in various Islamic countries? What are their rights as minorities? What kinds of discrimination do they experience? How should they respond, for example, to pressures for further implementation of *shari'a* law?

■ How are Muslims treated as minorities living in non-Muslim countries? What kinds of discrimination do they experience? What should be the Christian response to complaints about the way they are treated in this situation?

279

In order to begin to answer these questions, we need to trace the development of Islamic teaching about the treatment of non-Muslims since the time of the Prophet to the present day. Only against this background will we be able to consider what might be distinctive about Christian attitudes and responses to these aspects of the challenge of Islam.

30.1 Islamic theory and practice past and present
Muhammad – prophet and statesman

As we have seen, for the first twelve years of his ministry, Muhammad was essentially a prophet calling the people of Mecca to renounce idolatry and worship the one true God and gathering around him a small group of disciples. The *Hijra*, the 'migration' of Muhammad and his followers from Mecca to Medina, however, marked a turning-point in his life, since it meant that he now became both prophet and statesman. From now on he led the Muslims into battle and claimed to receive from God all the detailed legislation required for the establishment of the Islamic community in Medina.

The Islamic concern for the life of the community, therefore, together with all the political interest that is part of that concern, springs ultimately from the example of the Prophet. This is how Kenneth Cragg sums up the significance of this 'progression from preaching to ruling':

> So it was that he grew steadily more and more pre-occupied with the ultimate issues of how his truth would succeed . . . His life came to a watershed in what is the central issue of all religious history, namely the relation of truth to power. The city of Islamic origins, Mecca, is linked with another city of Islamic statehood, Medina . . . The search for religious recognition became a quest for political power . . .
>
> The student is here at the heart of the deepest issue in the psyche of Muhammad. It used to be assumed, in some quarters, that his character underwent a certain declension and that an initial sincerity came to be undermined by baser motives. But this is to miss the real point. The real problem is deeper. The urge for power is more truly seen here, not as a lapse but a logic,

not something now less sincere and idealist, but more so in a different guise. How is a prophet sincere if he becomes reconciled to non-success, or refuses to undertake what success requires when his words, long sustained, have failed of response?

There may have been other factors in Muhammad's reach for power. There were economic and social motives. There was also that Arab 'manliness' and the tradition of battle in the picture. But, in the last analysis, Islam sees the militancy of Muhammad as the legitimate and appropriate progression from preaching to ruling, and all within the will of God.[2]

Qur'anic teaching about the treatment of Jews and Christians

While the Qur'an is generally very critical of Jews, some verses are remarkably positive about Christians:

Thou wilt find the most vehement of mankind in hostility to those who believe (to be) the Jews and the idolaters. And thou wilt find the nearest of them in affection to those who believe (to be) those who say: Lo! We are Christians. That is because there are among them priests and monks, and because they are not proud.

When they listen to that which hath been revealed unto the messenger, thou seest their eyes overflow with tears because of their recognition of the Truth. They say: Our Lord, we believe. Inscribe us among the witnesses (5:82–83; cf. 2:62; 5:55–60; 22:40).

Other passages reflect the kind of dialogues which Muhammad must have had with Jews and Christians, and the argument and appeals he used to persuade them to accept his message:

Say: O People of the Scripture! Come to an agreement between us and you: that we shall worship none but Allah, and that we shall ascribe no partner unto Him, and that none of us shall take others for lords beside Allah . . . (3:64).

O People of the Scripture! Why disbelieve ye in the revelations of Allah, when ye (yourselves) bear witness (to their truth)? (3:70; *cf.* 3:19–20; 5:14–19; 29:46–47; 57:27).

In other verses, however, there is a more critical attitude towards Jews and Christians, which no doubt developed in the context of their coolness towards him, and later, their rejection of his message:

O ye who believe! Take not the Jews and Christians for your friends. They are friends one to another. He among you who taketh them for friends is (one) of them. Lo! Allah guideth not wrongdoing folk (5:51).

Fight against such of those who have been given the Scripture as believe not in Allah nor the Last Day, and forbid not that which Allah hath forbidden by His messenger, and follow not the religion of truth, until they pay tribute readily, being brought low.
And the Jews say: Ezra is the son of Allah, and the Christians say: The Messiah is the son of Allah. That is their saying with their mouths. They imitate the saying of those who disbelieved of old. Allah (Himself) fighteth against them. How perverse are they! (9:29–30).

These last verses are particularly important because the words for the 'tribute' (*jizya*) in 9:29 is the word that was used for centuries for the tax paid by non-Muslim subjects living under Muslim rule. A. Yusif Ali comments on the word as follows:

Jizya: the root meaning is compensation. The derived meaning, which became the technical meaning, was a poll-tax levied from those who did not accept Islam, but were willing to live under the protection of Islam, and were thus tacitly willing to submit themselves to its ideals being enforced in the Muslim State, saving only their personal liberty of conscience as regarded themselves. There was no amount fixed for it, and in any case it was merely symbolical – an acknowledgment that those whose religion was tolerated would in their turn not interfere with the preaching and progress of Islam.[3]

The treatment of Jews and Christians by the first Muslims

Jews and Christians who refused to submit to Islam were allowed to continue to practise their own religion. This system was given the name *dhimma*, which means literally a contract or obligation. The assumption was that the Muslim community accepted responsibility for these Jews and Christians, who, as *dhimmis*, constituted tolerated and protected minorities living under Muslim rule.

Early Muslim tradition records the text of treaties which Muhammad made with Jewish and Christian communities in Arabia. This, for example, was the agreement made with the Christian communities in Najran in the south of Arabia (the modern Yemen):

> This is a letter from Muhammad the prophet, the Messenger of God, to the people of Najran. To him belonged the decision upon them in respect of every fruit, yellow, white, or black, and every slave; but he was gracious to them and left (them) all that for the payment of 2,000 suits of clothes, namely, suits of ounces, of which a thousand are to be handed over each year ... Najran and their followers have protection of God and the *dhimmah* of Muhammad the prophet, the Messenger of God, for themselves, their community, their land, and their goods, both those who are absent and those who are present, and for their churches and services (no bishop will be removed from his episcopate, no monk from his monastic position, and no church-warden from his church-wardenship) and for all, great or little, that is under their hands ... On the terms stated in this document (they have) protection of God and *dhimmah* of the prophet for ever, until God comes with His command, if they are loyal and perform their obligations well, not being burdened by wrong.[4]

In spite of these agreements, however, the Christians and Jews were expelled from Arabia some years later, during the time of the caliph 'Umar, on the basis of a saying reported to have come from Muhammad himself. This is how these expulsions are recorded in the *Life of the Apostle of God* by Ibn Ishaq:

> When God took away His prophet, Abu Bakr continued the arrangements (with the Jews of Khaybar) until his death, and so did 'Umar for the beginning of his amirate. Then he heard that the apostle had said in his last illness, 'Two religions shall not remain together in the peninsula of the Arabs' and he made enquiries until he got confirmation. Then he sent to the Jews saying, 'God has given permission for you to emigrate,' quoting the apostle's words: 'If anyone has an agreement with the apostle let him bring it to me and I will carry it out; he who has no such agreement let him get ready to emigrate.' Thus 'Umar expelled those who had no agreement with the apostle.[5]

The so-called 'Code', 'Ordinance' or 'Pact of 'Umar'

This is the name of a document which purports to be a response from 'Umar, who ruled as the second caliph between 634 and 644, to the Muslims who were demanding that the lands of Iraq and Syria (Palestine) should be shared out among the Muslim conquerors. It is likely that the document is a compilation which reflects a later stage in the codification of Islamic law concerning conquered peoples. It is significant for our purposes, however, because it summarizes what came to be regarded as Islamic practice, if not law, concerning Jewish and Christian *dhimmis* for centuries. In return for toleration and protection from the Muslim rulers, these are the requirements laid down for Jews and Christians:

■ All non-Muslim males had to pay a poll-tax (*jizya*) to the Muslim state as an expression of their submission to Muslim rule. (Many documents say they should experience some kind of humiliation while making the payment – *e.g.* by being struck on the neck.) If they owned land, they also had to pay a land tax (*kharaj*).

- Non-Muslims could not engage in military service, since this would involve them in *jihad*, Holy War.

- Jews and Christians were not allowed to build new churches or synagogues or repair those in areas occupied by Muslims.

- They were not allowed to display the cross outside churches or to hold public religious processions outside.

- Their houses could not be built taller than those of Muslims.

- Their clothes should be different from the clothes worn by Muslims. Often they had to wear a badge to mark them out from Muslims, and sometimes they were required to shave their heads.

- They were forbidden to ride on horses, and had to ride on mules or donkeys.

- They must show respect to Muslims – for instance by giving up their seats to them.

While these requirements were not always enforced, there were times when they were enforced rigidly in different parts of the Islamic Empire. Michael Nazir-Ali explains the legacy of the Code of 'Umar:

Emancipation from the provisions of this pact came only gradually and often painfully, for the non-Muslim populations. It was not until the early years of this century that the pact as such ceased to be operative in most Muslim lands. Vestiges of it survive, however, in the way *expatriate* non-Muslims are treated in the State of Saudi Arabia and in the Gulf. Even in the relatively tolerant parts of the Gulf States, church buildings have to be away from the centres of towns, many congregations must share one building (24 in one instance), no display of Christian symbols is allowed and the ringing of church bells is not permitted. In Saudi Arabia . . . no church buildings are allowed at all and even services in the homes of Christians are liable to be broken up by the religious police.[6]

Jews and Christians were in a special position because they were regarded as 'People of the Book'. 'Idolaters' had no such special privileges, and it seems that in the early years they were offered the simple choice between submission to Islam and death. Later, however, when Muslims found themselves ruling over large numbers of peoples of other faiths who refused to accept Islam, the protected status given to Jews and Christians was extended to include people such as Zoroastrians, Buddhists and Hindus.

Classical statements of 'jihad'

This word, which means literally 'effort', came to be a technical term referring to the effort of Muslim believers for the rule of God and the supremacy of Islam in the world. Many Muslims in recent times have distinguished between *jihad* in this sense and the more inward and spiritual struggle in which all believers seek to overcome all that is unworthy within themselves. In spite of these more recent developments in the meaning of the word, however, we should be aware of how Muslim thinkers of the past have understood this concept. The following statement comes from Ibn Khaldun (1333–1406), the famous Arab historian:

> In the Muslim community, the holy war is a religious duty, because of the universalism of the (Muslim) mission and (the obligation to) convert everybody to Islam either by persuasion or by force. Therefore, caliphate and royal authority are united (in Islam), so that the person in charge can devote the available strength to both of them (religion and politics) at the same time.
>
> The other religious groups did not have a universal mission, and the holy war was not a religious duty to them, save only for purposes of defense. It has thus come about that the person in charge of religious affairs (in other religious groups) is not concerned with power politics at all. (Among them) royal authority comes to those who have it, by accident and in some way that has nothing to do with religion. It comes to them as the necessary result of group feeling, which by its nature seeks to obtain royal authority, as we have mentioned before, and not because they are under obligation to

gain power over other nations, as is the case with Islam. They are merely required to establish their religion among their own people.[7]

He names the main groups of Christians in his day and continues with this comment:

> We do not think that we should blacken the pages of this book with discussion of their dogmas of unbelief. In general, they are well known. All of them are unbelief. This is clearly stated in the noble Qur'an. (To) discuss or argue those things with them is not up to us. It is (for them to choose between) conversion to Islam, payment of the poll tax, or death.[8]

Such a statement needs to be understood in its fifteenth-century context. And Christians need to be aware that some Christians in the past have had similar aspirations about the supremacy of Christianity as a force in the world. But Ibn Khaldun's statement is particularly significant because of the way he underlines the theological reasons for the difference he perceives between Islamic and Christian ideas about political power.

Some contemporary Muslim views

We need here to recognize the wide variety of views represented among Muslims.

This, for example, is a contemporary statement of how one Nigerian Muslim leader of the Qadiriyya Order understands the concept of *jihad* today:

> If you are living with a non-Muslim in your area and you want him to go, you simply call him and tax him. You tell him three times that he will live in your neighbourhood but only on condition that he pays tax . . . If he refuses to pay tax and still insists on living with you, on your own land, then you have to advise him on three occasions that I will be coming at so, so, so date to wage a war against you. Only when he consistently proves obstinate are you allowed, in Islam, to wage war against him. The intention is to ensure that he is well prepared.

In particular countries (such as Pakistan) some Muslims have been calling for the Code of 'Umar to be reintroduced as the basis for dealing with non-Muslim minorities in Muslim states.

Professor Mohamed Talbi, a Tunisian Muslim historian, believes that the *dhimma* system must be regarded by Muslims as a thing of the past:

> We face here an extremely complex history. In seeking to overcome this historically contentious question we need, today, to approach this problem with much realism, departing from our respective traditions and in accordance with our present aspirations. Today we live in a world where *dhimmis* no longer should exist. It has become imperative and absolutely indispensable to shelve this notion in the cupboard of history, something which from the point of view of Islam I deem absolutely possible. We face here an evolution which, according to my point of view, is part and parcel of the very meaning of Islam which today subscribes – with certain reserves – to human rights.[9]

In a book entitled *The Struggle within Islam: The Conflict between Religion and Politics*, Rafiq Zakaria writes out of his experience of the Muslim community in India. The book traces 'the continuous fight between the holders of power and theologians', and is a sustained protest against the many different forms that fundamentalism has taken through the centuries. It commends the secularist approach as the only one that is true to the spirit of Islam and appropriate in the world today:

> In their muddled zeal the modern fundamentalists forget that it was not Hasan al-Banna, Maududi, and Sayyid Qutb who freed the Muslims from colonial exploitation and gave them a better and more secure future, but Ataturk, who despite his heresies, saved Turkey from the clutches of European power; Jinnah, a non-practising Muslim, who single-handedly created the most powerful Muslim state in the world; Nasser, who liberated the Arabs from the foreign yoke and gave them new strength and hope; Sukarno, who brought

freedom to more Muslims than any other leader and united the Indonesians under one banner; Tenko Abdul Rahman, who breathed new life into the Malaysian Muslims and made them a force in South-East Asia; Mujibur Rahman, an avowed secularist, who founded the second biggest Muslim state (Bangladesh) in the world; Qaddafi, whom the fundamentalists disown, but who challenged the might of America in North Africa; Boumedienne, who fought the imperialists and provided a socialist system to their people. These and many more in the secular mould were the real builders of modern Islam. Without them the Muslims would not have breathed the fresh air of liberty and equality; without them they would not have been able to hold their heads high in the comity of nations; without them they would have continued to be hewers of wood and drawers of water. These leaders might not have been pious and puritanical, orthodox and traditional; some of them might not have offered their prayers regularly; most of them did not fit into the straitjacket of scholastic theology; but they all brought Muslims out of the sloughs of despondency and despair and made them once again a power to reckon with ... despite their lapses and faults they have taken Islam ahead and by their secular outlook ensured the future of nearly a billion Muslims all over the world.[10]

30.2 Christian responses

How then should Christians respond to the wide variety of ways in which they experience the challenge of Islam on the political level? Much will depend on the local situation. But if there is an opportunity for Christians to stand back from their immediate situation, these are some of the most important principles which should determine their response. Taken together, they can at least provide a framework within which Christians can decide how to face the challenge in particular contexts.

Accurate information and responsible publicity

Part of our problem is that people in all communities are influenced by impressions, prejudices and stereotypes, especially as they are communicated by the media; and our information is often one-sided, misleading or hopelessly out of date. It is therefore essential that we determine to be scrupulously accurate and honest in our reporting of what is happening in different countries. We need to avoid making generalizations, recognizing that no two countries are the same, and that situations are constantly changing.

In its work on religion in what used to be known as 'the Communist world', the research centre Keston College has provided an excellent model of accurate and honest reporting, which should be emulated in all reporting about relations between Christians and Muslims in different countries. It is significant that Keston College was reporting on the position of people of *all* faiths in the Communist world, including Jews, Christians and Muslims.

United local protest

In some situations where they have reason to be concerned, Christians of all denominations must get together to make their voices heard. The following extract from a pastoral letter from the Roman Catholic Archbishop of Khartoum and three other Sudanese Catholic bishops (dated 16 November 1991) is an example of such united protest:

> Although the government professes and advertises that all Sudanese are equal on human rights . . . we see the real situation differently. The government policies are intended to create one nation under Islamic-Arab culture, regardless of other religious, ethnic and cultural considerations. These policies are manifest in the below-mentioned areas . . .

The areas discussed in the remainder of the document are education, freedom of religion, worship and conscience, and evidence of the containment and restriction on Christians.

United protest from international bodies

Whether or not the Christians in any situation are able to say anything publicly about their situation, there is often a need for the protest to come from international bodies *outside* the country.

This point is made in the following paragraphs of the Report *Christian Witness to Muslims* from the Lausanne Conference held at Pattaya, Thailand, in 1980:

> We have noted that Christians in Communist countries have generally welcomed publicity that has been given to particular cases of unjust treatment of individuals and communities. When the reporting is known to be scrupulously accurate, it has strengthened the position of those who are unable to defend their own rights. The situation of Christian minorities in Muslim countries is not exactly comparable. And some Christians are afraid that any publicity about their situation could make it even worse. Others, however, are confident that they would benefit from pressure that is brought to bear on their governments when it is based on thoroughly reliable and accurate information.
>
> We recognise the need for the world-wide church to speak out against all forms of oppression and social injustice. If we cannot do this through representative church bodies (such as the World Council of Churches), through independent church agencies (e.g. Keston College), or secular bodies (e.g. Amnesty International), we need to explore other effective means of voicing these concerns on behalf of *both* Muslim *and* Christian communities.[11]

Lessons from history

Many Christians today hold strongly to the need for the separation of church and state. It is, then, easy to assume that the majority of Christians have always held views like these. It therefore comes as something of a shock when we discover that, in the Christianity which Muhammad and the early Muslims knew in several of the countries surrounding Arabia, church and state were one.

One might even have to say that Muhammad learned the model he followed from the Christians, since the code he established to regulate relations between Muslims and their non-Muslim subjects has close parallels with the codes adopted by the Christian Roman emperors, Theodosius and Justinian, for

291

dealing with pagans, Jews and heretics. As Michael Nazir-Ali points out,

> In many parts of the world, Muslim rule succeeded theocratic Byzantine imperialism ... it is paradoxical that the Byzantine Church itself became subject to these provisions when they became part of the Muslim legislation on the *dhimma*.[12]

This pattern of church–state relations was also followed in medieval Europe.

Turning the other cheek

It is often suggested by Christians and others that true Christian obedience to the teaching of Jesus in the Sermon on the Mount demands passive acceptance of every insult and injustice. The following paragraphs from John Stott's exposition of these verses, however, suggest that this can hardly have been the real intention of Jesus:

> Jesus' illustrations and personal example depict not the weakling who offers no resistance .... They depict rather the strong man whose control of himself and love for others are so powerful that he rejects absolutely every conceivable form of retaliation ...
>
> So the command of Jesus not to resist evil should not properly be used to justify either temperamental weakness or moral compromise or political anarchy or even total pacifism. Instead, what Jesus here demands of all his followers is a personal attitude to evildoers which is prompted by mercy not justice, which renounces retaliation so completely as to risk further costly suffering, which is governed never by the desire to cause them harm but always by the determination to serve their highest good.[13]

The Golden Rule

The Sermon on the Mount contains another vital principle which should be fundamental to Muslim–Christian relations in every context. The Lausanne Report on *Christian Witness to Muslims* points out the continuing relevance of Old Testament commands as well as the teaching of Jesus:

> We have no right to point the finger of accusation at Muslim communities and governments, if we are blind to the ways in which Muslim minorities suffer from unfair discrimination in so-called Christian countries in the West. Christians in this kind of situation are called to take seriously the words of the Mosaic Law, 'You shall not oppress the alien, for you know how it feels to be an alien; you were aliens yourselves in Egypt' (Exodus 23:9). We also need to take very seriously Jesus' warning about the danger of judging others, 'Why do you look at the speck in your brother's eye and pay no attention to the log in your own eye? . . . You hypocrite! . . .' (Matthew 7:3, 5). Only if and when we have taken this warning seriously can we begin to draw attention to situations in the Muslim world in which Christian minorities feel that their religious freedom is being threatened, not only by subtle forms of discrimination, but also by new Islamic constitutions which affect the status of minorities.
>
> We urge Christian leaders in all walks of life to use their influence to encourage governments and business organizations to follow as far as possible the principle, 'Do for others what you want them to do for you' (Matthew 7:12). This would mean, for example, treating other communities in the same way that *we* would like to be treated if we were in a similar situation. It might mean putting pressure on governments and companies not to deny or restrict freedom in their own country which they themselves enjoy in other countries. It is hypocritical for governments to subscribe to the UN Declaration of Human Rights and for their citizens to enjoy those rights when they are living in a foreign country, but to deny those rights to foreigners living in their own country.[14]

A Christian leader from the Middle East today makes this strong plea for western governments to recognize the relevance of the principle of reciprocity:

If only the West could persuade the Muslim world to grant its religious minorities the same treatment that Muslim minorities in the West enjoy.[15]

Appealing to Islamic principles

The following extracts are taken from a paper by Michael Nazir-Ali, written while he was living in Pakistan, in response to a request for advice from a Christian Member of Parliament who was serving on the Parliamentary Constitution Committee in Pakistan. It is a good example of a Christian response *from within the situation* to political questions about the place of Christians and other minorities within an Islamic state, based on the principle of working 'for the good of the entire nation':

> The Christian minority in Pakistan does not wish to become a disenfranchized, segregated group which has little or nothing to contribute to national life ... We would continue to wish to be treated as equal citizens with freedom of worship and proclamation; free to build, maintain and manage our own institutions. In particular, any move to reinforce the so-called 'Ordinance of '*Umar*' is to be resisted.
>
> We would hope that in any future polity, our country would acknowledge the ultimate sovereignty of God which is exercised through the people ... Granted that the polity of Pakistan will be in accordance with Islamic ideals and aspirations, the basis of such a polity should then be the *Qur'anic* conception of human beings as vice-regents of God fulfilling the trust which they have undertaken. Only in such a broad and liberal system would the minorities feel at home ... Which nomenclature we use for our polity is of secondary importance. What is important is to safeguard the principle of popular, representative government and enfranchize all sections of the population. We must beware of serving only our own community interest. We must work for the good of the entire nation and especially of the poor, the weak and the oppressed.[16]

Appealing to international law

We have already cited Article 18 of the Universal Declaration of Human Rights, which speaks of the right to freedom of thought, conscience and religion.

It is, of course, far easier to state these principles than to know how to apply them in every situation. It requires serious study of the Bible, of Christian and Islamic history, and of national and international politics. Christians need to be thoroughly informed of the facts and aware of the particular issues involved.

Those who look on from outside the situation have a special responsibility to stand by their fellow Christians who have to live with all the pressures. If there is any sense in which Islam wants to 'win the world', Christians all over the world will need to work out how to respond to the political challenge – and to do so in ways that are not Islamic, but distinctively Christian.

Resources for further study

Jens Christensen, *The Practical Approach to Muslims* (Arab World Ministries, 1977)

Kenneth Cragg, *Muhammad and the Christian: A Question of Response* (Darton Longman and Todd, 1984)

Hamid Enayat, *Modern Islamic Political Thought* (Macmillan, 1982)

Edward Mortimer, *Faith and Power: The Politics of Islam* (Faber, 1982)

Michael Nazir-Ali, *Islam: A Christian Perspective* (Paternoster, 1983)

——, *Frontiers in Muslim-Christian Encounter* (Regnum, 1987)

Phil Parshall, *The Cross and the Crescent: Understanding the Muslim Mind and Heart* (Tyndale House, 1989)

Bilquis Sheikh, *I Dared to Call Him Father* (Kingsway, 2nd edn., 1983)

Part 5

Sharing our faith

We need the *song* note in our message to the Muslims . . . not the dry cracked note of disputation, but the song of joyous witness, tender invitation.

Temple Gairdner[1]

We believe not in words, but in the Word made flesh, a Word which only the Spirit of God can interpret to us. To argue is to turn it into mere words.

Roger Hooker[2]

If Christ is what Christ is, he must be uttered. If Islam is what Islam is, that 'must' is irresistible. Wherever there is misconception, witness must penetrate; wherever there is the obscuring of the beauty of the Cross, it must be unveiled; wherever persons have missed God in Christ, he must be brought to them again . . . In such a situation as Islam presents, the Church has no option but to present Christ.

Kenneth Cragg[3]

Do not deceive yourself; proclamation is NOT child's play. It is not a thing every gossipping layman can do. Serving the Word as a preacher is the most exacting charisma in the Church, and besides faith and humility, patient, wearisome and continual effort and struggle are needed on the part of those whose gift it is to serve the Church in this way.

Jens Christensen[4]

In Part 5 we consider different ways of sharing our faith with Muslims. Assuming that we have understood and begun to practise what is involved in the four stages described in parts 1 to 4, we now ask: what does it mean to bear witness to Jesus? If we want to share with Muslims our understanding and experience of God as he is revealed to us in Jesus, how do we do it? Is there anything special about the way we share our faith with Muslims?

The following chapters offer several different models, none of which should be seen as a blueprint for Christian witness. It can hardly be emphasized too strongly that the most effective Christian witness usually arises naturally out of any situation, and is backed up by actions and by a lifestyle that are genuinely Christian. There are no simple techniques that are bound to make our witness easy or effective. All we can do here is try to learn from the experience of others, noting what they have found to be appropriate ways of sharing the Christian faith in different situations, and trying to understand what is involved in making the gospel intelligible and relevant to Muslims.

31

Natural openings in everyday life

It is not possible for us to prepare in advance what we should say in different situations. It may be helpful, however, to begin to reflect on the kind of situations in which there will be opportunities to share our faith.

The following conversation is taken from the book *What Shall I Say to my Muslim Friends?* by Margaret Burness. The conversation takes place at the time of Id, *i.e. Id al adha*, the Muslim feast celebrating Abraham's sacrifice of a ram in place of his son (whom Muslims believe was Ishmael, not Isaac). The celebration of this festival has several similarities with Christmas as it is celebrated in the West and in certain other parts of the world; for example, it is a public holiday in Muslim countries, and there are family parties, greeting cards and presents. The typical greeting between Muslims is *Id mubarak* ('May this feast be blessed').

There is a knock on Elizabeth's door; and when she opens it, she sees her neighbour's daughter Fatima with a bag of cakes.

ELIZABETH   Hello, Fatima. Do come in.

FATIMA   Good evening, Mrs Twining. No, I can't, thank you. I have to go and help mother – she's very busy preparing food for all our guests tomorrow. She sent me to bring you these special cakes – she would be very glad if you and Mary could come to see us tomorrow evening, and my father would be glad to welcome your husband – it's our Id.

ELIZABETH   Thank you very much. We'll come tomorrow if we can. What does Id mean?

FATIMA   It's a festival – people come from miles away to greet their families and friends. We exchange special greeting cards, and presents. We dress up in our best clothes, and eat special food. It's not as good as it was at home, though – we're not allowed to kill a ram here – you have some law against it, I think. It's just like your Christmas, no difference.[1]

What is Elizabeth to say to Fatima? How appropriate are the following possible responses?

1. 'Of course there's a difference – we don't kill rams!'

2. 'It does sound rather like Christmas. I hope you have a very happy day tomorrow with your family and friends!'

3. 'There is something more to Christmas than turkeys and presents – we are celebrating a very special present God has given to us all, Jesus Christ, our Lord and Saviour. It's his birthday we remember at Christmas. I would love to hear some time what you are celebrating tomorrow – but it's not the same thing, is it?'

4. 'Yes, the cards, presents and the family parties *are* much the same, but there is another connection too. We Christians, remember, like you, how Abraham was prepared to sacrifice his son, and how God made a greater sacrifice – Jesus Christ, the Lamb of God who died to take away the sins of all the world. At Christmas we celebrate the birthday of Jesus, the Lamb of God.'

32

Christian responses to 'folk Islam'

Chapter 14 contained a description of several major aspects of 'folk Islam' or 'popular Islam', and discussed the relationship between 'folk Islam' and 'ideal Islam'. We now consider three guiding principles in the way Christians may want to respond to these aspects of Islam.

1. We need to recognize the felt needs that are being met through these practices.

All these different practices and phenomena are responses to basic human needs which we all feel as human beings in one way or another. The following diagram comes from an article entitled 'Popular Islam: the Hunger of the Heart' by Bill Musk,[1] and suggests what are the felt needs that underlie the different practices of popular Islam:

Felt-Needs in Popular Islam	Animistic Answers to Felt-Needs Not acceptable . . . More acceptable			Christian Answer to Felt-Needs
fear of the unknown	idolatry stone worship	fetishes talismans charms	superstition	security in Christ as Guide Keeper
fear of evil	sorcery witchcraft	amulets knots	exorcism (?)	exorcism, protection in Christ
fear of the future	angel worship	divination spells (?)	fatalism fanaticism	trust in Christ as Lord of the future
shame of not being in the group	magic curse or bless	hair/nail trimmings		acceptance in fellowship of believers
powerlessness of individual against evil	saint worship		baraka saint/angel petitioning	authority and power of the Holy Spirit
meaninglessness of life		familiar spirit (?)		purpose in life as God's child
sickness	tree/saint worship	healing magic (?)		divine healing

Musk's approach is developed in greater detail in his book *The Unseen Face of Islam: Sharing the Gospel with Ordinary Muslims.*

2. *Where appropriate we can point to Jesus as the greatest mediator.*

We can bear witness to Jesus as the one through whom the power of God is available, and the one who has overcome all the powers of evil. In the diagram above, the column on the right suggests how basic felt needs are met within the Christian faith.

In this context the gospel accounts of Jesus driving out evil spirits can be specially significant for Muslims. (See chapter 33.3.)

3. *We should recognize that we may be involved in 'spiritual warfare'.*

It is important that we should avoid some of the more extreme positions over this question. Some Christians see almost everything to do with Christian witness (especially to Muslims) in terms of 'spiritual warfare'; they therefore try to find spiritual explanations for any resistance to the Christian message, and see the whole of life as part of a confrontation between God and supernatural forces of evil.

Others go to the opposite extreme and deny the reality of any kind of 'evil spirits' or 'evil powers'. What is needed is a balance between these two extremes which recognizes the need for special approaches in particular situations.

Vivienne Stacey describes in detail an experience in Muscat in the Sultanate of Oman where a house occupied by a missionary nurse was said to be 'haunted', and required exorcism:

> My first task had been to find out what was really wrong with the house. Diagnosis is all-important. I asked the Lord to show me and I took practical steps to find out where evil particularly dwelt. I meditated and prayed in various parts of the house – in the kitchen, the sitting room, on the stairs. Several nights I was driven out of my bedroom by satanic forces. Even kneeling by my bed I found it too terrifying to stay. One night I called my companion. We prayed together and I spent the rest of the night sleeping on the floor in her room. Throughout the eight days I rarely slept for more than an hour at a time and never for more than five out of twenty-four hours. The Lord gave me extra strength

and I was able to pray and meditate and carry out my normal programme of Bible teaching and evangelistic meetings with Pakistanis in the areas around. One night all hell seemed to be let loose and I decided that I would read in the sitting room Isaiah's servant song about the death and victory of the Lord Jesus Christ (Isaiah 52:13 – 53:12) and praise God whatever happened. I knew that the local people claimed that sometimes they 'saw' spirits on the roof and so another day I set out to watch and pray on the roof.

At that moment the Lord clearly warned me that if I went on the roof I would be killed. Then the words of the communion service came to my mind: 'Preserve thy body and soul unto everlasting life' and I knew I was safe provided I did not go on the roof at that time. For some days I had prayed specifically that I might know what spirits inhabited the house and its environs (it had a small garden). The answer was clear – spirits of suicide, depression and fear. I commanded them in Jesus Christ's name that they should go. There was no clear proof that the spirits had gone and there were still other manifestations of demonic activities. One night I found my companion nearly choking. I asked her permission to put my hands on her throat and neck and to pray in Jesus' name. Immediately she was all right. She had heard a strange noise between her bedroom and the sitting room. The next day I dusted all the objects in the wall cupboard of the sitting room, some of which were souvenirs from Africa. She enquired what I was doing and I explained that I was praying over each object that it would be cleansed through the blood of the Lord Jesus Christ. She then joined me in this exercise. Some weeks later she wrote to explain that she had found one object that was probably the cause of some of the trouble in her room – a curved Omani dagger which had been used to ward off evil spirits from a mother and baby. She had taken it from the patient, hidden it in her room and forgotten about it.[2]

33

Using the Bible

33.1 The parable of the two lost sons (the prodigal son)

What is so unique about this parable in the context of Christian witness to Muslims? There are at least five reasons why it can be specially valuable as a way of introducing them to the message of Jesus:

1. *It is a story told by Jesus himself.* Whatever Muslims believe about the corruption of the Bible, many of them are curious to know what the Christian version of the *injil* actually says. We can tell them that this story is given in our *injil* as a story told by Jesus, and that it summarizes much of what was unique in his teaching.

2. *It presents the message of Jesus in the form of a story.* Those of us in the habit of trying to share the gospel by explaining a series of abstract, theological propositions (such as 'All people are sinners; Christ died for our sins', *etc.*) may get further if we can learn the art of telling stories. A story is something that can be told, elaborated and dramatized. A series of pictures will be printed on the minds of those who hear it. Their imagination will be stirred, and there will be something that we can discuss together. Long after they have forgotten us and what we have said, they may remember this vivid story.

3. *The parable teaches the essence of the good news proclaimed by Jesus.* Kenneth Bailey, in his study of the parables of Jesus, believes that Jesus' basic message can be summed up as *the costly demonstration of unexpected love.*[1]

- God *loves* all people.

- His love is *unexpected*, since we would not expect him to love his rebellious creatures.

- Not only does he proclaim his love, however, he actually *demonstrates* his love in action.

- This demonstration of his unexpected love is *costly* for him, since in a sense he suffers in the process of forgiving sins.

The parable of the prodigal son expresses all these points with special force. The father loves his sons – both the rebellious one who wants to leave home and the older one who has such a cold and formal relationship with him – and goes on loving them, even when we might expect him to want to punish and reject them. He demonstrates his love to both of them in ways that would have been considered surprising, if not shocking, to his original hearers. And the father suffers in the process of demonstrating his love for them.

Bailey summarizes the significance of the prodigal's homecoming as follows:

> On his return, the prodigal is overwhelmed by an unexpected visible demonstration of love in humiliation. He is shattered by the offer of grace, confesses unworthiness, and accepts restoration to sonship in genuine humility. Sin is now a broken relationship which he cannot restore. Repentance is now understood as acceptance of grace and confession of unworthiness. The community rejoices together. The visible demonstration of love in humiliation is seen to have clear overtones of the atoning work of Christ.[2]

4. *The parable comes out of a culture which is similar to the culture of much of the Muslim world.* The strong emphasis in Islam on the unity of the family and family loyalties, and the fact that most of the Muslim world is in Africa and the East, should make it easy for Muslims to understand what is happening in the story. In these cultures, who could imagine a younger son asking for his share of the inheritance while his father is still alive? Should a father not punish his sons when they dishonour the name of the family? Has an elder brother got to swallow his pride and welcome home a younger brother who has disgraced himself?

5. *The teaching of the parable is specially appropriate for the Muslim mind.* Muslims are taught to think of themselves as 'servants' who relate to God as their Master. When the prodigal thinks of coming home, his face-saving plan is that he will ask his father to accept him back as a *servant* or *slave*, so that he can earn his wages and at least have something to pay back to his father. Such a solution, however, is unthinkable to his father, who wants to welcome him home as a *son*. Jesus, who spoke of himself as 'the Son' who enjoyed a specially intimate relationship with God as Father, brought the good news that all his disciples can approach God as Father and have all the privileges and responsibilities of being full members of God's family, and not just servants.

One surprising thing about the parable is that it does not have an ending. Perhaps this is because Jesus wanted his readers or listeners to put themselves into the shoes of the elder brother and ask, 'What would *I* do if I were in his place? Would I listen to my father's pleading and join in the party to welcome my brother home? Or would I be so angry with him that I would take the nearest stick and beat him in full view of all the guests? And if God is like the father, and wants me to know and love him as a Father, how am I going to respond to his love?'

If the parable can be used in a context in which there can be genuine discussion, it can be followed up with gently probing questions such as these:

■ Have you been taught to believe that God is like a loving Father?

■ What is your picture of what God is like?

■ Do you believe that God loves you and loves all people?

■ Do you think there is any difference between saying 'God is merciful' and saying 'God is loving' or 'God is love'?

■ How do you think God shows his mercy or his love to us?

A leaflet containing the parable and its interpretation can be obtained from the Bible Society, Stonehill Green, Westlea, Swindon SN5 7DG, UK.

33.2 The gospel of Luke

We have already seen (in chapter 21) that the gospel of Luke may be the most appropriate one to give to Muslims. There are three further reasons for choosing Luke's gospel:

1. The christology of Luke may be a little easier for Muslims to appreciate than that of the other gospels. In 1:32, for example, 'Son of God' is associated with the idea of Jesus as a descendant of David, and in 1:35 with the Holy Spirit coming upon Mary. As in the other synoptic gospels, it is only very gradually that the disciples come to realize that Jesus is 'more than a prophet' (Luke 2:76).

2. The fuller birth narratives may be of special interest to Muslims, showing that there is some common ground between the Qur'an and the New Testament. They will certainly, however, become aware of some significant differences between the two accounts.

3. If, as is likely, Luke was the author of the Acts of the Apostles as well as of his gospel, it makes a great deal of sense for Muslim readers to go on to read Acts after the gospel. The gospel is about 'all that Jesus began to do and to teach' (Acts 1:1), while Acts records what Jesus continued to do and teach through the church. Muslim tradition has much to say not only about the life of Muhammad but also about his immediate successors (the caliphs), who played a very significant role in the history of Islam (see chapter 11). Christians similarly attach a great deal of importance to the life of the early church as recorded in Acts. Thoughtful Muslims can hardly fail to notice the contrast between the way in which Christianity spread in the early years after the ministry of Jesus and the way in which Islam spread immediately after the death of the Prophet.

One particularly helpful edition of the Gospel of Luke is the 'Study Edition', published by the United Bible Societies (Asia Pacific Regional Centre, 1001 South Seas Centre, Tower 1, Tsim Sha Tsui East, Hong Kong), which explains words, customs and ideas that may need some special explanation for Muslim readers.

33.3 *The Message of the Tawrat, the Zabur and the Injil*

In 1981 the Bible Society in Lebanon (PO Box 11–747, Beirut, Lebanon) published a folder of selected Bible passages, specially chosen for Muslim readers, under the title *The Message of the Tawrat, the Zabur and the Injil*. It was initially distributed in Arabic, French and English, and since then has been translated into other languages in the Muslim world.

The following are the main ideas which lie behind these selections:

1. The title uses the Qur'anic names of the three main Scriptures which Muslims believe were revealed before the Qur'an: the *tawrat* revealed to Moses, the *zabur* to David, and the *injil* to Jesus (see chapter 8). In the Qur'an God says that the message revealed to Muhammad contains the same message as that revealed in the previous Scriptures. Jews and Christians are invited to believe Muhammad's message because it is no different from the message contained in the Scriptures which they have in their possession.

The title is therefore intended to convey something like this to the Muslim reader: 'You believe that these are Scriptures which were revealed by God to the Jews and Christians, and that the Qur'an was simply confirming the message that was contained in their Scriptures. But do you know what these Scriptures contain? The following passages give an idea of the central message of these Scriptures which are in the same form today as those in the hands of Jews and Christians in the time of Muhammad . . .'

2. The Introduction explains briefly what the Bible is. Since the Qur'an for Muslims consists of what God revealed to one man in the course of twenty-three years, it is not easy for them to grasp the idea that the Bible is like a library of books containing history, stories, prayers, letters and visions, written by many different writers over a period of up to 2,000 years. For the same reason each passage has an introduction to explain what it is that we are about to read. Is it history? Is it a letter? Who recorded these words? Who was he or she addressing? And what is the main point of what is said in this passage?

3. We need to avoid controversy as much as possible. Thus, for example, the word 'Trinity' is not mentioned, although the claims that Jesus made about himself are clearly presented. We avoid any emphasis on Jesus as the Son of God, because of possible misunderstanding in the mind of Muslims, and because it is possible to draw attention to the claims of Jesus in different ways.

4. We start on common ground. The first studies therefore deal with God as Creator and human beings as creatures, and with God who reveals his laws to them. In this way we are trying to build bridges with Muslims by studying truths which they also believe, even if they express them in a slightly different way. We are also trying to lay foundations for the later studies. Thus long before we come to the delicate question of the crucifixion, we have tried to prepare the way by looking at sacrifice and forgiveness in the Old Testament, and the tension between the holiness and the love of God.

5. The terminology needs to be as Islamic as possible, provided there is no compromise of Christian belief. For this reason we use the Qur'anic names for Jesus, John the Baptist and the devil.

6. The most important theological assumption made in the studies is that we can present the gospel in the way that is unfolded in Paul's letter to the Romans. Law must come before grace. We need to know that we are sinners under the judgment of God before we can see Jesus as God's answer to our need. When, by the application of the law, sin has been shown to be sin (Romans 7:13), we are compelled to turn to the one through whom God has done something to deal with that sin.

In this respect the approach differs quite radically from that implied in the parable of the prodigal son. There, and in other parables of Jesus, as Kenneth Bailey has pointed out, the emphasis is on God demonstrating his unexpected love in costly ways. Sinners turn to God in repentance and faith in response to this unexpected demonstration of love. They become fully aware of their sin *after* they have seen how much God loves them and how much he has done for them to win their love.

7. The passages are grouped under ten themes, with each one on a separate paper. Christians who are able to study the passages with interested Muslims should proceed slowly and take one subject at a time.

Each study ends with a prayer from the Bible, which can be read aloud together. This is intended so that even if there is discussion or controversy in the study of the passages, it is possible to end in a spirit of prayer and worship rather than of controversy. It would be quite wrong to put words into the mouths of Muslims which they cannot in all honesty say. But in many cases there is nothing in the prayer which is likely to offend Muslims and which they could not say with conviction.

The following sections summarize these studies, introducing each passage for Muslim readers. Christians working through the studies with Muslims need to understand how Muslims may respond to these passages, and discuss them in a way that is intelligible to them.

1. God is one and has created us to serve and love him

We begin with passages which speak about the oneness of God and the rejection of idolatry. We want to assure Muslims that *we believe in the oneness of God as strongly as they do.*

The Ten Commandments (Exodus 20:3–5) begin with a condemnation of idolatry and what the Muslim calls *shirk* (the sin of associating anything created with God the Creator).

Jesus' summary of the OT law emphasizes the oneness of God and our obligation to love him (Mark 12:29–30).

Other parts of the Bible warn against idolatry in different ways: Paul condemns idolatry along with other serious sins (Galatians 5:19–21); John includes idolatry among the sins which deserve judgment in hell (Revelation 21:8).

Psalm 33:1, 4–9 and Psalm 105:1–6 call us to worship God as the one who has revealed himself through his mighty acts in creation and in history.

Psalm 95:1–7 and 139:1–6, 13–14 are prayers of worship, which express the believer's joy and thankfulness, his reverence for God and his confidence in him as a personal God.

2. God gives us his laws

The Tawrat includes the Ten Commandments, which God revealed after he had delivered the children of Israel from slavery in Egypt: *Exodus 20:1–17.*

Jesus the Messiah summed up the Ten Commandments in two basic commandments: love God and love your neighbour: *Matthew 22:34–40.*

Jesus the Messiah taught that God's laws do not simply apply to outward actions, but also to our inward thoughts and motives: *Matthew 5:21–24.*

Jesus the Messiah taught that God sometimes sets much higher standards than those which people set for themselves: *Matthew 5:43–45.*

In the Zabur the prophet expresses his desire to obey the law of God: *Psalm 119:1–16.*

3. God warns us of the consequences of failure to keep his laws

The account of the Garden of Eden is found near the beginning of the Tawrat. God warned Adam and Eve that if they disobeyed his command, they would die; this meant that their physical death would be a symbol of their spiritual death and their separation from God: *Genesis 2:8–9, 15–17.*

The devil (Iblis) used the serpent to tempt Eve, and she and Adam then disobeyed God's command: *Genesis 3:1–13.*

God then expelled Adam and Eve from the Garden to show that they no longer had any right to have fellowship with him: *Genesis 3:22–24.*

The prophet Ezekiel explains to the people that God holds every person responsible for his or her own sins. We cannot blame Fate or our parents or anyone else: *Ezekiel 18:1–4, 30–32.*

The apostle Paul declares that all people have broken the law of God and are therefore under the power of sin. The word 'sin' is used often in the Bible to describe human disobedience and failure to live up to the law of God: *Romans 3:9–20, 23.*

In the Zabur the prophet confesses his sins to God and asks for forgiveness: *Psalm 51:1–9.*

4. God is merciful and loving and wants to forgive

In the Zabur the prophet says that God is like a Father who loves and cares for his children: *Psalm 103:8–14.*

In the Tawrat God revealed to Moses that Aaron and the priests were to offer certain sacrifices or offerings to purify the people from their sins. The full meaning of these sacrifices was not revealed until the coming of Jesus the Messiah: *Leviticus 9:7.*

In addition to the daily sacrifices, there was one day every year called the Day of Atonement when special sacrifices were offered: *Leviticus 16:5–10, 21–22.*

Jesus the Messiah told the following parable about the need for humility and repentance before God. Although the Pharisee (a teacher of the Jewish law) was careful to obey the law, he was *not* forgiven by God because he was proud of himself and his achievements. The tax collector, however, who was probably dishonest and unpopular in his society, *was* forgiven because he knew he did not deserve God's mercy and could do nothing to earn forgiveness: *Luke 18:9–14.*

But *how* does God forgive? If he is a just Judge, how can he simply forgive the guilty? Speaking through the prophet Jeremiah he reveals that it is not an easy or light thing for God to forgive people who have turned away from him: *Jeremiah 5:7, 9.*

Speaking through the prophet Hosea, however, God reveals that because of his love for human beings, he does not want to judge and condemn them in the way that they deserve. This tension between the holiness and love of God is only resolved in what God did through Jesus the Messiah: *Hosea 11:8–9.*

In the Zabur the prophet expresses the joy that comes from knowing that his sins have already been forgiven: *Psalm 32:1–7.*

5. God revealed to his prophets that he would come among us

God comes to people through his Word. The prophet Isaiah speaks of how God acts in the world through his Word: *Isaiah 55:10–11.*

In the Tawrat God commanded Moses to make a tabernacle (tent) for worship as a sign of his presence among his people. God is the sovereign Lord; but He also wants to be in a close relationship with his people. These are the commands which were revealed by God to Moses: *Leviticus 26:1–2, 11–12; Exodus 29:44–45.*

God revealed through the prophet Ezekiel that he would one day come to live among his people in a new way: *Ezekiel 37:26–27.*

Similarly God declared to the prophet Malachi that he would come to his temple: *Malachi 3:1.*

God revealed through the prophet Isaiah that he would reveal his glory to all humankind: *Isaiah 40:3–5.*

The Old Testament includes many promises and prophecies that God is going to reveal himself more fully to the world. The prophet Micah, for example, prophesies that God will raise up a descendant for David to be ruler over the people: *Micah 5:2.*

In the Zabur the prophet is full of joy because God is going to come to rule the world with justice: *Psalm 96:10–13.*

The prophet Isaiah confesses the sins of the people; he longs that God should reveal himself in a dramatic way as he has done in the past: *Isaiah 64:1–9.*

6. God sent Jesus the Messiah as his Word through a miraculous birth and gave him miraculous powers

After Joseph became engaged to Mary, God sent an angel to reveal to him in a dream that Mary would give birth to Jesus the Messiah by the Holy Spirit: *Matthew 1:18–25.*

The story of the birth of Jesus the Messiah: *Luke 2:1–20.*

Jesus the Messiah received a special call from God to begin his public ministry when he was about thirty years old. These were some of the miracles he performed as signs of God's love and care for people:

■ He calmed the storm: *Luke 8:22–25.*

■ He fed the five thousand: *Luke 9:10–17.*

■ He drove out evil spirits: *Luke 4:31–37.*

Jesus was given the title 'The Messiah', which means 'The Anointed One', *i.e.* anointed by God as a special and unique Messenger. When John the Baptist (Yahya) was in prison he began to have doubts and sent his disciples to ask if Jesus really was the promised Messiah: *Luke 7:18–23.*

Mary offered this prayer when it was revealed to her that she was going to give birth to Jesus the Messiah: *Luke 1:46–65.*

7. God gave Jesus the Messiah the message of the Injil (the Gospel)

Jesus the Messiah spoke of his message as 'the Good News from God' – *i.e.* the 'Gospel' or 'Injil'. The Good News he announced was that through him God was going to establish his kingdom on earth: *Mark 1:14–15.*

At the beginning of his public ministry, Jesus the Messiah quoted words from the prophet Isaiah to describe the work that God had called him to do: *Luke 4:16–19.*

One of the most surprising things in the teaching of Jesus the Messiah was that he claimed to be able to forgive sins: *Luke 5:17–26.*

The message of the Injil is summed up in one of the best-known parables of Jesus the Messiah, which is called 'The parable of the two sons' (or 'the parable of the prodigal son'). The parable gives a picture of the love and compassion of God who longs for all people to return to him and be welcomed as members of his family: *Luke 15:11–32.*

Jesus the Messiah encouraged his disciples to pray to God as sons and daughters addressing a loving Father. This is the prayer known as 'the Lord's Prayer', which he taught his disciples to pray: *Matthew 6:9–13.*

8. God demonstrated his love for sinful people through the death of Jesus the Messiah

The Jewish authorities wanted to kill Jesus the Messiah because he spoke of God as 'my Father', as though he had God's Spirit in a special way or was a special Word from Him. This happened after Jesus the Messiah had healed a man on the Sabbath (the day of rest): *John 5:15–18.*

When Jesus the Messiah realized that the Jews were trying to arrest him, he prayed that God would save him from suffering and death; but if it was God's will, he was willing to suffer and die: *Luke 22:41–44.*

When Jesus was arrested he rebuked Peter for trying to defend him, explaining that if he wanted, he could ask God to send angels to rescue him: *Matthew 26:51–54.*

When Jesus was tried by the Supreme Jewish Court, the High Priest accused him of blasphemy: *Luke 22:66 – 23:2*.

The Jews persuaded Pilate to have Jesus crucified: *Luke 23:20–26*.

Jesus was nailed to the cross: *Luke 23:32–43*.

Jesus gave his life on the cross: *Luke 23:44–49*.

The prophet Isaiah many years earlier had spoken of someone whom God calls 'my Servant' who, in his death, bears the sins of many: *Isaiah 53:4–6*.

In this prayer from the Zabur the prophet feels that God has abandoned him, but prays that God will rescue him. The first sentence was spoken by Jesus as he hung on the cross. God *did* rescue him – not only from his enemies, but also from death itself. In a profound and glorious way he lifted him up in resurrection from the dead: *Psalm 22:1–19*.

9. *God raised Jesus from death*

The body of Jesus was taken down from the cross and placed in a rock tomb: *Luke 23:50–56*.

On the third day the disciples discovered that the body of Jesus had disappeared from the tomb; an angel explained that he had been raised from the dead: *Luke 24:1–12*.

The risen Jesus appeared to two of the disciples and explained to them from the Scriptures why it was necessary for the Messiah to suffer before being raised by God: *Luke 24:13–35*.

The risen Jesus appeared again to the other disciples, and told them to preach the message of forgiveness of sins to all nations: *Luke 24:36–47*.

The writer of a letter to the Hebrews explains that because Jesus was willing to die on the cross, he has by his death broken the power of death and of the devil (Iblis). He is now able to help us in all our temptations and suffering because he was identified with us right to the end: *Hebrews 2:14–18*.

In the Zabur the prophet expresses his trust in God, because he knows that God will protect him from the power of death and let him enjoy his presence for ever: *Psalm 16:1–11*.

10. *God gave his Spirit to the disciples who recognized Jesus as God's Messiah and God's Word*

Before Jesus the Messiah was taken up to heaven, he told his disciples that God would send the Holy Spirit to live in them in a new way: *Acts 1:2–5, 8–9*.

After he was taken up to heaven, the angels told his disciples that he would one day return to the earth: *Acts 1:10–11*.

Some time later the Holy Spirit came on the disciples: *Acts 2:1–4*.

When the Spirit of God was given to the disciples, the apostle Peter explained to the Jews what had happened to Jesus the Messiah in this way: *Acts 2:22–36*.

The apostle Paul explained that when we receive forgiveness of our sins through the death of Jesus, we also receive the Holy Spirit who enables us to live up to the standard of God's law: *Romans 8:1–17*.

In the Zabur the prophet confesses his sins to God (see Study 3, Psalm 51:1–9) and asks for complete restoration to the presence of God: *Psalm 51:10–17*.

34

Rethinking and restating the gospel, starting from the Qur'an

Whenever there is resistance to the gospel among Muslims, it is easy to find reasons on *their* side for such rejection. But what if some of the responsibility is on *our* side? If the Christian church has contributed to the misunderstanding and rejection, we need to recognize that we have an obligation to look again more carefully at the way we articulate our message.

This challenge is described in the Report of the 1980 Pattaya Consultation, *Christian Witness to Muslims*, in the following way:

> As soon as we begin to listen to Muslims and try to share the gospel, we begin to realise how difficult it is to express ourselves in a way that Muslims understand. The painfulness of this experience ought to drive us back to the Bible, in order to learn new ways of understanding our faith and relating it to the Muslim mind.[1]

After giving several examples of areas in which we need to rethink and restate our faith it goes on to say:

> If the gospel was first given to us in an eastern context, it ought to be possible for us to get behind the Graeco-Roman patterns of thought through which we have interpreted it, and express it once again in ways that make more sense to the eastern mind.[2]

The three studies in this chapter attempt to take up this challenge by studying an important theme in the Qur'an before turning to study how that same theme is handled in the Bible. The value of this method is that it forces us to understand the mind of well-taught Muslims. Instead of simply restating Christian doctrines in a very traditional way, we will first of all have to understand what the Qur'an teaches on these themes and only then turn to the Bible. Our restatement of Christian teaching *after* such a study of the Qur'an should then be more intelligible to the Muslim mind.

34.1 God and his prophets

Here is a theme which is fundamental to Islam: God responds to human ignorance by sending prophets and messengers or apostles. As we explore how Muslims think about these prophets, we will want to recognize all the common ground we can find between the two faiths, working within that area where the two overlap. (See chapter 24.4.) Or, to change the metaphor, we will want to see how far we can walk along the same road with the Muslim before we come to the fork where our paths diverge.

When after this we turn to the Scriptures, we will be trying to look in a fresh way at how they describe the relationship between God and his prophets. We will want to see if we can correct any Muslim misunderstandings of Christian beliefs, and find new ways of restating the gospel that really engage with the Muslim mind.

But why choose Jeremiah as our example of a biblical prophet (see pp. 320–323)? One reason is that he is not entirely unknown to Muslims, although he is not mentioned in the Qur'an . *Sura* 2:259 speaks of a doubting man who passes by a ruined town and exclaims, 'How shall Allah give this township life after its death?' Allah's response is to cause him to be dead for a hundred years and then bring him back to life. Some of the early commentaries on the Qur'an identify this man with various Old Testament characters, including Jeremiah.

Another reason is that we know more about the life and personality of Jeremiah than about almost any other prophet in the Old Testament. Just as 2 Corinthians lays bear the heart of Paul and reveals much of his thinking and feeling, so the book of Jeremiah reveals much about him as a man and as a prophet, and in particular about the inner agonies that he faces in his ministry. A third reason is that since Jeremiah stands half-way between Moses and Jesus, he may have something to say to those who cannot make such a huge leap immediately from the prophet on Mount Sinai to the Prophet in the Garden of Gethsemane.

God and his prophets in Islam

The following summary of Islamic teaching is based largely on that given by B. D. Kateregga in *Islam and Christianity: A Muslim and a Christian in Dialogue*:[3]

1. A messenger/apostle (*rasul*) is sent with divine Scripture to guide and reform humankind. The four most important are those through whom Scriptures were revealed: *i.e.* Moses, David, Jesus and Muhammad.

A prophet (*nabi*) carries information or proclaims God's message, but is not given Books like the messengers. Thus all messengers are prophets, but not all prophets are messengers.

2. Both prophets and messengers were given a message by God through revelation (*wahy*) for the guidance of a group or nation. They all brought essentially the same message – the message of Islam. Almost every nation has had its messenger or prophet. Twenty-five are mentioned in the Qur'an (*e.g.* 16:36 and 2:136), and 124,000 in tradition.

3. All God's prophets were trustworthy, knowledgeable, and most obedient to God. They were the best examples of moral trust. They were all human beings, but protected by God from serious sin and bad diseases. They set very good examples with their own lives, although (according to strictly orthodox teaching) they were not sinless.

4. We must accept *all* God's prophets and messengers. Denying any one of them, therefore, constitutes unbelief (4:150–151). Some prophets were more highly endowed than others (especially Moses and Jesus, 2:253), but it is sinful to elevate any one prophet and put him on a higher level than the others.

5. Many prophets were mocked and rejected (15:11; 17:94). Some prophets were delivered by God, *e.g.* Noah (21:76; 26:118; 29:15; 37:76), Lot (21:71, 74; 26:170), and Moses (28:20–22; 26:65). It is worth noting that in several of these passages the word used is *najjainahu* ('we delivered him'), where the verb is the same as that used in the Arabic Lord's Prayer for 'deliver us'. It seems to be understood that God is in some way *obliged* to rescue his prophets; he *must* intervene to save them from the hands of those who want to destroy them:

> Then shall we save Our Messenger and the believers, in like manner (as of old). It is incumbent upon Us to save believers (10:104).
>
> Allah delivereth those who ward off (evil), because of their deserts. Evil toucheth them not, nor do they grieve (39:61).
>
> In Allah we trust . . . of Thy mercy save us from the folk that disbelieve (10:85–87).

6. Some of the prophets, however, were killed 'wrongfully' (*e.g.* Abel, Zecharias, and Yahya (2:61, 87, 91; 3:21, 112; 4:155; 5:70). Those who were responsible for killing the prophets were later punished by God (2:61; 3:21).

7. Muhammad is 'the seal of the prophets' (33:40). In receiving what was revealed to him, he was to recite the stories of the previous prophets, partly as a warning to unbelievers (46:30–34), and partly as an encouragement to himself to persevere with patience in the face of opposition (46:35).

A study in the life of Jeremiah

Here we can note briefly some of the main characteristics of the ministry of Jeremiah, observing where there is anything similar or significantly different in the ministry of Muhammad.

1. The prophet has a clear call from God at the beginning of his ministry (Jeremiah 1:1–19), in which he feels that God has laid his hand on him (verse 5), and promises to give him the words to speak (verse 7) and to rescue him from enemies (verse 8). Later in his ministry, when experiencing hostility from the people, he questions several elements in the original call he has received (15:11–18). It is interesting to compare this language with that of the Qur'an and the early accounts of the call of Muhammad in the early *siras* (Lives of the Prophet), some of which speak of a nocturnal vision in a dark cave, while another speaks of a vision received in clear daylight.

2. Jeremiah receives God's message in different ways, and there is considerable variety in the language used to describe the process of revelation. Sometimes he is said to recite the words that are given to him by God (1:7). Elsewhere the reception of the message is compared to drinking (23:9). In another place he listens to the words he is to convey (23:18). In one case he receives the message during a dream (31:23–26; but contrast 23:29).

This language is of special interest when we appreciate how Muslims think of the process of revelation and inspiration. Muhammad is simply the human vehicle through which an eternal message is delivered to humankind. He is almost like a typewriter used by God to deliver his word, or a pipe through which words are conveyed like liquid.

3. Jeremiah declares the judgment of God which will fall on a stiff-necked, stubborn and disobedient people (*e.g.* 11:9–17; 19:15). Similarly Muhammad speaks of the judgment of God which is imminent, and tells many stories of God's judgment on sinful people in the past.

4. The prophet calls for repentance (*e.g.* 11:1–8). Muhammad likewise has a message of judgment to proclaim. But whereas Jeremiah is recalling his people to obedience to a law revealed centuries before through Moses, Muhammed claims to bring a new revelation for the Arabs which is basically the same as that revealed through previous prophets.

5. The prophet Jeremiah is identified with his people, and because of his identification with them confesses their sins and prays for them (8:18 – 9:1; 14:7–9; *cf.* Lamentations 3:1–52, especially 40–47).

6. At the same time Jeremiah the prophet shares the anguish of God over his sinful people (6:9–12; 14:17–18); it is not always clear whether the 'I' refers to God or the prophet. The Qur'an never uses language of this kind to describe God's response to evil; anguish is far too human an emotion to be ascribed to God. It is therefore inconceivable that Muhammad as prophet should identify himself with God in this way.

7. Jeremiah's message is rejected, and *he* is rejected (11:18–23; 12:6). Gerhard von Rad makes the significant comment that in Jeremiah we see 'a shift in the centre of interest from the *message* to the *messenger'*. As a result he suffers great indignities and is treated cruelly. For example, he is put in the stocks (20:2); he is imprisoned (32); left in a muddy cistern, ignored by the leaders and humiliated by the king (38); finally he is bound and taken to Babylon, but later freed (40). In his agony he pours out his complaint to God (especially 15:10–18 and 20:7–18), asking for judgment and vengeance on his enemies (20:12; *cf.* Lamentations 3:58).

When Muhammad is persecuted, he is given, in the Qur'an, examples of prophets who have suffered before him, and have been patient in their sufferings. Richard Bell, an Islamic scholar, believes that the example of Moses leading his people out of bondage and suffering in Egypt may have made a strong impression on Muhammad. The idea would therefore be that if God brought his people out of Egypt, surely he can also deliver the Muslim community; in this way the pattern of the exodus is repeated in the Hijra, the migration from Mecca to Medina.

8. Jeremiah has a message of hope – but only after judgment (30 – 33, especially 30:3, 18; 31:2, 16–17). He is even told to buy a field to demonstrate the certainty that there will be a future for the people in the land (32). His life ends, however, in misery and shame, as he is taken down to Egypt (43:1–13, especially 4–7). At the end of the book, we are left asking: 'Did God keep his original promise to deliver Jeremiah?'

9. Jeremiah can be compared with Jesus. Whereas Jeremiah is called to take the cup of the wrath of God and make all the nations drink it (25:15–31), Jesus in the Garden of Gethsemane finds that *he himself* is being called to drink the cup of wrath. What makes the prospect of his coming death so much more intolerable, therefore, is that he knows that those who *should* drink the cup are 'all the wicked of the earth' (Psalm 75:8).

10. Jeremiah can be compared with Paul. In Luke's account of the conversion of Paul, there are clear echoes of the call of Jeremiah (Acts 9:15). When Paul writes about his own conversion, he uses language similar to Jeremiah's account of his call (Galatians 1:15–16).

In such ways as these the story of how God dealt with this particular prophet in the Old Testament, and how the people treated him, may give some clues about the Christian understanding of prophethood. It may offer the opportunity to put to Muslims questions such as these:

- Do you as Muslims take seriously enough the perversity of humans in their rejection of the Word of God? You say that people are created 'weak', and suggest that all we need is law and admonition, combined with the example of the Prophet. But look at the way the people of Judah treated the prophet Jeremiah! Isn't there something more seriously wrong with human nature than mere 'weakness' and 'forgetfulness'?

- What do you understand about the inner experience of the prophet or of any prophet? In the light of the experience of Jeremiah, do you accept that suffering may be a necessary part of the prophetic experience? And how do you explain the fact that God doesn't always seem to deliver his prophets?

- What does it mean if the prophet is willing to suffer? Could it not say something about how God deals with evil? Could it not suggest that judgment is not the only response God can make to evil? If this can be so, the prophet's suffering can become a kind of mirror of the suffering of God himself. *The prophet's suffering* can indicate the way that *God himself suffers* as he bears with his people and forgives them.

- How do you understand God's involvement in this prophet? Is there not a sense in which the honour of God is tied up with his prophet, so that what the people do to *him*, they are doing to *God*? If so, is God bound to deliver his prophet? If he is bound, why the exceptions? Why did he allow some to be humiliated and killed? What does it say about God that when the preaching of his Word draws out the worst in human nature, he doesn't rescue his servant, but allows him to suffer?

These questions can be answered only by Christians when they have been with Jesus in Gethsemane, and begun to understand that 'God was in Christ . . .' (2 Corinthians 5:19). But if the followers of the Prophet can see Jeremiah as being half-way between Moses and Jesus, perhaps they can catch a glimpse of what the fuller answers to these questions can be in Jesus.

34.2 God and his Word

The choice of this theme arises out of the fact that Jesus is given the title 'Word' in both the New Testament and the Qur'an:

> In the beginning was the Word, and the Word was with God, and the Word was God (John 1:1).

> The Messiah, Jesus son of Mary, was only a messenger of Allah and His Word which he conveyed unto Mary, and a spirit from Him (4:171).

Although we have here some obvious common ground, the same title is interpreted differently in the two communities. Do we therefore simply have to accept that we are poles apart, or is there any possibility of building bridges?

Jesus as 'Word' in the Qur'an

The following verses describe the annunciation of the birth of Jesus to Mary:

> (And remember) when the angels said: O Mary! Lo! Allah giveth thee glad tidings of a word from him, whose name is Messiah, Jesus, son of Mary . . . (3:45).

Another important verse in which Jesus is spoken of as God's Word comes in the context of an appeal to Christians not to exalt Jesus too highly:

> O People of the Scripture! Do not exaggerate in your religion nor utter aught concerning Allah save the truth. The Messiah, Jesus son of Mary, was only a messenger of Allah, and His Word which he conveyed unto Mary, and a spirit from Him. So believe in Allah and His messengers, and say not "Three" – Cease! (it is) better for you! – Allah is only One God (4:171).

If we go on to ask how the title 'Word' is interpreted in the Qur'an, a later verse in *sura* 3 gives the answer:

> Lo! The likeness of Jesus with Allah is as the likeness of

Adam. He created him of dust, then He said unto him:
Be! and he is (3:59).

The traditional Muslim interpretation of the title has therefore been that Jesus is the Word of God in the sense that he was *created by the Word of God*. Thus the thirteenth-century Qur'anic commentator Baidawi says: 'Jesus is called "a word", because he came into existence by God's command without a father, so that he resembled the new creations.'[4] Another commentator, Razi, gives a different explanation: Jesus is called 'a word' because he was the fulfilment of the word spoken by the prophets.[5] Yusuf Ali's comment on 3:39 is: 'Notice: "*a* Word from God", not "*the* Word of God", the epithet that mystical Christianity uses for Jesus . . . Jesus was created by a miracle, by God's word "Be", and he was.'[6]

What then do we do when faced with these Islamic interpretations? One natural response on our part is to investigate sources and ask where Muhammad might have heard these ideas. Although the title is found in only five verses in the New Testament (John 1:1, 14; 1 John 1:1, 10; and Revelation 19:13), the idea of Jesus as the eternal Word of God was developed by certain theologians between the second and fourth centuries, notably by Clement of Alexandria.

It is significant, however, that the title was used much less after this time, and was not used in any of the major creeds. Geoffrey Parrinder suggests this may have been because the Logos idea had also been used by various Gnostic sects. The example he gives is the apocryphal Acts of John, written about the second century AD, which describes the disciples taking part in a dance, 'going round in a ring', and saying to Jesus:'Glory be to thee, Lord: Glory be to thee, Grace: Glory be to thee, Spirit.'[7] The fact that this same document says that Jesus was only crucified in appearance (*cf.* 'They slew him not nor crucified, but it appeared so unto them', 4:157), suggests that Muhammad may well have found the title 'Word' as well as the Qur'anic idea of the crucifixion in heretical Christian sources like these.

This kind of enquiry about sources makes sense to many, because it helps us to understand how Muhammad may have come in contact with these ideas in either Arabia or Syria. It needs to be recognized, however, that it is anathema to Muslims, because they believe that the words of the Qur'an were revealed directly from God. Their concept of divine revelation rules out the possibility that what is recorded in the Qur'an could have come to Muhammad from any human sources.

Another possible response is to use the kind of argument first developed by St John of Damascus in the seventh century. In his treatise *On Heresies* he speaks of Islam as 'the Heresy of the Ishmaelites', and gives a clear idea of how he must have engaged in discussion with Muslims in Damascus less than a hundred years after the death of the Prophet. He suggests that when Muslims accuse Christians of *shirk* (*i.e.* of associating a created being with God the Creator), we should reply that in our eyes Muslims are guilty of *mutilating* God by refusing to believe that the Word of God is fully divine.

> Since you say that Christ is Word of God and Spirit, how is it that you revile us as *Hetairiastai* (Associators)? For the Word and the Spirit are not separated from the one in whom they are by nature. If therefore His Word is in God, it is evident that the Word is also God. But if the Word is outside of God, then according to you God is without reason and without life. And so, fearing to provide an Associator for God, you have mutilated Him. It were better for you to say that He has an Associate than to mutilate Him, and to treat Him as stone, or wood, or some insensible thing. Wherefore you speak falsely of us when you call us *'Hetairiastai'* but we call you *'Koptai'* (Mutilators) of God.[8]

Whether or not these two approaches bring us any nearer together, our main desire should be to come back to the gospels to see what light they shed on the title 'Word'. We want to say to the Muslim: 'We understand what *you* mean when you say that Jesus is the Word of God or a Word of God. But will you allow us to explain what *we* understand by the title?'

Jesus as the 'Word' in the gospel of John

We will need to begin with the prologue to John's gospel, and say something about the background of ideas which must have influenced John. Greek philosophers centuries before had thought of the *logos*, word or reason, as the rational principle by which the universe is sustained. And the Jews, probably under the influence of Greek philosophy, had reflected on the role of the creative word of God in Genesis 1, and of the Wisdom of God described in Proverbs 8:22–31. Thus when John spoke of Jesus as 'the Word', most of his readers would have connected the title with one or both of these ideas which were common in the first century. But they would not fail also to take note of John's incredibly bold claim that the eternal *logos* of God 'was God' (John 1:1), and that he 'became flesh and made his dwelling among us' (1:14).

Words of command can 'get things done' and achieve certain ends. Thus when John speaks of Jesus as the Word of God, he means that it was through Jesus that the universe was created: 'Through him all things were made; without him nothing was made that has been made' (1:3). Whereas the Qur'an speaks of Jesus as created by the Word of God, John believes that God created the universe through Jesus the eternal Word. But words also reveal a person's mind and character. So when John thinks of Jesus as the Word of God in this sense, what he means is that Jesus reveals God in the fullest possible way: 'No-one has ever seen God, but God the One and Only, who is at the Father's side, has made him known' (1:18).

If then the title is used by only one writer in the New Testament, and this is what he seems to understand by it, where else do we need to look? Much can be gained from looking at the synoptic gospels, which give us a different kind of account of the life and teaching of Jesus. We may then see how the apostle John, writing in the nineties of the first century, and reflecting on all that he and the other apostles had seen and heard of Jesus of Nazareth, could have come to think of him as the eternal Word of God.

We notice first of all examples of how the words of Jesus affect the created order (the so-called 'nature miracles'). We then look at healing miracles, in which the words of Jesus bring about a cure. Finally we see examples of Jesus pronouncing words of forgiveness. All the examples are taken from Mark's gospel. In each case we note in the column on the right in italics the recorded words of Jesus, and in several cases we also note significant parallels in the Qur'an.

1. The word of Jesus working in creation

He calms the storm	*'Quiet! Be still!'* (Mark 4:35–41)
He feeds the 5,000 after giving thanks (Mark 6:30–44)	

This second miracle is of special significance for us, since it is referred to indirectly in the Qur'an. In the *sura* entitled *The Table Spread*, the disciples are reported as praying. 'Send down for us a table spread with food from heaven' (5:114).

It is also helpful to notice the verse in the Qur'an in which Jesus speaks of his miracles: 'I fashion [*akhluqu*, create] for you out of clay the likeness of a bird and breathe into it and it is a bird, by Allah's leave' (3:49). One Muslim's pilgrimage to faith in Jesus began when he thought about the implications of the word 'fashion' or 'create'; surely only God can create – so how can Jesus here speak of himself creating something?

2. The word of Jesus in healing

The man possessed by evil spirits	*'Be quiet! Come out of him!'* (1:21–23)
The man with leprosy (*cf.* in the Qur'an: 'I heal . . . the leper; 3:49.)	*'Be clean!'* (1:40–45)
The paralysed man	*'Your sins are forgiven.'* (2:1–12)
Legion	*'Come out of this man, you evil spirit!'* (5:1–13)
The sick woman	*'Go in peace and be freed from your suffering.'* (5:25–34)
Raising the dead girl (*cf.* in the Qur'an: 'I raise the dead, by Allah's leave', 3:49.)	*'Talitha koum! Little girl . . . get up!'* (5:21–24, 35–43)
Healing the deaf and mute man	*'Ephphatha! Be opened!'* (7:31–37)
Healing the boy with an evil spirit	*'You deaf and mute spirit, I command you, come out of him and never enter him again.'* (9:14–32)

Healing of blind Bartimaeus	'Your faith has healed you.' (10:46–52)
(cf. in the Qur'an: 'I heal . . . him who	
was born blind', 3:49.)	

3. The word of Jesus in forgiving

| The paralysed man | 'Son, your sins are forgiven.' (2:5) |

One reaction of the Pharisees to these words ('He's blaspheming! Who can forgive sins but God alone?' 2:7) is exactly the same as that of the orthodox Muslim who knows that the Qur'an says, 'Who forgiveth sins save Allah only?' (3:135).

With the memory of these events and these words indelibly printed on his mind, the apostle John recognizes that the words of Jesus have power to still the storm – which is something that only God can do ('He stilled the storm to a whisper', Psalm 107:29). He remembers also how his words brought healing and forgiveness – which once again is the prerogative of God himself (he 'forgives all your sins and heals all your diseases', Psalm 103:3). If therefore the words of Jesus have the power to do things that only God can do, Jesus must be the one through whom God has spoken and acted in a special way.

The title 'Word', which John gives to Jesus, is therefore firmly grounded in all that John remembers of Jesus. For if the words of Jesus were in effect the words of God in these different situations, is it not natural to think that Jesus is himself the Word of God? And if the historical Jesus spoke and acted in this way, speaking the creating, healing and forgiving word of God, then the risen and ascended Jesus can still speak these words to us today. The Word of God cannot be less than, or other than, God himself.

34.3 God and his mercy

'In the name of God, the Merciful, the Compassionate . . .', says the Muslim in the Fatiha. 'How can I find a merciful God?' cried Luther in his despair. It is one thing to proclaim the mercy of God, but another to be sure of experiencing that mercy. Thinking about the mercy of God, therefore, brings us nearer the heart of the matter. For how do we benefit from God's prophets and his Word, unless they communicate not only *teaching about God's mercy*, but also *an experience of that mercy*?

God and his mercy in the Qur'an

The Qur'an's teaching about mercy can be summarized in the following way:

1. God is merciful and forgiving (*rahman, rahim, ghafur*).

> Your Lord is a Lord of all-embracing mercy, and His wrath will never be withdrawn from guilty folk (6:148).

> Despair not of the Mercy of Allah, who forgiveth all sins! Lo! He is the Forgiving, the Merciful (39:53; *cf.* 23:118).

2. God loves certain kinds of people; those who do right (3:134; 3:148; 5:13, 93), those who turn to him (2:222), the pure (2:222), the God-fearing (3:76; 9:4, 7), the patient (3:146), the trusting (3:159), the equitable (5:42; 49:9; 60:8), and those who do battle for his cause (61:4).

3. God does *not* love certain other kinds of people: aggressors (2:190), the corrupt (5:64; 28:77), the evil unbelievers (2:276), the ungrateful (22:38), the braggart boasters (31:18), the prodigals (6:142; 7:31), the proud and boastful (4:36), the unbelievers (30:45), the wrongdoers (3:57, 140; 42:40), the treacherous (4:107; 8:58; 22:38), those of harsh speech (4:148), the transgressors (5:87).

4. Forgiveness is associated with obedience to God and his Prophet.

> If you love Allah, follow me. Allah will love you and forgive you your sins. Allah is forgiving, Merciful (3:31; *cf.* 8:29; 20:73; 46:31; 57:28; 61:11–12; 71:3–4).

5. God's forgiveness is inscrutable; he forgives whom he wills.

> He [Allah] will forgive whom He will and He will punish whom He will (2:284; *cf.* 3:129; 5:18).

> Knowest thou not that unto Allah belongeth the Sovereignty of the heavens and the earth? He punisheth whom He will, and forgiveth whom He will. Allah is able to do all things (5:40; *cf.* 48:14).

6. We cannot be sure of forgiveness; God will show mercy on the day of judgment.

> We ardently hope that our Lord will forgive us our sins because we are the first of the believers (26:51).

> . . . and who, I ardently hope, will forgive me my sins on the Day of Judgment (26:82; *cf.* 14:41; 66:8).

7. There is *no* forgiveness for certain sins, such as *shirk* (association).

> Allah pardoneth not that partners should be ascribed unto Him. He pardoneth all save that to whom He will . . . (4:116; *cf.* 4:48, 137, 168, 9:80; 47:34).

God and his mercy in the teaching of Jesus

One of the clearest expressions of the teaching of Jesus about the mercy of God is found in the parable of the two lost sons (also known as the parable of the prodigal son; see chapter 33.1). If we put the teaching of the parable alongside the teaching of the Qur'an, we can note how the teaching of Jesus compares with each point of our summary of the Qur'an's teaching.

1. Here we have no difference, since the whole message of this parable is that God is merciful and forgiving.

2–3. God loves not only those who love him. The father in the parable loves *both* sons and shows the same kind of forgiving love to both of them.

4. God's forgiveness is associated with the one who proclaims and declares that forgiveness to people. The father himself welcomes his son and reinstates him in the family. When Jesus declares, 'Your sins are forgiven', it is because he speaks with the authority of God himself. So what Jesus does, God does; and what God does, Jesus does.

5. God does indeed show mercy on whom he wills (Romans 9:18); but we *can* know where we stand before him. The way the father shows his love for both his sons shows how God's love extends to us all. It also shows how he takes the initiative and comes to meet us and welcome us home.

6. We *can* be sure of God's mercy and forgiveness. We do not have to wait until the day of judgment before we know how we stand before him. The prodigal knows that he is forgiven because his father goes out of his way to show that the wrongs of the past are forgiven and forgotten.

7. The only unforgivable sin in the teaching of Jesus is what he calls 'the sin against the Holy Spirit' (Mark 3:23–30), that is, attributing the work of God to Satan and calling what is good evil. If the older son in the parable refuses in the end to accept the mercy shown to him by his father, he is spurning his father's love, and the breach in their relationship looks as if it must be final. But this is only *after* the father has demonstrated his love for his son in a way that is beyond all doubt.

The teaching of Jesus therefore reveals an understanding of the mercy of God which, while it has something in common with the teaching of the Qur'an, is distinctively different. Daoud Rahbar has had to grapple with the similarities and differences in his own experience. Writing in 1960 as a well-known Muslim scholar, he made a thorough study of the justice of God in a book called *God of Justice*. Some years later, he explained his conversion to the Christian faith, pointing out that the distinctive thing about the New Testament is the way God's love is related to his justice:

> When I read the New Testament and discovered how Jesus loved and forgave His killers from the Cross, I could not fail to recognize that the love He had for men is the only kind of love worthy of the Eternal God.[9]

35

Strategies for the church:
what can we do together?

Individuals reading this book on their own will no doubt be trying to work out the implications for themselves. But any group – in a church, a theological college, or a missionary college – using this material for study will probably want to reflect on what they can and should be aiming to do *together*. These are the kinds of question they may need to explore. As you read them, ask yourself: 'Should *I* be doing any of these things to follow up what I have been studying? Should *my church* be doing any of them? Should the *churches in this area* be doing any of them *together*?'

(Note: Some of the questions here are relevant primarily to situations in Europe and North America, and will need to be omitted or adapted in other situations.)

Meeting Muslims

■ How well do we know our Muslim neighbours? How much personal contact do we already have with Muslims?

■ What can we do to encourage more face-to-face meeting with neighbours, colleagues, *etc.*?

■ What kind of visiting could we do – homes, mosques, *etc.*?

Service

■ Are there any ways in which we and others can help to serve the Muslim community, through teaching English, through voluntary organizations, through local community projects, *etc.*?

■ Are there ways in which we can work *with* Muslims in serving the community?

Political action

■ What does the Muslim community feel are the important issues for them in the local area – for instance, housing, schools, permission to establish mosques?

■ Are there any ways in which it would be right for Christians to work with Muslims on any of these issues?

■ Are there any national issues of concern to Muslims in which we need to be involved – for instance, the aftermath of the Rushdie affair, immigration, the question of state-funded Muslim schools?

Teaching in the church

■ What are we teaching about other faiths and our relations with other-faith communities? What should we be teaching?

■ Do we need to plan a programme which will include teaching in Sunday School, youth fellowships, wives' groups, house groups, Sunday sermons, *etc.*?

■ What books do we know of that could be recommended for people to read? What material is being produced by different denominational and interdenominational bodies on the subject of other faiths in general and Islam in particular?

Relating to Muslim leaders

■ Is it appropriate for church leaders, ordained and lay, to meet with leaders of the Muslim community from time to time? If so, how should it be done?

Schools

■ How many pupils in our local schools belong to other-faith communities?

■ What, if any, are the particular issues that concern the local Muslim community about schools?

■ How is religious education being taught in schools in our area? What is the approach to the teaching of Christianity and other faiths?

Finding people with special gifts

We need to be aware of the danger of 'passing the buck', of thinking that we are not properly equipped to do the things we have been talking about, and should therefore leave it all to the 'experts'. But are there people in our churches who have special gifts in this area (perhaps because they have worked with Muslims overseas and can speak one of their languages), and could *help* us (but not do it all for us)?

- Which individuals and groups do we know who are already involved in work with Muslims?

- Do we need to set aside other individuals to work either part-time or full-time in this task?

Prayer

- How should we be praying about our relations with people of other faiths in general, and Muslims in particular? If we were to pray regularly about this subject, how should we do it? What should we be praying for?

- Is the question of multi-faith worship an issue in our area? What should be our response?

Sharing the gospel

We should be able to assume that some of the other activities already discussed will provide opportunities for sharing our faith. But are there any other initiatives that we can or should be taking? For example:

- Are Bibles, New Testaments or other portions of Scripture in different languages easily available for sale in local shops?

- Is there a correspondence course, particularly appropriate for Muslim enquirers, that could be advertised?

- How could one get hold of a video (such as *Jesus*, produced by Campus Crusade) in different languages to lend to friends who may be interested?

Concern for the church overseas

- How can we learn from the experience of the church in predominantly Muslim countries?

- How can we support the churches in these countries? What should be our response to reports of the different kinds of pressures on these churches (*e.g.* the imprisonment of individual Muslims who have become Christians; see chapter 30)?

Resources for further study

Margaret Burness, *What Shall I Say to my Muslim Friends?* (Church Missionary Society, 1989)

John Gilchrist, *The Christian Witness to the Muslim* (Jesus to the Muslims, 1988)

Abdul Haqq, *Sharing Your Faith with a Muslim* (Bethany Fellowship, 1980)

Don McCurry, *The Gospel and Islam: A 1978 Compendium* (MARC USA, 1979)

C. R. Marsh, *Share Your Faith with a Muslim* (Moody, 1975)

Phil Parshall, *Beyond the Mosque* (Baker, 1985)

Vivienne Stacey, *Christ Supreme Over Satan* (Masihi Isha'at Khana, 16 Ferosepur Road, Lahore 16, Pakistan, 1986)

J. Dudley Woodberry, ed. *Muslims and Christians on the Emmaus Road: Crucial Issues in Witness Among Muslims* (MARC USA, 1989)

Conclusion:
Walking the way of the cross

The missionary among Muslims (to whom the Cross of Christ is a stumbling block and the atonement foolishness) is driven daily to deeper meditation on this mystery of redemption and to a stronger conviction that here is the very heart of our message and our mission.

Samuel Zwemer[1]

Wherever there is the obscuring of the beauty of the Cross, it must be unveiled.

Kenneth Cragg[2]

Throughout our study we have been exploring what might be a genuinely Christian way of responding to the challenge of Islam. Perhaps the most vital clue to this response in every area can be found in the symbol at the heart of the Christian faith. What will it mean to walk the way of the cross in all our thinking about Islam and our relating to Muslims?

Walking the way of the cross in our relationships with Muslims will mean following the example of the one who was willing to cross barriers of race, class, sex and religion, in order to meet people where they were in their joy, their pain and their need. For some of us this may mean surrendering any power and privilege that are part of our history and culture, and 'taking the very nature of a servant' (Philippians 2:7). The cross will constantly call us to leave the safety of our own circle and to reach out to that other community or that other individual in love and hope.

Walking the way of the cross in understanding Islam will mean trying to get inside the mind and heart of Islam. Our desire will not be to judge or condemn, but to 'sit where they sit', and to show that words such as 'identification' and 'empathy' can be more than easy slogans. Sooner or later, however, we will have to understand why, from the Muslim point of view, the cross is a symbol of weakness, shame and defeat. In their way of thinking it is both a stumbling-block and foolishness, and can never be the final clue to the working of an all-powerful God.

Walking the way of the cross in discussion and dialogue will mean patient and attentive listening, which understands the words and appreciates the total worldview and the feelings that they express. The more keenly we feel the sins and shortcomings of the Christian church of the past and present, the more we will feel compelled to say, 'We have sinned, even as our fathers did' (Psalm 106:6). The example of Jesus will teach us how to respond to scorn, anger and ridicule, and also to recognize the searching of a Nicodemus or the faith of a Syro-Phoenician woman. We shall continually be praying that stumbling-blocks will be removed, so that through our words and deeds, and through the free working of the Holy Spirit, Muslims can begin to see why the Christ had to suffer (Luke 24:26).

Walking the way of the cross in facing fundamental issues will mean testing everything in Islam not by the standards of our own history and our culture, but by the measure of the crucified and risen Christ. Whether we are talking about revelation or salvation, law or the state, our goal will be to try as far as possible to seek 'the mind of Christ' (1 Corinthians 2:16; *cf.* Philippians 2:5ff.). Sometimes we may need to hear the rebuke that says, 'Away with you, Satan . . . you think as men think, not as God thinks' (Mark 8:33, NEB). Much of the time we may be dealing with misconceptions and misunderstandings. But where there is rejection of the real *injil*, the real gospel, we will be driven, in the words of Zwemer, 'to a deeper meditation on this mystery of redemption'.

Walking the way of the cross in our witness will mean testifying as best as we can how it is 'in the face of Christ' that we see 'the light of the knowledge of the glory of God' (2 Corinthians 4:6). However weak our efforts to bear witness to Christ crucified as the very heart of our message, we shall find that for 'those whom God has called' – of whatever community and whatever faith – Christ on the cross will be recognized as the supreme revelation of 'the power of God and the wisdom of God' (1 Corinthians 1:23–24).

Notes

Part 1: Relating to our Muslim neighbours

1. Roger Hooker, *Uncharted Journey* (Church Missionary Society, 1973), pp. 22, 21.
2. Robert Bruce, quoted in *History of the Church Missionary Society*, vol. iii (Eugene Stock, 1899), p. 125.

1. Meeting face to face

1. Roger Hooker, *Uncharted Journey*, p. 21.

2. Appreciating Islamic culture

1. Anonymous.
2. Stan Nussbaum, in an unpublished lecture at Selly Oak, Birmingham.
3. L. J. Luzbetak, *The Church and Cultures: An Applied Anthropology for the Religious Worker* (William Carey Library, 1970), p. 60.
4. The Willowbank Report, *Gospel and Culture* (Lausanne Occasional Papers 2, Lausanne Committee for World Evangelization, 1978).
5. Lesslie Newbigin, *The Open Secret* (Eerdmans, 1978), p. 159.
6. Ghulam Sarwar, *Islam: A Brief Guide* (leaflet) (Muslim Educational Trust, 130 Stroud Green Road, London N4 3RZ, 1993).
7. Albert Hourani, *Europe and the Middle East* (Macmillan, 1980), p. 15.

3. Examining our attitudes

1. Bilquis Sheikh, *I Dared to Call Him Father* (Kingsway, 2nd edn., 1983).

5. Facing immediate issues

1. From a case study written by a Kenyan pastor at the London Institute for Contemporary Christianity (now Christian Impact).

Part 2: Understanding Islam

1. Roger Hooker, *Uncharted Journey*, p. 26.
2. Jens Christensen, *The Practical Approach to Muslims* (North Africa Mission, 1977), p. 369.
3. Ninian Smart, *The Religious Experience of Mankind* (Collins Fount, 1982), p. 12.
4. D. B. Macdonald, quoted in Michael Shelley, *The Life and Thought of W. H. T. Gairdner, 1873–1928: A Critical Evaluation of a Scholar-Missionary to Islam* (PhD dissertation, University of Birmingham, 1988), pp. 111–112.

6. Muslims at prayer

1. Constance Padwick, *Muslim Devotions: A Study of Prayer Manuals in Common Use* (SPCK, 1961), pp. xi, xiii.
2. Kenneth Cragg, *The Call of the Minaret* (Collins, 1986), p. 26.
3. M. M. Pickthall, *The Meaning of the Glorious Koran* (Mentor, no date), p. 31.
4. W. Montgomery Watt, *Companion to the Qur'an* (George Allen and Unwin, 1967), p. 13.

340

5. Kenneth Cragg, *The Event of the Qur'an* (George Allen and Unwin, 1971), p. 74.
6. Roger Hooker, *Uncharted Journey*, pp. 24–25.
7. *Ibid.*, p. 25.

7. Basic Muslim beliefs and practices

1. Ghulam Sarwar, *Islam: A Brief Guide*.
2. *Ibid.*

8. The Qur'an

1. Wilfred Cantwell Smith, *Islam in Modern History* (Princeton University Press, 1957), pp. 17–18.
2. Ghulam Sarwar, *Islam: A Brief Guide*.
3. A. J. Arberry, *The Koran Interpreted* (Oxford University Press, 1972), p. 161.
4. Kenneth Cragg, *The Call of the Minaret*, p. 66.
5. In W. Montgomery Watt, *Bell's Introduction to the Qur'an* (Edinburgh University Press, 1970), pp. 87–88.
6. Jan Slomp, *To Understand the Muslim Approach to Scripture* (unpublished paper delivered to a seminar of the United Bible Societies in Holland, January 1993).
7. A. Guillaume, *The Life of the Prophet: A Translation of Ibn Ishaq's Sirat Rasul Allah* (Oxford University Press, 1970), p. 259.
8. In W. Montgomery Watt, *Bell's Introduction to the Qur'an*, pp. 87–88.
9. A. Yusuf Ali, *The Holy Qur'an: Text, Translation and Commentary* (The Islamic Foundation, 1975), pp. 233–234.

9. Muhammad

1. Gai Eaton, *Islam and the Destiny of Man* (George Allen and Unwin, 1985), pp. 96–97.
2. Ghulam Sarwar, *Islam: A Brief Guide*.
3. A. Guillaume, *The Life of the Prophet*, p. xxiv.
4. *Ibid.*, pp. 79–81.

10. Tradition

1. Kenneth Cragg, in W. Foy (ed.), *Man's Religious Quest*, (Croom Helm/Open University Press, 1982), p. 512.
2. Alfred Guillaume, *The Traditions of Islam* (Oxford University Press, 1924), p. 15.
3. Ghulam Sarwar, *Islam: A Brief Guide*.
4. Gai Eaton, *Islam and the Destiny of Man*, pp. 186–187.

11. Law (*shari'a*) and theology (*kalam*)

1. Joseph Schacht, *Introduction to Islamic Law* (Clarendon Press, 1964), p. 1.
2. Kenneth Cragg, *Islam and the Muslim* (Open University Press, 1978), p. 49.
3. H. A. R. Gibb, in R. C. Zaehner (ed.), *The Hutchinson Encyclopedia of Living Faiths* (Hutchinson, 1988), p. 172.
4. Trevor Ling, *A History of Religion East and West* (Macmillan, 1982), pp. 292–293.
5. H. A. R. Gibb, in *The Hutchinson Encyclopaedia of Living Faiths*, p. 196.
6. Michael Nazir-Ali, *Islam: A Christian Perspective* (Paternoster, 1983), p. 50.
7. Hammudah Abdalati, *Islam in Focus* (The World Assembly of Muslim Youth, Riyadh, 1980), pp. 196–197.
8. Al-Ghazali, *The Ninety-Nine Beautiful Names of God*, translated with notes by David B. Burrell and Nazih Daher (The Islamic Texts Society, Cambridge, 1992), pp. 35–41.

12. Sub-groups in Islam

1. W. Montgomery Watt, *The Muslim Intellectual: A Study of al-Ghazali* (Edinburgh University Press, 1963), p. 80.
2. Table from Richard Tames, *Approaches to Islam* (John Murray, 1982), pp. 51–52.

13. Sufism

1. H. A. R. Gibb, in *The Hutchinson Encyclopedia of Living Faiths*, p. 190.
2. *Ibid.*, p. 194.
3. Shaykh al-'Alawi, in W. Foy, ed., *Man's Religious Quest*, p. 520.
4. Kenneth Cragg, *Islam and the Muslim*, p. 74.
5. *Ibid.*, p. 75.
6. Ninian Smart, *The Religious Experience of Mankind*, p. 520.
7. Quoted by H. A. R. Gibb, *Mohammedanism* (Oxford University Press, 1969), p. 90.
8. Quoted in *ibid.*, p. 90.
9. Abu-l 'Abbas al-'Alawi, quoted by Kenneth Cragg in W. Foy, ed., *Man's Religious Quest*, p. 521.

14. 'Folk Islam' or 'popular Islam'

1. Bill Musk, *The Unseen Face of Islam: Sharing the Gospel with Ordinary Muslims* (MARC, 1989), pp. 15–16.
2. Samuel Zwemer, quoted by Bill Musk, 'Popular Islam: The Hunger of the Heart' in Don M. McCurry, ed., *The Gospel and Islam: A 1978 Compendium* (MARC, California, 1979), p. 209.
3. Detmar Shuenemann, quoted by Bill Musk, 'Popular Islam: The Hunger of the Heart', pp. 209–210.
4. Paul Hiebert, 'Power Encounter and Folk Islam', in Dudley J. Woodberry, ed., *Muslims and Christians on the Emmaus Road* (MARC California), extracts from pp. 45–61.
5. Michael Nazir-Ali, *Islam: A Christian Perspective*, p. 65.

6. Al-Bushiri, in James McL. Ritchie, 'The Prophet's Mantle (*Qasidatu-l-Burda*): Translation and Presentation', *Encounter* 171–173 (Pontifical Institute for Arabic and Islamic Studies, January–February 1991), pp. 3–16.

15. The spread and development of Islam

1. Kenneth Cragg, *The Call of the Minaret*, p. 219.
2. Hammudah Abdalati, *Islam in Focus*, p. 150.
3. Michael Nazir-Ali, *Islam: A Christian Perspective*, pp. 35–36.
4. John Taylor, *Introducing Islam* (Lutterworth, 1971), p. 33.
5. Trevor Ling, *A History of Religion East and West*, p. 300.
6. *Ibid.*, p. 302.
7. Albert Hourani, *Europe and the Middle East*, p. 4.
8. *Ibid.*, p. 9.
9. Kenneth Cragg, *Islam and the Muslim*, pp. 78–79.
10. Trevor Ling, *A History of Religion East and West*, p. 300.
11. *Ibid.*, p. 384.
12. *Ibid.*, p. 387.
13. *Ibid.*, p. 395.

16. Islam and Muslims in the world today

1. Kenneth Cragg, *Islam and the Muslim*, pp. 78–79.
2. Zaki Badawi, *Islam in Britain* (Ta Ha Publishers, 1981), pp. 26–27.
3. Amir Taheri, *The Cauldron: The Middle East Behind the Headlines* (Hutchinson, 1988), p. 254.
4. Kenneth Cragg, *The Call of the Minaret*, p. 19.
5. Wilfred Cantwell Smith, *Questions of Religious Truth* (Gollancz, 1967), pp. 48–49.
6. Rafiq Zakaria, *The Struggle Within Islam: The Conflict Between Religion*

and Politics (Penguin, 1988), p. 295.
7. Kenneth Cragg, *The Call of the Minaret*, p. 24.
8. Ronald Nettler, *Islam and the Minorities: Background to the Arab–Israeli Conflict* (Israel Academic Committee on the Middle East, Jerusalem, 1978), p.11.
9. Amir Taheri, *The Cauldron*, p. 257.
10. Rafiq Zakaria, *The Struggle Within Islam*, p. xiii and back cover.
11. Khurshid Ahmad, in John L. Esposito, ed., *Voices of Resurgent Islam* (Oxford University Press, 1983), p. 228.
12. *Ibid.*, pp. 228–229.
13. Zaki Badawi, *Islam in Britain*, p. 26.

17. Women in Islam

1. Alfred Guillaume, *Islam* (Penguin, 1983), p. 71.
2. W. Montgomery Watt, *Muhammad: Prophet and Statesman* (Oxford University Press, 1975), pp. 233–234.
3. John Gilchrist, *Muhammad and the Religion of Islam*, vol. 1 (Jesus to the Muslims, Benoni, 1986), pp. 88–89.
4. Gai Eaton, *Islam and the Destiny of Man*, pp. 122–123.
5. Vivienne Stacey, *The Life of Muslim Women* (Fellowship of Faith for Muslims, 1980), pp. 34–35.
6. *Ibid.*, pp. 18–20.
7. *Ibid.*, pp. 24–25.
8. Amir Taheri, *The Cauldron*, p. 255.
9. Abdur Rahman I. Doi, *Women in Shari'ah (Islamic Law)* (Ta Ha Publishers, 1989), p. 175.
10. Fatna Sabah, quoted in Fatima Mernissi, 'Femininity as Subversion: Reflections on the Muslim Concept of *Nushuz*', in D. L. Eck and D. Jain, eds., *Speaking of Faith: Cross-Cultural Perspectives on Women, Religion and Social Change*
(The Women's Press, 1986), pp. 88–89.
11. *Ibid.*, p. 98.
12. *Ibid.*, p. 100.
13. Abdur Rahman I. Doi, *Women in Shari'ah*, p. 169.
14. *Ibid.*, p. 175.
15. *Ibid.*, pp. 175–176.

Part 3: Entering into discussion and dialogue

1. Roger Hooker, *Uncharted Journey*, p. 23.
2. W. Montgomery Watt, *Times Literary Supplement*, insert on Islam (30 April 1976), p. 513.
3. *Journals and Letters of Henry Martyn*, ed. S. Wilberforce (Seeley and Burnside, 1837), vol. 2, p. 373.
4. Sam Schlorff, *Discipleship in an Islamic Society* (North Africa Mission, 1978).

22. A deeper look at the main Muslim objections

1. David Brown, *The Cross of the Messiah* (SPCK, 1969), p. 31.
2. *Ibid.*, pp. 29–30.
3. Kamel Hussein, *City of Wrong (Qaryatu Zalimah)*, translated with an introduction by Kenneth Cragg (Djambatan, 1959), p. 222.
4. Kenneth Cragg, *The Call of the Minaret*, pp. 265–268.
5. Geoffrey Parrinder, *Jesus in the Qur'an* (Faber and Faber, 1965), p. 109.

23. Learning from the controversies of the past

1. Jean-Marie Gaudeul, *Encounters and Clashes: Islam and Christianity in History* (Pontifical Institute for Arab and Islamic Studies, 1984), pp. 89–90.
2. *Journals and Letters of Henry Martyn*, vol. 2, journal 26 (1811), p. 371.
3. Constance Padwick, *Temple*

Gairdner of Cairo (SPCK, 1929), pp. 148–149.

24. Exploring dialogue

1. Isma'il al-Faruqi, in *Christian Mission and Islamic Da'wah: Proceedings of the Chambésy Consultation* (The Islamic Foundation, 1982), pp. 47–48.
2. Private letter to author.
3. Roger Hooker, *Uncharted Journey*, pp. 26–27.

Part 4: Facing fundamental questions

1. Arne Rudvin, preface to Jens Christensen, *The Practical Approach to Muslims*, p. vii.
2. Muhammad Hamidullah, *Introduction to Islam* (Centre Culturel Islamique, Paris, 1969).
3. Kenneth Cragg, *The Call of the Minaret*, p. 220.
4. Abul A'la Mawdudi, *Murtaddki Saza Islami Qawmi Mein* (Islamic Publications, Lahore, 8th edn., 1981).

25. Theological questions

1. Michael Nazir-Ali, *Frontiers in Muslim–Christian Encounter* (Regnum, 1987), p. 20.
2. Charles Kraft, *Christianity in Cross-Cultural Perspective: A Study in Dynamic Biblical Theologizing* (Orbis, 1981), p. 402.
3. Jean-Marie Gaudeul, *op. cit.*, p. 130.

26. The Islamic view of Jesus

1. Kenneth Cragg, tr., *Readings in the Qur'an* (Collins, 1988).
2. M. Ali Merad, 'Christ According to the Qur'an', *Encounter* 69 (Pontifical Institute for Arabic and Islamic Studies, November 1980), p. 7.
3. *Ibid.*, p. 15.

4. Samuel Zwemer, *The Muslim Christ* (Oliphants, 1912), p. 157.
5. Kenneth Cragg, *The Call of the Minaret*, pp. 219–220.
6. Henri Michaud, quoted in G. Parrinder, *Jesus in the Qur'an*, p. 166.

27. Crucial differences

1. Michael Nazir-Ali, *Frontiers in Muslim–Christian Encounter*, p. 20.
2. Isma'il al-Faruqi, in *Christian Mission and Islamic Da'wah*, pp. 47–48.
3. Jens Christensen, *The Practical Approach to Muslims*, pp. 379–380.
4. Kenneth Cragg, *Muhammad and the Christian: A Question of Response* (Darton Longman and Todd, 1984), p. 51.

29. Counting the cost of conversion

1. Abul A'la Mawdudi, *Murtaddki Saza Islami Qawmi Mein*.
2. Kenneth Cragg, in *Christian Mission and Islamic Da'wah*, p. 92.
3. Al-Baidhawi, quoted in Samuel Zwemer, *The Law of Apostasy in Islam* (Marshall Brothers, 1924), pp. 33–34.
4. A. Yusuf Ali, *The Holy Qur'an: Text, Translation and Commentary* (The Islamic Foundation, 1975), pp. 207.
5. Maulvi Muhammad Ali, *The Holy Qur'an: Arabic Text with English Translation and Commentary* (Ahmadiyyah Anjuman-i-Ishaat-i-Islam, 1920), pp. 98–99.
6. Al-Bukhari, quoted in Samuel Zwemer, *The Law of Apostasy in Islam*, p. 38.
7. H. A. R. Gibb and J. H. Kraemers, eds., *Shorter Encyclopedia of Islam* (Brill, 1961), article *Murtadd*, p. 413.
8. *Ibid.*
9. Abdullahi Ahmed An-Na'im, 'The Law of Apostasy and its Modern

Applicability: A Case from the Sudan', *Religion* 16 (1986), p. 211.

10. *Shorter Encyclopedia of Islam*, p. 413.

11. Rafiq Zakaria, *Muhammad and the Qur'an* (Penguin, 1991), pp. 86–87.

12. Isma'il al-Faruqi, in *Christian Mission and Islamic Da'wah*, pp. 92–93.

13. Syed M. Darsh, *Impact International* 24, no. 2 (February, 1994), p. 29.

14. Isma'il al-Faruqi, in *Christian Mission and Islamic Da'wah*, p. 92.

15. Abdullahi Ahmed An-Na'im, 'The Law of Apostasy', p. 213.

30. Facing the political challenge of Islam

1. Jens Christensen, *The Practical Approach to Muslims*, p. 53.

2. Kenneth Cragg, *Islam and the Muslim*, p. 17.

3. A. Yusuf Ali, *The Holy Qur'an: Text, Translation and Commentary*, p. 447.

4. W. Montgomery Watt, *Muhammad at Medina* (Oxford University Press, 1977), pp. 359–360.

5. Ibn Ishaq, *Life of the Apostle of God*, p. 525.

6. Michael Nazir-Ali, *Martyrs and Magistrates: Toleration and Trial in Islam* (Grove Ethical Series 73, Grove Books, 1989), p. 12.

7. Ibn Khaldun, quoted in Bat Ye'or, *The Dhimmi: Jews and Christians Under Islam* (Associated University Presses, 1985), p. 162.

8. *Ibid.*

9. Mohamed Talbi, 'Christian–Muslim Encounter in the Middle East', *Middle East Perspectives* 4/5 (Middle East Council of Churches, July/August 1985), p. 10.

10. Rafiq Zakaria, *The Struggle Within Islam*, pp. 300–301.

11. *Christian Witness to Muslims* (the Thailand Report) (Lausanne Occasional Papers 13, Lausanne Committee for World Evangelization, 1980), pp. 23–24.

12. Michael Nazir-Ali, *Martyrs and Magistrates*, p. 14.

13. John Stott, *The Message of the Sermon on the Mount* (Inter-Varsity Press, 1978), extracts from pp. 107–113.

14. *Christian Witness to Muslims*, p. 23.

15. Confidential source.

16. Michael Nazir-Ali, *Frontiers in Muslim–Christian Encounter*, pp. 144–145.

Part 5: Sharing our faith

1. Temple Gairdner, quoted in Constance Padwick, *Temple Gairdner of Cairo* (SPCK, 1929), p. 158.

2. Roger Hooker, *Uncharted Journey*, p. 24.

3. Kenneth Cragg, *The Call of the Minaret*, pp. 304–305.

4. Jens Christensen, *The Practical Approach to Muslims*, p. 145.

31. Natural openings in everyday life

1. Margaret Burness, *What Shall I Say to my Muslim Friends?* (Church Missionary Society, 1989), pp. 11–12.

32. Christian responses to 'folk Islam'

1. Bill Musk, 'Popular Islam: The Hunger of the Heart', p. 219.

2. Vivienne Stacey, *Christ Supreme Over Satan: Spiritual Warfare, Folk Religion and the Occult* (Masihi Isha'at Khana, Lahore, 1986), pp. 4–8.

33. Using the Bible

1. Kenneth Bailey has written about the parable in three books: *The Cross and the Prodigal* (Concordia, 1973), *Poet and Peasant and Through Peasant Eyes* (Eerdmans, 1983),

and *Finding the Lost: Cultural Keys to Luke 15* (Concordia, 1993).
2. Kenneth Bailey, *Poet and Peasant and Through Peasant Eyes*, p. 206.

34. Rethinking and restating the gospel, starting from the Qur'an

1. *Christian Witness to Muslims*, p. 13.
2. *Ibid.*, p. 16.
3. B. D. Kateregga and D. W. Shenk, *Islam and Christianity: A Muslim and a Christian in Dialogue* (Paternoster, 1980), pp. 34–37.
4. Quoted in Geoffrey Parrinder, *Jesus in the Qur'an*, p. 45.
5. Quoted in *ibid.*, p. 46.
6. Yusuf Ali, *The Holy Qur'an: Text, Translation and Commentary*, p. 133.
7. Geoffrey Parrinder, *Jesus in the Qur'an*, pp. 45–48.
8. *The Apology of John of Damascus*, translated by John W. Voorhis (The Muslim World, 1934), pp. 394–395.
9. Daoud Rahbar, *Letter to Friends* (unpublished).

Conclusion: Walking the way of the cross

1. Samuel Zwemer, *The Glory of the Cross* (Baker, 1982), p. 6.
2. Kenneth Cragg, *The Call of the Minaret*, p. 304.